UP BEAT AND DOWN DALE

MIKE PANNETT

HODDER &
STOUGHTON

First published in Great Britain in 2012 by Hodder & Stoughton
An Hachette UK company

1

A CIP catalogue record for this title is available from the British Library

Trade paperback ISBN 978 1 444 72060 0
Ebook ISBN 978 1 444 70899 8

Typeset in Sabon MT by Palimpsest Book Production Limited,
Falkirk, Stirlingshire

Printed and bound by Clays Ltd, St Ives plc

Hodder & Stoughton policy is to use papers that are natural, renewable
and recyclable products and made from wood grown in sustainable
forests. The logging and manufacturing processes are expected to conform
to the environmental regulations of the country of origin.

Hodder & Stoughton Ltd
338 Euston Road
London NW1 3BH

www.hodder.co.uk

For Lol, Rhoda, Christine, Gillian, Philip.

With special thanks to Alan Wilkinson
and my beautiful wife Ann.

Contents

tHe DA LeS
The Moors
Lealholm
Rosedale
Farndale
Newtondale
Bilsdale
Bransdale
Kirkbymoorside
Thirsk
Helmsley
A 170
Sutton Bank
River Derwent
POLICE
Hovingham
Castle Howard
Whitwell Hill
Kirkham Priory
HAr roG Ate
A64
Stamford Bridge
York
A166

Whitby

Н169

Scarborough

Pickering

Ganton

Filey

Malton The Wolds

Norton

Leavening
The Jolly Farmers

Dri
ffie
LD

Hanging Grimston

As in my previous books about policing in North Yorkshire, all the cases I deal with actually happened. I have changed the names of the characters – police as well as villains – and altered the locations and certain details but only when absolutely necessary to protect people's identities.

Policing procedures are always being updated; what you read here accurately reflects the way we operated at the time each event took place – which in every case is within the last ten years.

Mike Pannett
North Yorkshire
2012

Chapter 1

Doves Might Fly

'There you are, cock-bod.' Soapy watched as the last of the stout poles rolled down the trailer bed and clattered onto the pile. Then he peeled off a glove and held out his hand. 'That'll be thirty smackeroos. And I tell you what, matey, you've got yourself a bargain. Nicely seasoned logs. I can get twice that if I take 'em to town.'

'If this weather keeps up much longer you want to set up a stall in the Saturday market.' I dipped my hand into my hip pocket and felt for my wallet. 'Hang on,' I said. 'I must've left it in the house. Won't be a minute.'

'Well, put your skates on,' he called after me. 'I've no cab on this tractor and I'm frozen half to death as it is.'

It may have been springtime by the calendar, but the weather was still stuck in a wintry rut. We were all fed up with it. An easterly wind had been blowing since the end of March, and the central heating had been working overtime. Ann and I had been lighting the open fire night after night, and now, for the first time since we'd moved into Keeper's Cottage, I'd got to the bottom of our logpile. Normally, I'd expect to replenish our stocks over the summer months. I knew one or two landowners who'd let me go into their woods from time to time and thin out a few ailing trees, but this cold spell had caught me on the hop. Still, it's an ill wind and all that, and it was good to be able to throw a bit of business Soapy's way.

As I prepared my chainsaw he stuffed the money in his jeans and grinned at me. 'Another bit in the kitty,' he said.

'You mean for the wedding?'

He frowned and shook his head. 'That book,' he said, 'is closed.'

'Oh. Sore point, eh?'

'I've told her straight. If there's owt else she wants she can pay for it herself.' He climbed up onto the tractor and fired it up. 'I'm done wi' spending.'

'All sorted then, is it?' I was shouting above the noise of the engine. 'The church, the choir, the cake?'

'You said you were providing the cake, cock-bod. Or was it Walt's sister? And Ann's aunt's doing t'flowers, isn't she?'

'Aye, that's right. You don't need to have any worries there, matey. That's all in hand. What happened about the white doves then?'

As soon as I mentioned them I wished I hadn't. Soapy switched off the engine and slumped in his seat. He sat there with a face like a fiddle. 'Don't talk to me about white doves,' he said. His jaw slackened and his brow was suddenly lined with creases. He looked about ten years older. 'I'm up to here with them.'

'Oh, so you're not sorted after all?'

'Look, Mike, don't get me wrong. She's a grand lass is Becky, and she deserves her special day, but she's pushing me to t'brink with this one. She got it into her head she wanted them bods releasing outside the church and she won't budge. I've tried to tell her, there's more to it than you'd think – and it'll cost a bloody fortune. There's . . . well, there's issues.'

'What, between you and her?'

'No no no – issues to do wi' doves. All sorts. First off there's the weather. You're talking about homing bods here, mate, and they won't fly – leastways, the owners won't let 'em, not if it's foggy, or raining. Or if it gets too late and the light's fading.'

'No, I s'pose not. Might get lost.' I thought for a moment. 'But we're talking late April, mate. High noon you kick off, don't you? Weather'll be perfect. Daffodils, blue skies. You've no worries.'

He ignored me, held out his hand and started counting the points off on his fingers. 'No fog, no high wind, no heavy rain. Then there's distance. I mean, how far have they to fly from t'church, back to their loft? And will they mek it for bedtime? It all has to be accounted for.'

'Blimey. Complicated business.'

Soapy tapped his head. 'Teks a lot of thinking about, my friend. And when you read the small print – cos I've been looking 'em up, don't you worry – there's special clauses for if you're running late.'

'Come again?'

'Well, supposing you're delayed – like if t'bride shows up late, as they have been known to, or t'car breaks down. And don't forget, she's arriving at the church in a 1934 Frazer Nash with a dodgy service history. Why, you fetch them bods back after hours and you've a stonking great surcharge on top. I'm telling you, Mike, it's a bridge too far.'

As he was speaking, I'd been looking into the trees at the top of our drive. A pair of pale doves was perched on a slender branch, billing and cooing. 'Pity you can't—' I began, but Soapy was checking off his list again.

'Then there's are you going to release them yourself or are you having a handler to do it for you? And if it's a handler, who's to provide t'gloves? And what's your dress code for the handler? A dress code, mate. Have you ever heard owt so daft? Does he have to have a special costume?' Soapy reached forward and turned the key in the ignition. 'Mike,' he said, 'I've told you before, mate, if you and that lass of yours ever tie the knot, pop down the registry office, then invite everyone out for a drink when it's all over. Pass round a slice of cake and a few crisps, lad, and slip away quietly.'

'Tell you what,' I said, 'why don't you let me have a think about it. I don't reckon you should be paying through the nose for all this stuff. You need all your spare cash for the honeymoon.'

'No, that's all paid for. I'm saving up for t'stag night now.'

'Aye, that. I'm looking forward to our big night out. When did you say it is?'

'Friday week.'

'In York, right?'

'Aye, and they'd better batten down the hatches, cos we'll tek the place by storm.'

'Soapy,' I said, 'we're going to town for a few drinks. You, me, one or two of your mates, you said.'

'Aye. And Algy boy, and Walter. Should be a fair few of us.' He rubbed his hands and started the tractor up again. 'Out on the town, eh? We'll tear the place apart.'

'Steady on, Soapy lad. I mean, check out the age profile. Who exactly is going to take what apart?'

'Aye well. We can dream.'

'This is true,' I said. 'Anyway, mate, it's very good of you to be treating us all.'

Soapy snorted. 'Dream on, my friend. Dream on.' He'd perked up now that he'd got the white-dove business off his chest. He gave me a wicked grin as he shouted above the roar of the engine. 'It's you lot to treat me, Mike. Me last night as a free man, remember? So – brace yourself. I might just go mental.'

I watched as he drove down the lane, bouncing up and down at the wheel of Algy's old grey Fergie, ducking as the bare branches of the larch trees brushed against his head. Then I started up the chainsaw and sliced through the first of the poles, savouring the sweet scent of fresh ash chippings.

I only had an hour or so before I had to get ready for my late shift, but it was enough time to pile up a decent stack of logs against the side of the garage and wheel a barrowload to the back door. Surely the weather would pick up before we got through this lot. Before I put the saw away I had a look at the huge old log that Ann and I had used as a garden bench these last couple of years. She'd often complained that it was all knotty and uncomfortable, and every chance she got she'd grab the one smooth patch where I'd scooped out a seat for myself before she moved in. I revved up the chainsaw one more time and took out a neat slice, carving a second seat right up against mine. I stood and looked at it for a minute; then it was time to get myself cleaned up and off to work.

The first person I bumped into at the station was Jayne. She'd been down south for a week, and of course the first thing she wanted to know was, had I heard anything?

'You mean about the exams?' I said.

'What else? Couldn't stop fretting about it all the time I was away. I was hoping there'd be something waiting for me when I got back.'

'Be a while yet,' I said. We'd walked through into the parade room to await the briefing. She sat down and started chewing the nail on her middle finger. 'You're not worried, are you?' I said.

'No, not about passing as such. But I want to get a decent mark, don't I?'

'You'll be fine,' I said. 'Anyway, it's part two you wanna be thinking about. All that role-play malarkey. They really put you through the mill. I've heard some right horror stories.'

'Can hardly wait.'

'Course,' I said, 'the good news is that we can apply for acting sergeant.'

'You mean if we pass.'

'When we pass.' Ed and Fordy had come in and sat down.

Chris Cocks would be in any moment. 'Positive, Jayne. Always think positive.'

'That what you gonna do then?'

'What, go for acting sergeant? Depends whether anything comes up in our neck of the woods.'

'You mean you wouldn't move away?'

'Not me. Now that Ann's settled in York.'

'Yeah, I s'pose so.'

'And besides, we're very attached to our little place in the country. Best bit of business we ever did, buying that place.'

'Oh, right. D'you know, I've never even seen it. Wass it like?'

'Secluded. We're tucked away in the woods, a few miles out of town. An island of peace in a sea of turmoil. Wouldn't suit everyone, but . . . Listen, you should drop by some time. Take a look at it. Might even get a cup of tea if you catch us right.'

'See how the other half live, eh?'

'As far as us country folk are concerned, Jayne, it's you townies that's the other half. Nothing but trouble, the lot of you.'

She didn't answer, just carried on chewing her nail. Usually it's easy to wind her up, but she wasn't having any today. 'So,' I said, 'how's that young man of yours, the teacher? Was it him you were visiting?'

'Yeah. Matter of fact he might be coming to live up here.'

'What, moving in with you?'

'Maybe. If he behaves himself. He's applying for a job in York.'

'Blimey. He must be keen.'

'And why wouldn't he be?'

'Oh yeah, fair point. Sure.'

Before she had time to respond Chris came in and started the briefing. It didn't take long. There had been a couple of reports of possible sheep rustling, and the intelligence unit were warning us of an upswing in country house break-ins, possibly the work of an organised gang. Sometimes at briefing you get bombarded with information and you know you're not going to take it all on board. The trick is to make notes, and read them over when you get a bit of downtime. But Chris's style was short and sweet, and for that I was grateful.

Ten minutes later I was on the road. I drove through town and out towards the Wolds, slowing to pass a string of racehorses that were spread out halfway across the road in a ragged line, one or two with riders, the rest being led by the reins. Some people get fed up with having to make way for them day after day. Not me. They're a beautiful sight, a reminder of the area's rich racing tradition.

As I cruised slowly past I wound the window down. It wasn't such a bad day. At least the sun was out, and the fields were greening up, looking drier than they had for months. Here and there the hedges were already splashed with white blossom. I grinned, thinking about the fun and games we'd had last year with the sloe gin. I dropped down to Langton crossroads and carried on towards Birdsall, braking sharply to avoid a gaggle of hens and guineafowl that had wandered across the road from a smallholding.

I was on my way to see a farmer who was worried about travellers camping on his land. They came through every year, he said, parked on the verge alongside his fields, and sometimes left a bit of a mess for him to clear up. He wanted to fence off the strip of grass in the hope that they'd move on elsewhere. Having said that, this fellow was more restrained than some. I've had people dump a row of boulders along the roadside to keep travellers off a possible campsite, or throw up a pile of rooted-out hedging to form a barrier. This was one of those problems that's best tackled before it gets out of hand. I needed to make sure this fellow wasn't about to break the law, or cause unnecessary upset. Maintaining the peace in the countryside is all part of a rural cop's job.

I drove on through Birdsall village and out the other side. It doesn't consist of much now: a disused post office with a letter box in the wall, a telephone kiosk, a village hall and a scattering of houses. Plus, of course, the rather grand and imposing Hall. There's a steep climb out the other side, which takes you right into the beech trees at the top of the Wolds. There I turned left through the woods and started the long slow descent towards Thixendale village. I'd only gone half a mile or so when my mobile rang. I pulled over and dug it out of my pocket.

'Mike Pannett,' I said.

'Oh, thank God I got you, Mike. It's Jim, Jim Stevens.'

'What's up Jim?'

'We've had a vehicle stolen. We're on our way home from the livestock market. Just coming up to Buttercrambe bridge and there's our bloody Land Rover sailing past.'

'Come again?'

'We're on our way home from Murton, right? Pulled in at the bridge, as you do. There's a stream of cars to let through and in amongst them's our Land Rover. Some bugger's nicked it. Two of them inside, far as we could see.'

'You got a look at 'em, did you?'

'Hell, aye. They passed within two feet of us at fifteen miles an hour, cheeky buggers.'

'Right, where are you now, Jim?'

'Why, we're still at the bridge. I didn't want to move in case I lost the signal. You know what it's like out here.'

'And the Land Rover?'

'They shot off towards Gate Helmsley.'

'OK Jim, let's have the details.'

'It's a Discovery; silver-grey, four years old.'

'Strewth, so it's worth a fair bit.'

'We paid twenty thousand for it, Mike. Or let's say the bank did. We owe them most of that, plus interest.'

'Give us the registration number so I can get it circulated

straight away – and what about the occupants? You say you got a good look?'

'One was bearded, dark, maybe forty years old . . .' I could hear Jim's wife in the background, prompting him. 'Aye, and heavy-set. The other was just a youth. Fair hair, long . . . baseball cap . . .' He tailed off. 'No, that's about it, Mike. Sorry.'

'No, that's plenty. Right, you get yourself off home and check things back at the farm. I'll get all this out and see if we can't track them down. Can't have got far.'

I put the phone down and got on the radio. '1015 to control, active message.'

Brian came back straight away. '*Go ahead Mike.*'

'Just had reports of a stolen Land Rover; registration – with two male occupants heading west towards Gate Helmsley. Could you get on to York and Humberside to get units on the A166?'

'*All received Mike, will do.*'

I got my foot down and headed down into Thixendale. I wanted to cut across to Fridaythorpe to cover the 166 just in case they doubled back on themselves. At this stage there was every chance of spotting the stolen vehicle. The suspects would most likely be making their way to York, from where they could go on towards the West Riding. Either that or they could be making for the coast.

But despite the best efforts of a Humberside car, and a unit from York, we drew a blank. Within half an hour I was turning the car around and calling control again. 'I'm on my way to the owners' farm,' I said. 'See what the score is over there.' I could leave the wider area search to the other units.

As I drove back I thought things over. I didn't like the feel of this case, at all. Had whoever nicked the vehicle been watching the farm, checking Jim and Helen's movements? Or had they just got lucky? I dismissed that last thought. The chances of them just turning up at a farmhouse in the middle of the afternoon, finding nobody home and deciding to nick a Land Rover seemed pretty remote. They must've been keeping an eye on the place, and that wasn't a comfortable feeling.

I wasn't far from the farm now. I was having to slow right down. The house was at the end of a long, narrow private road, and spotting the turn-off was always tricky. Now my phone was ringing. I pulled over.

'Mike, been trying to get you.' Jim sounded breathless, distressed.

'What is it, mate?'

'We're back at the house. I can't believe this. They've forced the front door.'

'I see. Have you been inside?'

'Aye, we've had a look around. Can't see anything obvious missing. Helen's taking a closer look. She's right upset. We both are.'

'You will be. But listen, Jim. Tell her not to touch anything if she can avoid it – especially door handles and suchlike. Don't disturb anything either. If there's a mess, leave it for now, OK? And listen,' I said, 'I'm not far off you. So hold tight. I'll be there in just a couple of minutes.'

This didn't sound good at all. It had all the hallmarks of a well worked, professional job. It sounded like a 'two-in-one burglary', as we call them. Breaking into people's homes to steal vehicle keys, then making off with the car. Years ago it used to be a pretty simple affair to steal a car, but nowadays, with sophisticated locking devices, a thief will want the keys. Hence this new type of crime. I got back on the radio and asked control to make a request for Stuart, the scene of crime officer, to attend.

I was making my way down the long track, squinting against the bright sun as I weaved to left and right, dodging the ruts of dried mud, the sunken half-bricks and random stretches of tarmac, straddling the strip of coarse grass that ran down the middle of this typical farm drive. Away to the west the rooks were busy in the woods that made up a part of Jim and Helen's land, putting the finishing touches to their nests. Perhaps a third of a mile ahead of me was the pale brick double-fronted house, overshadowed on one side by a clump of cypresses, to the other by a tall Dutch barn. Theirs was an attractive looking set-up, and you could be forgiven for assuming that they were living off the fat of the land, but the fact is they were just typical North Yorkshire farmers. Always working, never seeming to get their noses in front, and, as they liked to say, 'worth more dead than alive'. They were also recent recruits to my Country Watch scheme. Yes, they ran a decent vehicle, but they needed it, and they paid the bank for the privilege. Banks will always lend money to farmers; it's one of the safest bets in the business. If things go belly up, they've got the best collateral you can have: productive land and a nice big detached house. I always remember what a farmer told me one time; that he was rarely more than a couple of poor harvests away from complete failure. But these are the kind of people who keep farming because they love it, and for no other reason. Sometimes you can't help wondering why they aren't treated with more respect.

I parked in the yard and got out. Jim was there, edging out from the front door, which was hanging at an awkward angle, barely half open. A black and white Border collie was at his heels. 'Now then,' he said. 'Glad you got here.' He looked at me from under a cap pulled low over his eyes, and jerked his head towards the house. 'She's in a bit of a state.'

'Not surprising. You can do without uninvited people tramping around your house, can't you?'

'We couldn't believe it, Mike. Just driving home like that after a morning at the market and there's your blooming Landie coming right at you. Worst of it is, that's the one she likes to take the kids to school in. I mean, there's all sorts of personal stuff in there. Coats, gloves, boots, car seats . . .' He paused as Helen came out to join us.

'Aye, not just ours either. We had a pile of the children's schoolbooks,' she said. 'All their homework. They won't be happy when they come home tonight. Nor will their teachers. Games kit as well. It'll all want replacing.'

I approached the door. It was an old wooden thing and it looked heavy enough, with its black metal studs, but whatever they'd attacked it with they'd managed to pull the hinges clean out of the frame.

'Have you got an alarm system?' I asked as we went through the doorway and into the hall. Helen looked at Jim and Jim looked at the ground. 'Nah,' he said. 'We haven't got one. I mean, who's gonna hear it out here? Besides,' he added, 'the dog always barks the minute anyone comes into the yard.'

'Trouble was he was out with us,' Helen added.

I went outside to look at the door. It only had a single Yale type lock on it. When we went back inside and into the kitchen, I could see that the dresser drawers had been opened, but apart from that the place looked relatively undisturbed.

'Do you think anything's been taken?' I asked.

'Doesn't look like it,' Jim said. 'Not that we've had a proper look around yet. You said not to disturb anything.'

'I did pop upstairs,' Helen said, 'just to check my dressing table. I've a few bits and pieces in there – old jewellery. Nothing too fancy. Sentimental value, mostly.'

'And?'

'No, they haven't touched it. Don't think they've even been up there.'

'Doesn't make sense, does it?' Jim said. 'I mean, breaking in and taking nowt.'

Unless it was a recce, I thought; but I didn't say anything. As well as the car keys theory, there was the possibility that this was the sort of gang who might come back to take anything else that had caught their eye – whether that was from the house or the farm. The fact is, you do get different types of burglars.

As well as the two-in-one thieves, for example, you get those who target residential homes for cash, jewellery and electrical goods. They might even do a total house clearance, although that's not very common. Then you get the ones who target pubs or other non-residential properties: outbuildings, sports clubs, shops, churches and factories. This job didn't seem to fit in with the trend Chris had outlined at briefing.

What struck me as slightly odd in this case was that the house was mostly furnished with fairly nondescript stuff: modern, most of it. There was little that looked to be of any antique value, just a nice big flat-screen TV and a couple of computers. As daft as it seemed I found myself hoping that this was the kind of gang who were only after the vehicle keys.

'Where did you keep the Land Rover?' I asked.

'In there, look.' Jim was at the window pointing across the yard to an open garage. 'Next to the Dutch barn, d'you see?' There was a quad-bike tucked away in the far end.

'Not locked up, then?'

'The garage? No, but we always lock the vehicle, and bring the keys in.'

'And where do you keep them?'

'Over there,' Helen said. 'Just inside the door.' There was a little side window, and on the side of the cupboard next to it a length of wood, maybe nine inches long, with a row of brass hooks on it and various keys hanging from them. Jim followed me outside. 'Plain as day,' I said, pulling a face as I tapped the window with my hand. 'That explains them smashing the door – although they could almost have reached them from the window. Anyway, point is . . . your keys are on display for all the world to see, I'm afraid. You need to sort that out right away. Tuck 'em away somewhere where they can't be spotted.'

'I suppose it was a daft place to put them,' Helen said. 'But you don't think. You want them convenient, don't you?'

I was about to answer when the radio cut in.

'*Control to 1015.*'

'Go ahead, Brian.'

'*Mike, I've got the SOCO on his way. Should be there in a quarter of an hour, over.*'

I turned to Jim and Helen. 'That's to say our scene of crime officer's coming through. Stuart. He's a decent lad, and very good at his job. He'll go over everything with a fine-tooth comb, see if there's any fingerprints, fibres or marks of any kind. If we can find some forensic evidence, it could help us identify the offenders.'

While we waited for Stuart I talked them through a few security pointers. If someone really is determined to break into your house, I told them, they will do so. But they knew that. The object, I said, is to make it as hard as possible for the intruder to gain access. That'll help see off the opportunist, or the amateur. I also pointed out that even for people living in a remote area, having a good alarm system is a great deterrent. It can be linked to an alarm-handling centre, and staff there can alert the police as soon as it's activated. And the criminals, I pointed out, know it.

By the time I'd finished they agreed that they would fit a solid front door with a stout mortise lock, and a set of good-quality window locks, as well as security lights. And, despite the costs involved, they would look at some alarm systems.

'Reckon I may as well put a gate in too,' Jim said, sitting down at the table. 'But I tell you what, it's an expensive business this security lark.'

Stuart had arrived by now and set straight to work. The main area he worked on was around the door. On his hands and knees he used a little brush to apply a greyish powder, then used adhesive tape to lift any fingerprints. It's laborious work, but it suits a fellow like Stuart. He's not the type of chap to be rushed.

While he worked I glanced out at the yard. It was unfenced,

bounded only by the house and outbuildings. 'Where you going to put this gate, Jim?' I asked.

'Along the lane there. There's a sheep-proof fence cuts across it – about a quarter mile from the house, and a cattle grid. I could stick a metal gate across there and put a lock on it. Be a pain in the neck unfastening it every time we go down the lane, like, but . . .'

'Doesn't matter,' Helen said. 'Being broken into once is – well, it's once too many for me.'

'Hel-lo. What's this then?' Stuart said, on his knees by the front door.

'You found something?'

'I have. A nice impression of a shoe print, right on the door. Barely visible but looks about the right height for a kick. I'll take a photograph and then try to get some kind of lift. Won't be brilliant, but you never know.'

'Tell you what we haven't looked at,' I said, turning to Jim. 'Firearms. Where d'you keep your guns?'

'Oh hell. Clean forgot about them.' Jim led me through the kitchen into a passageway that led to the back of the house. 'In here,' he said, opening the door to a little cloakroom under the stairs. He unlocked a steel cabinet and showed me three guns, all neatly stored, the cartridges sitting in a carton on a shelf at the top.

'All as it should be?'

'Aye, thank goodness. Don't want them going missing, do we?'

'All done, gents.' Stuart had come through to join us. He'd completed his survey of the place. 'Not a lot, I'm afraid. Just that footprint. So – time I was on my way.'

'Right,' I said, turning to Jim, 'I'll leave you and Helen to tidy up. Where is she, anyway?'

'On the phone – to her sister, I expect.'

'Right, well, I'll make sure the station knows what's happened, and get it on the briefing. I'll also ring round the Country Watch members. And if the Land Rover turns up, I'll let you know straight away.'

'What d'you reckon?' Jim had followed me out to the car, leaving Helen inside. 'Was it just some opportunist, or are we to expect a return visit?'

I tried to reassure him that it was just the Land Rover they had been after. It was a classic two-in-one burglary, I explained, and I doubted that the thieves would return. I just hoped I was right.

Back at the station I circulated the details of what had happened to Country Watch, filled in a crime report on the computer and submitted a copy to intelligence. It was getting on for six o'clock by now, and time for my break. And I needed to get back to this farmer out at Thixendale before it started to get dark. I grabbed my lunchbox, got in the car and set off towards Leavening. Might as well get a free cuppa along the way.

By the time I'd driven back out to Walter's place the sun was down behind the sycamores and the wind was slicing through my uniform jacket, but there he was, in his vegetable garden, balanced precariously on a long plank, setting out his onions in an immaculately raked bed.

'Bit cold for that sort of work, isn't it?'

He readjusted his line and shifted his plank a foot or so to one side, ready to start another row. 'It has to be done, lad. And me shallots, and t'garlic and such-like.' He stood up and grimaced, holding a hand to his back. 'Should've had these in a few weeks since, but it's been so blinking wet.'

'Well, don't let me stop you, Walt. If you're busy . . . I've not got long.'

'There's just this row to do. Rest of 'em can wait while tomorrow. With a bit of luck I shall have me hands thawed out by then.' He walked along the plank towards me. Go on.

You get yourself inside and put t'kettle on. I'll be with you shortly.'

'Right you are, mate.'

Five minutes later we were sitting at his kitchen table enjoying a brew, and talking about . . . wedding dresses.

'Tek me sister,' Walt was saying. 'When she got wed all she had to buy were the material for her frock. Cost her eleven shillings and sixpence – old money, that is – from that haberdashers in town. 'Tisn't there now, of course. And her mother, as used to be a seamstress, like, she made it up for her on her old treadle sewing machine. And d'you know, she still has that dress in her attic, all folded up wi' tissue paper in a suitcase.'

'That's really interesting, Walt, but what I asked you was, how're we going to get Soapy through this wedding caper without him losing his sanity – and his life savings?'

'Well of course the daft bugger shouldn't have said yes in t'first place, should he?' Walt wrinkled up his nose and sniffed. 'I told you what me dad used to say about marriage, didn't I?'

'You did,' I said, 'several times.' But he took no notice. It was one of his favourite sayings and he loved to repeat it at every opportunity.

'Why give half your food away to get the other half cooked, eh? There's a lot of truth in that, lad.'

'Yeah yeah yeah, but the point is, he's made his mind up. He's getting spliced. And there's no going back. By his reckoning he entered into the agreement voluntarily, too. I just want to see that he doesn't put himself in the poorhouse – permanently. Thing is, he's provided every last item Becky's asked him for, all bar one thing.'

'Aye? And what's that?'

'He still hasn't managed to sort out any white doves.'

'Can't they have pheasant?' Walt asked. 'I've plenty pheasants in my freezer. He could have 'em casseroled. They go further if you stew 'em up, y'know.'

'Walt, we are not talking wedding breakfasts here. We are talking about snow-white birds to be released outside the church – as you well know. A symbol of beauty, purity and hope. So enough of your funny stuff, mate. It's time to put our thinking caps on. White doves. What we gonna do, eh? Cos I've told him not to worry. Told him you and me'll fix it.'

Walt just sat there and said nothing for a minute or two. 'That means me, doesn't it?' he said. Then he scratched his chin and screwed up his face. 'Well,' he began, then fell silent again. The only sound was the ticking of the clock, and Tess's tail thumping against the side of the dresser when she caught me looking at her.

After a few minutes Walt stood up. 'Aye, it's a proper poser,' he said, 'but I'll tell you what I'll do. I'll have a word wi' Gideon.'

'Gideon who has pigs and turkeys – and had a hernia?'

'Aye, him. He's always kept a few birds in an aviary, like. Wouldn't be surprised if he has what we're after.'

'You reckon so?'

'I do. He used to be a bit of pigeon fancier, and I remember he bought an old dovecote at one of them country house sales. I'll see what he reckons. Leave it to me, lad. If Soapy's daft enough to promise that lass of his . . . well, I s'pose it's up to them as care for her to give her what she wants.'

'Oh, cheers Walt. I know it's a big ask, and – well, tell you the truth I'm surprised Soapy didn't tell her it was a non-runner, but he wants to do his best for her. Desperate to please. You should've seen him when he came round this morning. Right wound up, he was. Good job he has his big night out to take his mind off things for a bit. By the way, you are coming, aren't you?'

'What, on his bachelor party?'

'Yeah. Friday week.'

Walt shook his head. 'Thought he were a North Yorkshire lad,' he said.

'He is. Born and bred. What're you saying?'

'Why can't he have his night out in North Yorkshire, then?'

'It's in York, Walt. What's the matter with that?'

'I don't reckon to go outside of the North Riding, that's what.'

'Don't be daft, mate. York's part of the North Riding, surely?'

Walt shook his head once more, and folded his arms across his chest. 'You go and read your history books, lad. It's never been one of t'three Ridings. It's always been the City and County of York. That's what they taught us in school, and I've never forgotten it.'

'I'm not sure about that, Walt. There's been a few changes since you were in short pants – like brave people venturing out on a night further afield than the little house at the bottom of the yard, for a start. Look, this is our mate's stag night. Think yourself lucky he isn't having it in Prague. Cos that's where they're going these days, y'know. Budapest, Vilnius, anywhere you can get a cheap flight and a decent drop of beer.'

'I've made me position clear. I'll not budge.'

'Are you serious?'

'I am.'

'I don't believe you. Or is it your age?'

'How's that?'

'Why, it's made you come over all cantankerous. Not to mention plain wrong. I know – I'm dead sure – you're wrong on this one and I'm going to show you. You've been overtaken by events, mate. And I'll prove it. Now then.'

'You do your worst, young feller. I'm not budging out of North Yorkshire and that's that. I don't see why we just can't go down the Spotted Cow in Malton. Nice and handy, and it'll be a sight cheaper.'

'Come on, Walt. Where's you sense of adventure?'

'Adventure lad, adventure? I don't need adventure at my age. Every day I get out of bed and mek it down them stairs, that's adventure enough for a feller my age.'

'I seem to remember you enjoyed that little expedition to York races not so many moons ago. Now then.'

Walt sat down in his chair and pushed his cap back, exposing his forehead. 'That were different, Mike.'

'Different?'

'That were a special occasion. And, more important – it was outside of the City walls. D'you see, lad?'

I didn't, but I hadn't the stomach for an argument. I grabbed my coat and left without another word. I don't often fall out with Walt, but there are times when he digs his heels in and won't listen to reason, and it makes me mad.

As I left I shouted over my shoulder, 'You're wrong, Walt, and I'm going to prove it.'

Chapter 2

The Micklegate Run

For its size, the bird seemed very light in my hands, maybe three or four pounds at most. Seeing the white head-feathers and the yellow around its beak, I had a shrewd idea as to what it was, and once I'd opened one of the wings I was sure. Its wingspan was a full three feet, and there indeed, on the underside and towards the outer end, was the broad splash of white feathers. Had I seen it in flight, I dare say the forked tail would have given me a clue, but then again maybe not: I've never been the best at identifying birds on the wing.

'Aye,' Baz said, reaching out to stroke the feathers, 'it's a handsome bird is the red kite. We've started seeing one or two of them these last couple of years. Since they started that release scheme.'

I was glad that Baz had called me out to his place. I'd heard about the red kites that were being released from locations such as Harewood, over near Leeds, and I'd heard one or two comments from gamekeepers about the advisability or otherwise of their reintroduction, but until now I'd not encountered one close up. All the more sad, then, that this one was dead.

'Where did you say you found it?'

Baz pointed to a thick thorn hedge across the far side of a

field sown with barley. 'It was under there. Can't have been dead long or something would've been at it.'

'What d'you reckon killed it?'

He didn't hesitate. 'Poison,' he said. 'That's the most likely.'

'But why?'

'Well Mike, if I wanted to be controversial I'd say that any bird with a hooked beak and a set of claws – gamekeepers don't like it. There now.' He looked at me, his mouth set in a straight line.

'Blimey.'

'It's only my personal view, mind. You speak to a keeper and he may tell you otherwise. In fact, I'm sure he will.' He placed the dead bird back on a cardboard tray and handed it to me. 'These birds don't do any harm. They're scavengers mostly. Eat carrion. I s'pose they might take the odd chick if they got the chance, and maybe that's why they aren't popular. There's a lot of value tied up in young pheasants and partridges and suchlike.'

'So why's it being reintroduced?'

''Cos it belongs here, Mike. That's one reason. It's native, like you and me. And – unlike you and me – it's beautiful, isn't it? So you could say there's a bit of sentiment behind the whole thing. Not that everyone feels that way, as you'll find out if you raise the subject in the pub.'

'So you think it might have been deliberately poisoned?'

Baz held his hands up. 'Listen Mike, I'm saying nowt. It could just as easily have eaten a rat that's been poisoned. But do you call that accidental? I don't. Anybody as lays down poison for rodents should be taking their responsibilities seriously. They've a duty to make sure the bait can't be taken by anything other than a rat – and they should make damned sure to pick up the dead ones, shouldn't they?' He sighed. 'Then again, it could as well have been a dead rabbit, laced with insecticide and left there for a scavenger to find.'

'That's nasty, that is.'

'It is. But you know, and I know: it happens. And of course it's completely' – he looked at the dead bird – 'completely indiscriminate.'

'Well, if it is a case of poisoning, that's a serious business. I'll need to get a postmortem carried out by a vet. I need to know one way or another.'

I made a search of the immediate area to see whether I could find anything linked with the bird's death. The trouble was, the kite could have flown some distance before the poison had taken effect – if, that is, it had in fact been poisoned in the first place.

I laid the bird in the back of my van and placed it in a clear plastic evidence bag. It really did seem a sad ending for such a beautiful creature. I closed the door and said, 'Well, I'd better take it back to Malton and get it preserved. Thanks for calling me out, Baz. I appreciate it.'

'Aye well, I'm all for eradicating pests, but this isn't a pest. In my book, what you're looking at is wanton killing. Just for the sake of it.'

As I drove to the station I cast my mind back to what I'd been taught on my wildlife course, four or five years ago now. The red kite had been persecuted for long enough before it was effectively wiped out in Britain. That was well over a hundred years ago, nearer two hundred. That much I knew. And I also knew that a number of pairs had been raised in captivity and released in selected areas over the past few years – although this bird lacked the identifying tag that you'd expect to find on one of them. I was also aware that the red kite has greater protection than almost any other bird. Not only is it an offence to kill or harm them, it's even an offence to disturb them when they're in or near their nests. If my memory served me right, the penalties allowed under the law are pretty severe: a fine of up to £5,000 or a six-month prison sentence. All you have to do is secure a conviction.

As Baz had suggested, opinions on the release scheme vary. Birdwatchers love to see them – and claim that they do a useful job, as any carrion species does, in cleaning up dead carcasses and so on. Other people tend to lump them in with vermin, and treat them accordingly. Well, I'd have to let the experts decide what the cause of death was in this case, and take it from there – although God knows, the chances of finding the culprit were pretty slim.

Back at the station I placed the dead bird in the freezer. I then entered the incident on the computer. I marked it as 'no press'; the last thing we wanted at this stage was to have details of the find circulated by the media. That could wait until I had a few more facts at my disposal. And that wouldn't happen today. I'd just about got to the end of my shift and I wanted to be away home. I'd call the vet tomorrow, see when I could get him to have a look at it.

As I drove home I was thinking about what the next day had in store. It was going to be a long one: an early turn followed by a few domestic chores and, after that, as I reminded Ann when she got home, Soapy's big night out.

'You do realise I'm on duty tomorrow evening, don't you?' she said. 'Late turn, through to about two o'clock?'

I was only half listening. I hadn't taken Henry out for his walk yet and it would be dark before long.

'What's the problem?' I asked, clipping Henry's chain to his collar. He made one more leap towards a cock pheasant that had wandered into the garden and was browsing among the gooseberry bushes. 'You weren't thinking of joining us, were you?'

'What, me? On a blokes' stag do? Wandering round town as they relive their youth? I don't think so, Mike.'

'Hey, that's a bit harsh.'

'OK,' she laughed, 'present company excepted. But my point is that I do not want you lot getting in any kind of trouble.'

'Us? At our age? Who's gonna cause trouble?'

'Look, you know very well who I mean. Algy, for one: daft as a brush once he's got a drink inside him. And Soapy: doesn't even need a drink to start acting the goat. As for Walter: well, he should learn to keep his opinions to himself. Listen, Mike, the last thing I want is one of you lot being brought in to the cells.'

'Oh hell,' I said. 'Walter. Nearly forgot about him. I need to drop by his place. I've some news for him.'

'I thought you said he wasn't coming? Something about the price of drinks in York?'

'I think that is a factor, yes. But it goes deeper than that. Anyway, trust me. We'll have a couple of beers, give the lad a spin around a club or two, then whistle up the cab before he starts getting too frisky. And talking of frisky, this dog needs his run. Now. See you in a bit.'

Henry was soon pulling me down the lane, pausing only to dive into the ditch now and then in pursuit of sounds and smells that were off my radar. We made our way out onto the road and started climbing the hill. It wasn't as cold as it had been lately, and the wind had dropped. It was a calm evening, still just light, with a perfect half moon poking through a veil of mottled cloud. Who knows, I thought, maybe spring's on the way at last.

At Walt's place I walked round to the back, opened the door and called out to him. No answer. I tied Henry to the cast-iron downpipe and stepped inside. The place was almost in darkness; just the glow of his fire reflected off the low ceiling in the hallway.

'In you come, lad. Don't be shy.' He was sat in his old armchair, leaning forward towards the hearth, his wire-framed spectacles on his nose, a magnifying glass in one hand and a copy of the *Countryman* in the other.

'Why don't you put the light on?' I said.

'You want to ask t'electricity board about that,' he said. 'It's them that keeps putting t'price up. Besides, I allus reckon when it's too dark to read it's too late to be up.'

'Yeah, I remember. You didn't like me burning my bedside lamp when I lodged here, did you, you old skinflint. Anyway, I've told you before, you want to get yourself a set of them low-energy bulbs, mate. Burn less and last longer.'

He snorted. 'I've seen the price of 'em, lad. Beggars belief.'

'Yeah, but the idea, Walt, is they don't keep popping – so you get your money back in the long run. The clue's in the name: long life. Get it?'

'There you are. That's what I'm talking about.'

'Walt, you're at it again, mate. Talking in riddles.'

'Think on, lad. I mean, what happens if I fill me under-stairs cupboard with these fancy bulbs you're on about and then – and then I pop me clogs? What then? It'd be a proper waste of money, wouldn't it?' He tutted and shook his head, as if he'd just had to explain some blindingly obvious point of economics to a schoolboy. 'No,' he continued, shuffling his seat nearer to the hearth, 'I've enough old-fashioned ones under the stairs there to see me out. We can't live for ever, y'know. Leastways, nobody has yet.'

'Have it your own way,' I said. 'Now listen, I'm not here to argue about cost-effectiveness. I'm here to put you right on another matter.'

'Oh aye?'

'Aye. Geography. And to tell you you are coming to York for Soapy's stag night.'

'I've told you, lad. I don't venture outside t'North Riding.' He sighed, looked into the dying embers of his fire and said, wistfully, 'Otherwise, d'you know, I might quite like a trip out.'

'Aha! Well, that's where I've done you a big, big favour.' I went and switched the light on, then sat down and put my hand in my pocket. 'He may not deserve it,' I said, 'but Walter shall go to the ball.'

He leaned forward and peered suspiciously at the notebook I now had in my hand. 'What's that in aid of?'

'I have been doing some digging, my friend. Research. I have been on the telephone, running your problem past a young lady at York Tourism.'

Walt snorted. 'Tourism? Bloody waste of taxpayers' money, always trying to rake in more visitors. What do they want tourists for? Place is crowded enough. From what I've seen on *Look North*, why, they haven't room to breathe.'

I ignored his comment. 'And not only that,' I said, 'but I have also consulted the Yorkshire Ridings Society. And don't tell me they're a waste of money . . .' I waited for a reaction, but there was none. Walt was looking at the light I'd switched on, and frowning. I carried on, holding my notebook close to it to get the full benefit of the 40-watt bulb. 'The Yorkshire Ridings Society,' I read. 'You'll like this bit, mate: actively working to protect the integrity of Yorkshire. How about that, eh?'

'They blooming want to, lad, else it'll disappear – like Rutland did, aye, and Westmoreland. They used to be counties, y'know, before they got swallowed up.' He put his magnifying glass down. 'Go on, then, what did them Ridings lot have to tell you that I can't?'

'That you're both right and wrong. York is indeed a separate entity.'

'Aye, I said so, didn't I? Everything within them bar walls.'

'But,' I let the word hang for a moment while he poked the fire and stirred up a few flames from the last of the coals. 'But – your North Riding extends all the way to Doncaster.'

'Does it now?'

'It does, since reorganisation. And do you know what that means?'

'Higher rates, I shouldn't be surprised.'

'It means, Walter, that it encircles York completely. You, my old mate, can come for a night out in York, to celebrate Soapy's upcoming nuptials, and never actually step outside the boundaries of the North Riding.'

'You mean, more like I step into a great gaping hole in the middle of it?'

'If you want to put it that way, yes.' I put my notebook away. 'Listen, it's a compromise. Saving face if you like.'

He didn't speak at first, just gave a little growl as if he was on the verge of making a painful decision. Finally he said, 'I'll mull it over. Let you know.'

'I'm taking that as a yes. We've a minibus all set up. We'll call by for you about six thirty or seven.'

I left Walt in the middle of another growl and set off down the hill with Henry pulling me all the way. 'Go on then,' I said, as I loped down the hill with giant strides, 'Sooner I get you home the better.' I'd picked up a nice bottle of red on my way home from work, and laid a fire. Ann and I were looking forward to a rare night home together.

The first voice I heard when I walked into the station at a quarter to seven next morning was Jayne's.

'I dunno. You country bumpkins. You go out with yer guns, you pop off at anything that moves . . .'

'Morning Jayne.'

'And if you dunno what to do with it you shove it in the bleeding freezer.'

'Except that that is not a gamebird, Jayne.'

'Well if it's not a gamebird, what is it then?'

'That bird is a parrot Jayne. In fact it is a Norwegian Blue Parrot.'

'Very funny, Mike. Very funny.'

'It is also, as you can see, dead. Lifeless. Kaput. It is no more.'

'Yeah, but dead or not I don't wanna come face to face with it when I'm putting me DNA samples in cold storage. Frightened the bleeding life outta me, that – that pterodactyl or whatever it is.'

'It's a red kite, Jayne. A rare and beautiful species. Nearly went the way of the pterodactyl, of course – but that was a bit before your time. Before mine, even. Anyway, it's off to the vet's shortly.'

'The vet's? Bit late for that, innit?'

'No flies on you, are there? Listen, joking aside, I need to know how it died. I've a strong suspicion it was poisoned. And I am not happy about it.'

'Neither's the bloody bird by the look of it.'

'Anyway, Jayne, you're out and about with me this morning. So no more tasteless jokes about endangered species, eh?'

Once we were out on patrol Jayne quietened down. She was still fretting about the exams, even to the extent of going over individual questions and telling me what she'd put for an answer.

'Listen,' I said, 'however many times you go over it you aren't going to change anything. Just put it out of your mind. The sooner you manage to forget about it, the sooner the results'll come plopping through your letter box.'

'Yeah, but . . . this is important to me.'

'And? Listen, don't think it's not important to me, Jayne. There's a lot at stake here – for both of us.'

'Yeah, but . . .'

I waited, but she didn't say anything more. I was starting to think that there was something serious troubling her, but I decided I'd better not push it. We went out along the A64, stopped in at the garage for a coffee and a natter with Jack, then made our way slowly back through Foxholes, Weaverthorpe and the Luttons, before heading up onto the top of the Wolds. I was explaining to her where Keeper's Cottage was, and was on the point of taking a ride down there, when the call came from control.

'*Reports of a man behaving erratically in a house in Norton . . .*'

I got on the radio right away. 'Yeah Brian, show me and Jayne dealing. I can be there in seven or eight minutes.'

As we sped down the hill towards town we got a few more details.

'*It's a semi-detached house, Mike. Owners live downstairs and the lodger has the upstairs. Twenty-two years old, no previous history of violence or drug abuse, but he's known to have minor mental-health issues. He's throwing furniture out onto the stairs and shouting, causing a general disturbance.*'

We arrived to find a middle-aged couple on the lawn in front of the house, looking at an upstairs window.

I got out of the car. 'Hello,' I said. 'What's going on? Was it you that called us?' As I spoke there was a loud crash from inside the house, and a muffled shout.

The man spoke first. 'He's never been any trouble before, but he suddenly started banging and crashing. Woke us up about eight o'clock and it just went from one thing to another.'

His wife cut in. 'Then he started throwing things down the stairs. We had to get out – for our own safety.' She was holding a thick cardigan tight around her. I noticed that they were both in their slippers.

'Right,' I said, 'is his accommodation self-contained? I mean, can he lock himself in?'

'Yes. Has his own key. What he's doing is opening the door at the top of the stairs, hurling stuff out and then locking himself back in again.'

'And these front windows, upstairs, are they his?'

'Yes, he has half of the top floor. It's converted into a flat. Single bedroomed.'

'Has he done anything like this before?'

It was the woman who answered. 'No. That's what took us by surprise. He's really quiet most of the time. Keeps himself to himself. Just the odd visit from his family. This is – I mean, it's totally out of the blue. He's on medication, you see . . .'

'Medication?'

'Well, he has some – you know, mental-health issues. But the tablets he takes – they keep things under control.' She hunched her shoulders as something crashed against the window. 'He's normally such a nice lad.'

'I see. Has he ever turned violent before?'

She looked at her husband, who shook his head. 'Not that we know of. He's lived here for six months – coming up to seven – and we've never had any problems with him.'

'What's he called?'

'Darren.'

'OK, thanks.' I moved a couple of steps away from them and looked around for Jayne. 'Oh, good lass.' She was standing behind me, putting her body armour on. 'I think we'll have to go in and try and speak to him,' I said. 'See what we can do. Gimme a moment to get me armour on. And could you do some checks? Update control with what we've got?'

As soon as I started putting my protection on I spotted the curtain in the upper window being moved to one side. I cupped my hands and shouted up.

'Darren? You there, Darren?'

Nothing. This is the problem with a call like this. You don't know how people will react to seeing the police, and you need a few answers. Has he stopped taking his medication? What state of mind is he in? Will he be violent to the police? Will he try to self-harm? Has he got any weapons? What I needed to do was get a feel for the situation, make an assessment, and try to establish what resources might be required to bring the incident to a safe conclusion. If I could speak to him – and get him to speak back – that would help.

The major factor in this sort of situation for a rural force is, naturally, manpower. It's not like it would be in a city, not at all. Getting properly equipped and trained officers to the scene to deal with things safely could take well over an hour – and in that time who knows what the individual might do.

I called up again. 'Darren, I just need to speak to you.' Still nothing.

'OK Jayne, you ready? Let's see what we're up against, shall we?'

I approached the front door of the house and opened it.

We entered the hallway and slowly started up the carpeted stairs, as quietly as we could. 'Keep your wits about you,' I said, 'just in case he confronts us.' Jayne gave me a nod, and I noticed she had her CS spray at the ready. As we turned the corner towards the top of the stairs we saw the landing was littered with various items: a broken plate, a couple of cushions, a stool, a computer keyboard, a deflated football. A pair of tracksuit bottoms was draped over the banister rail, along with a dirty towel. But the biggest object was a wardrobe. Somehow Darren had managed to shove it out of the flat, and it was now lying across the top of the stairs just outside his door. 'We need to get this out the way,' I whispered. But just as Jayne and I leaned into it and started shoving, there was a loud crash from outside and the sound of breaking glass.

'Bloody hell, Mike!'

I followed Jayne down to the front step just in time to see a television roll over and come to rest on the lawn. I looked up at the window above the front door. He'd hurled the TV straight through it. Shards of glass were lying all over the grass and on the concrete path.

'Darren!' I shouted. 'Come on, we need to speak to you.' I turned to Jayne. 'We're going to have to go very carefully here. We don't want anybody getting hurt.' A small group of onlookers had gathered outside the gate. 'Take care of that lot, will you.' Jayne went to ask them to keep away from the premises for their own safety. I turned to the householders. 'Just give me an idea of the layout up there, will you?'

'Well, it's like a conversion. That there's the bedroom.' The woman was pointing up to the broken window. Then there's a living room that's just to the back of it. And at the other side he has a little bathroom.'

'And is there a separate kitchen?' I asked.

She looked puzzled. 'No, but he has a sort of kitchenette at the back of the living room.'

'I see.' Details like that are vital if you're going to enter a place and confront someone in a disturbed state of mind, because the kitchen is the most dangerous room in any house. Knives, implements, heavy pots, kettles full of hot water: I've had all of those – and more – hurled at me or brandished in my face. You soon learn to enter with extreme caution.

'And you're quite sure he's alone?' I asked. 'Wouldn't have anybody up there with him?'

'I've not seen anyone going up.' The woman turned to her husband. 'Have you?'

He shook his head. 'No, he never brings anyone home – not that we know of, at any rate.'

'OK, thanks.' I took out my radio. '1015 to control.'

'*Go ahead, Mike.*'

'It looks like we have a young man who's suffering from some kind of breakdown. Could you get some other units down here with shields, just in case – over.'

'*All received. Have already got Ed en route. Will get Fordy to grab some shields and make his way.*'

Jayne was back at my side. 'You ready?' I asked her. She nodded. 'Right, let's go back in, I want us to make contact with him. We can use the wardrobe as protection until we get the shields.'

As soon as we entered the hallway we could hear shouting from the floor above. 'It's gotta stop, it's gotta stop.' He kept repeating the words, and hurling heavy objects about, kicking the door, then shouting again. 'It's gotta stop now or there's gonna be trouble. Big trouble. It ends right now.'

We were at the top of the stairs. We'd managed to ease the wardrobe to one side, leaving us with an easy escape route should we need it and at the same time offering us some protection should Darren come bursting out.

'What now?' Jayne was looking at me, waiting for the lead. Everything had gone quiet inside the flat.

'Whatever we do, we go carefully. What we don't want is him harming himself. That's probably the biggest danger right now.'

I reached out to the door, which had a Yale lock and a round ceramic handle. I put my hand on it, turned it and pushed gently, but it didn't budge. I heard Jayne swear under her breath. 'Well, he wasn't gonna leave it open, was he?' I whispered.

I leaned forward and put my ear to the door. I could hear footsteps, and the guy muttering to himself. I called out, 'Are you OK in there? Everything all right Darren?'

It went quiet again straight away. I stepped back from the door. Several seconds passed and I was about to call out again when Darren answered. 'Go away. I've had enough. Just leave me in peace, will you?' He seemed to be some distance away, probably in an inner room, but it was hard to tell. In any case, he didn't say anything else.

'I don't like this,' Jayne said.

'You mean the silence?'

She nodded. 'You wonder what he's up to. Just hope he doesn't kick off again.'

I looked at my watch. 'How much longer before those shields get here?'

'What if he's got a weapon?' Jayne's voice was a whisper, but I held up my hand. There was every chance that our man could be pressed up against the door, listening. I heard a sudden rattle that seemed to come from just the other side. It sounded like someone opening a bottle of pills. I looked at Jayne, who pulled a worried face. She'd heard it too.

Then I heard, quite clearly, the sound of a match being struck against a box. It was so close I could hear it flare. What the hell was he up to?

Next came a sudden hissing noise, prolonged, loud and steady. I raised an enquiring eyebrow. Jayne mouthed the word, 'Gas?'

At times like this you simply have to make a decision. If that was gas, and the rattle was a box of matches . . . Even as I took three steps back across the landing I was torn between breaking in to rescue him and retreating in order to save ourselves. Were we about to walk in on an explosion? Then I thought about what would happen if we backed off. We'd have to set up protective cordons around the property, clear the whole area, evacuate the neighbouring houses, and get the fire brigade and ambulance services down sharpish. It would be a right going-on. Followed by a blizzard of forms to fill in.

No, my mind was made up. While I stood there deliberating, this youth could be sitting there trying to blow the whole place to kingdom come – and all three of us with it. My heart racing, I turned to Jayne. 'I reckon we go in.' Jayne nodded. I stepped forward, leaned right back, and gave the door an almighty kick.

It flew open, slamming against the wall.

The lad – he barely looked eighteen – was sitting on the floor with a roll-up in his mouth, a huge plastic bottle of cola in one hand, and with the other he was dabbing himself down with a paper towel. When he saw us he gave the lid a twist, allowing the last of the gas to escape with a quiet hiss, then put the open bottle to his mouth and took a huge gulp from it.

I stepped over a pile of bedding, CDs and kitchenware and stood over him. He sat still for a moment looking at the cola bottle, then carried on dabbing his T-shirt, as if all this was the most natural thing in the world.

Whatever had fuelled the lad's rage and caused him to wreck

the place, it was all burned up. On some occasions with mental illness the very sight of a uniform can inflame the situation. But not this time. The lad sat there, limp, hunched, weary. He seemed barely interested in the fact that two uniformed police officers had kicked down his door and entered his home. He was more concerned at having spilled the cola down his front.

I walked through into the kitchen area, leaving Jayne to watch over the lad. I picked my way through a litter of pots, pizza boxes, dirty cutlery and clothes. I knew I'd better check, to be safe. On the stove was a saucepan with a spoonful of dried-up baked beans in the bottom, and beside it an empty can. The cooker was electric. There seemed to be no gas in the place.

The question now was, what to do with Darren? Thankfully he was calm – although for how long was anybody's guess. Clearly the lad was unwell. Our powers under the Mental Health Act, section 136, refer to people who are 'a danger to themselves or others in a public place.' This lad was clearly in need of help, but he wasn't in a public place. Therefore we had limited options and had to look at the alternatives. Whatever the law said, though, he wasn't fit to be left on his own. That much was clear. And we couldn't leave him with the couple whose house he lodged in. The way forward, as I saw it when I gave it some thought, was the angle of damage to property. We would formally arrest him for causing criminal damage. Then, when we got him back to the station, we could make a proper assessment of his state of mind. This way everybody would have a little time to think.

Darren put up no resistance. He didn't even argue, and for that I was mightily relieved. We took him back to Old Maltongate, where Jayne booked him into custody while I called out a doctor to examine him.

After the tension of an encounter like that what follows is, as often as not, a huge anticlimax. It's all about procedure, routine. But even before that there's the waiting. The doctor in this case took two hours to arrive, but it can often take longer. By the time she showed up we'd conducted a strip-search of the prisoner. Nobody likes that, least of all the officers who have to conduct it. But it's important to make quite sure that someone in a fragile mental condition, like this young man, isn't concealing anything with which he might harm himself. People who wish to do themselves damage can be unpredictable, often furtive and devious. They feel better if they have the knife or needle or whatever it is to hand, so they'll conceal it, often very cleverly. And as quiet as they might be upon being brought into custody, there's nothing to say they might not sit in a cell for a few hours and then decide they'd be better off dead. You don't take chances.

But this lad was clean. We brought him a cup of tea and left him to himself while we waited for the doctor, but his parents arrived from Scarborough before she got to us. They were saddened by his condition but not particularly surprised by what had happened. They told us that he'd left home and gone to live on his own when they all felt that his medication was working and he was more settled. They were pleased that he was able to live an independent life; previously, he'd been in and out of hospital, but had then been put on medication to control his moods. This possibly accounted for his landlords' assessment that they'd always found him to be a pleasant, quiet young man – and why they'd been so shocked at this outbreak of erratic behaviour.

I went to the cell and asked Darren about his medication. Was there something at the flat that he should be taking? He told me that, yes, he had been on something, but that he'd been feeling much better so he'd decided to stop. He reckoned he was cured. As the doctor later pointed out to us, that's the conclusion a lot of patients come to. However, it was her opinion, following a full consultation with the mental health team, that for his own safety the lad needed to be sectioned under the Mental Health Act.

He was taken to Cross Lanes Hospital, in Scarborough. Normally that would mean another job for us – escorting him down the A64 – but in this instance we were grateful for a brilliant ambulance crew. Often in situations where someone has been violent, they will insist on a police officer travelling in the back of the ambulance just in case of a problem. This team, however, were happy to take Darren on their own.

With him on his way to hospital we liaised with social services and got them to call on the landlords. They would have to make a decision as to whether they were happy to take him back in.

Before we knocked off, Jayne and I had a cuppa and a quick debrief with Chris Cocks. We talked about our breaking the door down and how big a risk it could have been. Also the massive relief of finding out it had been Darren opening his fizzy drink that we'd heard and not, as we'd first thought, gas. It was quite funny to look back on, and we all had a laugh about it, but at the time obviously we didn't know, and it could have been very serious. Things had worked out well in the end though, and we were mightily relieved we hadn't been blown up; that is, as Cocksy remarked, always a bonus.

Just before I left I had one more job I needed to attend to. I called one of the vets who I liaise with on a regular basis, and arranged to go round to see him with the red kite. He would be able to identify the cause of death and, if it had indeed been poisoned, give me a statement.

By the time I'd done that it was almost four, and I needed to be getting ready for the big night out. It was a lovely afternoon now, and at last the temperature was climbing. As I drove up to the cottage the grass – which I'd hoped to cut that afternoon – had that bright April sheen on it, the daffodils were all in bloom, the buds on the sycamores were swelling, and somewhere up in the trees a woodpecker was hammering away. Henry was at the gate of his little run, leaping up and down. 'Yeah yeah, gimme a chance to get my boots on,' I said.

I opened the back door and there on the mat was the usual clutter of junk mail and a couple of what looked like bills. I picked up a white envelope. It was addressed to us both, and handwritten in pink ink. I carefully opened it and read the contents. The paper was thick and somehow interwoven with dried rose petals. It was our invitation to Soapy and Becky's wedding. Very nice, I thought, turning it over in my hand and sniffing the exquisite perfume. No wonder you're always skint, Soapy lad.

Not surprisingly, I was in high spirits when the people-carrier came up the drive at half-past six. Soapy was already on board, along with Algy and a couple of his other mates. And as we drove up the hill there was Walter, standing outside his house in his tweed suit and trilby, a pale brown mackintosh folded neatly over his arm, his old leather brogues gleaming in the last of the sunlight.

'Bloody hell,' Soapy shouted out to him from the open window, 'this is the Micklegate run, cock-bod, not a charabanc ride to Filey!'

'Somebody has to maintain standards, young man. In my day when you visited the big city you made a bit of an effort.' Walt climbed into his seat. 'None of this jeans and T-shirt nonsense.' He patted his jacket pocket. 'Eh, packed me toothbrush, lad. Just in case.'

'In case what?' I said.

'In case I have to stay over. You cross over the borders of the North Riding, lad, and who knows what might befall you.'

I nudged Soapy. 'Aye, and I hope this young man's remembered to bring his wallet. That's if you've any money left after paying for those wedding invitations. They must've cost you a fortune, mate.'

'Only the best for my Becky. Well that's what she told me, any road. More to the point,' he said, feeling around in his trouser pocket, 'Have you got one of these? That's the question.'

'A tie? What would I want a tie for?'

'To get into t'clubs, mate. Look law-abiding and respectable.'

'Soapy,' I said, 'I don't know when you last went clubbing, but that rule went out with flared trousers and tank-tops.'

We made it to town in good time, got our driver to drop us just outside the city walls, then considered the challenge ahead.

'Right, lads,' said Soapy. 'The Micklegate Run. Eight pubs, a pint in each, and then' – he rubbed his hands and smacked his lips – 'we hit the clubs and get after them lasses.'

'No no no,' I said. 'What you want is one of these.' I handed everybody one of the stag-night passports I'd picked up in the stationers in Malton marketplace.

Algy laughed. 'Passports, old boy? So we're off to Prague after all, are we?'

'You needn't think I'm leaving t'country,' Walt said. 'I never bargained for no foreign travel.'

'It's all right, lads. Calm down and let me explain. What you do is get a drink from as many different countries from around the world as you can, then mark them all up on your passport. The one that's travelled to the most countries wins.'

'Aye, but what's the prize?'

'There's no prize, Soapy. You just do it for the satisfaction, the glory, the . . .'

'For the sheer hell of it, old chap. That what Mike's saying.'

'Right on, Algy!' Soapy was loving this, unlike Walter, who scowled darkly and said, 'You won't catch me supping owt that ain't brewed in God's own county.'

'Suit yourself, cock-bod,' Soapy said, 'but this could be my last night of freedom. I shall be globetrotting. It's a cracking idea, Mike.'

'Anyway,' Algy said, 'there's no reason why we can't still pay a call at all of these delightful establishments, and just have whatever takes our fancy.'

'That's sorted then,' I said. 'Right lads, best foot forward. I can feel some German lager coming on for starters.'

By the time we'd visited the first three pubs we were getting the hang of it – even Walter. After two pints of John Smith's and one of Black Sheep he announced he was ready to cast aside his inhibitions and go Continental.

'You sure, Walt?' Soapy asked him. 'Cos it's my round, cock-bod, and I reckon I've just the drink to send you somewhere you've never been.'

'In for a penny in for a pound, lad. Do your worst, I say.'

Soapy disappeared to the bar and lost himself in the scrum.

'Why, you've loosened up,' I said, nudging Walter in the ribs. 'You go on like this you might end up having a good time despite yourself.'

'That's the trouble wi' you youngsters,' he replied. 'You can't believe us old 'uns know how to let our hair down. You didn't invent fun, y'know. It's been around since before my time, and . . .' He paused in mid-sentence, and stared ahead of him. There was Soapy, weaving a path back to us with what looked like a smouldering test tube in each hand.

'Why, what have you got there, lad? It's on fire!' Walt exclaimed.

'Steady on, Walt. Russian vodka and dry ice. Cost me a bloody fortune.' He thrust a glass in Walt's face. 'Go on, get it down yer neck, and Mike'll stamp your passport, eh?'

I nudged Algy. 'He'll never swallow that,' I said. But I was wrong. Very wrong. Walt tipped his head back, raised the vessel to the light and downed it in one. Then he smacked his lips and said, 'I tell you what, Soapy, that weren't half bad – for a foreign concoction, like.' Then he fished in his pocket, pulled out a tenner and said, 'Go on, get us another – and one for yourself, eh?'

Twenty minutes later, out in the street, Algy and I each took one of Walt's arms and steered him towards the next pub.

'Right,' I said, 'What's next?'

Soapy had the answer. 'Karaoke time,' he said. 'Has to be.'

'You won't catch me eating any of that foreign grub,' Walter said. And with that he swayed across the road, dragging me and Algy with him. 'What's that big queue over there for?' he asked.

Algy winked at me. 'Ah,' he said, 'I do believe we seem to have washed up on the threshold of one of those – ah, establishments that require a special licence.'

'Eh up,' shouted Soapy, 'd'you mean it's one o' them laptop joints?'

'Algy laughed. 'My dear old fellow, a laptop is a computer. No no no, what I refer to is table dancing or pole dancing. A club for the discerning gentleman with a few pounds to burn, which rules out most of our party – including you, my boy.' He tugged my arm. 'I think it would be wise to sidestep this one, don't you agree, Michael?'

It took us a full three hours to complete the run. By the time we staggered into the 70s-themed club at the bottom of the hill, it was almost midnight and Soapy and his mates were in full cry, shouting endearments – and improper suggestions – to every passing female, of which there was no shortage. Algy, on the other hand, seemed to have peaked and had fallen strangely quiet. Walter was on his personal Grand Tour of Europe and sipping peach schnapps. I was starting to regret my passport idea, especially when Soapy got me on to something sweet, orange-flavoured and very, very potent. As for my own passport, I had long since parted company with that, and in any case I wasn't sure where in the world this latest drink came from. Still, Soapy was fine. It was Walter who was worrying me. He disappeared into a mêlée on the dancefloor, emerging half an hour later with a gang of Sheffield lasses out celebrating someone's divorce. I went to the bar and ordered him a mineral water, but by the time I'd got served he was on the floor again, moving about to the strains of Donna Summer. The poor lass he was dancing with couldn't keep pace. She staggered over to me and leant against the bar.

'Eh, he's a right little raver, your dad,' she shouted, cupping her hand to my ear.

'Me dad?' I repeated, lifting Walter's trilby off her head. 'Aye well, you know how they are. Give 'em a new hip joint and there's no stopping 'em. Seventy,' I added, 'it's the new forty – or so he says.'

An hour or so later I managed to round up Walter, reunite him with his trilby, his mac, and Algy and Soapy. Soapy's mates had moved on to another club down by the river and texted him to say they were already sorted for overnight accommodation, so about two o'clock the four of us decided to make our way back along Micklegate, through the Bar and down to the car park.

'I still don't get it,' Soapy said as we shoved a sleepy Walter into the back seat and piled in after him. 'How come he got more female attention than the rest of us put together? Me last night as a single man and I never got so much as a kiss.'

'I'd say you were well off out of it, mate. I mean, what do you want with a bunch of divorcees from South Yorkshire when you've got the lovely Becky at home? And besides, would you be interested in a lass who was chasing Walter?'

'Fair point, Mike, fair point.' Soapy settled down in his seat. 'Wake us up when we get home, won't you?'

By the time our driver dropped me off at Keeper's Cottage it was just coming up to three o'clock and Ann had arrived home off her late turn.

'So, did you leave the place as you found it?' she asked.

'You mean the City and County of York?'

'What else?'

'No worries, love. My little gang are all home, safely tucked up in their beds. Job's a good 'un. All we have to do now is get Soapy married.' As I put my arms round her and breathed on her face she grimaced. 'Smells like you've had a . . . colourful night out, Mike.'

'Oh yes. Very good. Did the whole of Europe in six hours flat. By the way, where does Cointreau come from?'

'What?'

'Well, I had two glasses of it. And it was two too many, let me tell you. Anyway . . .' I reached behind her and grabbed the envelope off the sideboard. 'You haven't seen this,' I said, pulling the letter out.

'What is it?'

'This, my dear, is our official invitation to the wedding of the year.'

'Hmm yes, really nice. Must have cost a packet though.' She took it from my hand and carried it over to the light. 'Mind you, that's the sort of thing I'd choose – if I were going to get married.' She glanced at me, then said, 'So – Soapy's wedding, eh? Yes, I'm looking forward to it.'

'Me too,' I yawned. 'Tell you what, I'm also looking forward to my bed.' I stopped halfway up the stairs. 'Here,' I said, 'I've just remembered. Crème de menthe? Where's that come from?'

'Oh God, you didn't, did you?'

'Think so. Not sure.'

Chapter 3

Soapy's Vow

I've never been massively superstitious. When something unexpected happens for no apparent reason I tend to shrug my shoulders. That's the way life is – full of coincidences. Some people look for explanations, but as far as I'm concerned they're wasting their time. The way I look at it, you just have to accept whatever life throws at you and move on. Having said that, I have noticed that no sooner do you get one piece of good news than another follows.

Ann and I had been enjoying a rare morning off together, and our first sleep-in for about a fortnight. We'd been at the Farmers the night before, enjoying a steak dinner and a bottle of wine. After putting away our desserts we'd sat there and talked about all the things we might do to Keeper's Cottage. By the time we got home we'd planted an orchard, bought a greenhouse, got a full-scale vegetable garden up and running, added a third bedroom, put in a cast-iron wood-burning stove, then bought the field next door and stuck a horse in it. As I drifted off to sleep Ann was debating whether to build a proper stable or buy a loose box. Now we were sitting there on the log enjoying our morning coffee. The sun was shining and the birds were singing, but the dream was starting to fade.

'Only trouble is . . .' I began, but Ann got there first.

'Precisely. Money.'

I was about to thank her for her positive and encouraging outlook when Henry started barking.

'Postie,' I said. 'Has to be.' And there was the red van, turning in at the end of the lane and bumping through the pot-holes towards us.

I got up, stretched, and went to meet him.

He handed me the usual collection of junk, plus a couple of bills and one white envelope with a window in it, addressed to me.

'Here we go.' I sat down beside Ann and handed it to her, my eyes fixed on the postie's van as it made its way back through the woods. 'We both know what that is, don't we?'

'You want me to open it?'

'Needs a steady hand, love.'

They send out two letters in notification of your exam results: one to your home address, another to your inspector. So it was a good job I was at home to receive the letter. At least I got to find out the news with Ann rather than sitting sweating in Birdie's office.

Ann was looking at me. 'Well, do I open it or what?' she said.

'Go on. Might as well know the worst.'

I hate moments like this. It's like when I'm standing behind the goal at Bootham Crescent and York City get a penalty at the Shippo end. I'm the one who always turns his back and waits for the crowd to roar – or groan. I can't bear to watch.

'Yesss!'

I turned round to see her grinning as she handed me the envelope. 'Not only did you pass,' she was saying, 'but you – here, see for yourself.'

I scanned the printed-out slip that confirmed my pass and showed my percentage score compared to what the other candidates had got. I slid off the log and punched the air. 'Bloody hell, I can't believe it. Me? In the top twenty per cent?'

Ann gave me a big hug and I danced her round the log with a perplexed Henry leaping up at us and trying to snatch the sheet of paper.

'Weird, isn't it?' I sat back down and reread the letter. 'I came out of that exam thinking, yeah, I'd done pretty well. Then the doubts set in – and it's been downhill ever since. The more I thought about it, the more I convinced myself that I'd screwed up. Hell, I'm relieved.' I looked at Ann. She gave me a big kiss and another hug. 'D'you realise,' I said, 'this is only the second exam I've passed. I mean in my entire life?'

'I'd say you're on a roll, Mike. So keep going.'

'Don't suppose we can go and celebrate again, can we?' I said.

She looked at her watch and started towards the house. 'Not this side of payday. Anyway, you seen the time? I've got to get to work. And so have you. But listen – I'll stop off on the way home and get something special to toast your achievement. But well done, Mike. I mean it. And enjoy your meeting with Birdie.'

'Yeah. Hey, I wonder how Jayne got on.'

'Well, she's a bright girl, let's hope she's passed too.' The back door swung to behind her.

Half an hour later Jayne and I were standing in Birdie's office. I nudged her and winked. She did not look happy. She'd left home before her post arrived and had no idea whether she was awaiting good news or bad. But she needn't have worried. Birdie was all smiles as he congratulated the pair of us and shook our hands. 'Well, that's a bloody relief,' she said as we made our way back across the yard from the wendy house. 'The old doubts were creeping in, I can tell you.'

'Yeah, same here. But it's behind us now, my friend. Onward to part two, eh?'

The meeting with Birdie was about more than just delivering

our exam results. He was already planning our next moves for us – or with us. Chris Cocks was about to be seconded to a team looking into reorganisation of the force and might be gone from Malton for several months, creating the perfect opening for me. As for Jayne, Birdie had her lined up for a post that would be coming up shortly at Pickering, mainly as cover for annual leave, sickness and so on – unless, of course, we planned to extend our search beyond the immediate area. The trouble with North Yorkshire is that it's such a vast county that unless you're prepared to move house, the travelling involved in a transfer does limit your options. Having not long moved in to Keeper's Cottage, I was happy to stay local. As for Jayne, with her boyfriend about to move up to York, she wouldn't want to move too far away either.

There was a lot to think about, and as ever, precious little time. Within a week, Chris had gone on leave and I was acting sergeant in his place. And I hadn't been at it many days when the inspector came to briefing with news of an outbreak of burglaries in the region – that is, in the wider policing area incorporating us and our neighbouring forces.

'We're pretty sure this is the work of a single gang,' he said. 'They're targeting large, isolated dwellings – farmhouses and the like. These aren't your regular burglars, making off with the usual electricals, jewellery and cash, et cetera. They're going in and systematically stripping these houses of everything worth taking. Furniture, fitments, rugs off the floors – and they're causing a huge amount of distress, as you can imagine. These are very well organised people who put a lot of care into their planning. Be aware that they're likely to be using larger vehicles to make off with their haul.'

Birdie went on to reiterate that we should all be aware of this crime trend. He reminded us that house burglary in Ryedale was very rare, and we wanted it to stay that way. He was determined that we should get on top of this. Everyone needed to be switched on, and vigilant.

I gave a lot of thought to what Birdie had told us at briefing. I clearly needed to bring my Country Watch people up to speed, and the quickest way of doing that was to get a message out on the telephone ring-round system. That's a handy bit of kit. Basically, it involves recording a single audio message onto the computer, pressing the correct button and bingo: out it goes to everyone on the list. I'd back it up with another newsletter – the old belt-and-braces approach. I would also do my best to get around my patch and spread the word in person – get the jungle drums beating throughout the rural community. It's all very well putting a notice in a single-sheet handout, but what guarantee is there that it'll be read? Most of the folk I dealt with responded best to a face-to-face approach. I could probably do more good walking around their houses and yards, pointing out ways in which they could improve security, for example. But where would I find the time for that? I had a lot on my plate these days.

As acting sergeant I still got out on my rounds, but at the start of every shift I tended to get caught up in various jobs around the station. This meant that I was spending more time on the computer, checking that all the jobs had been dealt with correctly, checking that crime investigations were up to date and being progressed, checking and signing off case files for court. Along with that, I had to answer any queries from the shift or at the front office. While covering those duties you also have to keep an ear open for the radio, listening out for where the troops are, what they're doing, and making sure they're safe. This particular day, however, it had been pretty quiet on all fronts. My team had all been out and about, working on their own initiative. After they'd come in for their various meal breaks Fordy asked me what the chances were of him getting to use the new speed gun. He'd had one or two complaints about cars speeding through the villages and, having just done the one-day course on the equipment, he was keen to practise what he'd learnt. Not everyone enjoys enforcing the speed restrictions

– apart from the traffic department, of course – but in Ryedale there are frequent complaints from virtually every village. The irony is that when you go and enforce the law, guess who's the first person you catch? Locals. Every time. So instead of leaving the village to a round of thanks, you generally leave with your ears ringing from abuse and complaints. As I like to say, you're damned if you do and damned if you don't.

I explained all this to Fordy, but he was still up for the challenge. 'Don't worry, Sarge,' he said. 'I'll put on the old charm. You wait and see.' So off he went, with his shiny new equipment and high hopes. I was just wondering whether to go out in the car myself when the mobile rang.

'Mike?'

'Speaking.'

'Mike, it's Helen.' I could tell by the way she spoke that she was upset. 'Jim's wife.'

'Yeah, go on Helen, what's the matter?'

'I've just come back from Malton, Mike – coming up our lane, you know . . .'

'Yes?'

She was breathless. She sounded as though she was crying. 'I was nearly at the house and this – this car shot out of the yard. I don't dare go in.'

'Oh my God, Helen. Are you OK?'

'Yes, I'm all right. I mean, nothing's happened to me as such. But this car, Mike. I think it's those people again. It came so fast, like a bat out of hell. I had to swerve off the road or it would've hit me. Mike, I'm scared to go home. What should I do? There were three of them in it, and . . . Oh God, what if I'd been a minute or two earlier and gone in the house . . . Just think.'

'Right, try to stay calm, Helen. I'll be on my way in just a second. Where are you right now?'

'I'm almost at the house. A hundred yards away? I had to

stop, they were coming so fast. They've only just disappeared, while I was dialling your number. You don't think they'll come back, do you?'

'No way. They know you'll be on the phone. Listen, Helen, did you see which way they went, I mean when they got to the end of the lane?'

'No, it's out of sight from here. There was nothing to be seen except a cloud of dust.'

'I see. OK then, just give me a few quick details, can you? If we can circulate something, you never know. What sort of car was it?'

'It was an Audi. Pale sort of colour – beige I'd call it.'

'New? Old?'

'Oh, it was an older model. Y registration. That's all I can remember.'

'OK. That's a start. Did you get a look at the occupants?'

'I did, Mike, and that's what really scared me.'

'Why's that?'

'Remember when we had our Land Rover taken the other week? And one of them had a beard?'

'Yeah. Of course I do.'

'Well, I'm sure it was the same man driving this Audi – only this time there was a woman sat next to him – younger; maybe twenty-five. She had real short hair, bleached blonde.' I could hear her shudder as she spoke. 'And there was someone else in the back. I think it was a man, but they were moving fast.'

'That's great, Helen. That's a massive help. Now listen, give me a minute or two to put these details out, will you, and I'll get to you as soon as possible. I'm only ten minutes away. Or there may be somebody nearer.'

'OK Mike. And thank you.'

'Hang on, Helen. Before you hang up. Did you pass any other vehicles – I mean, did you pass any others on your way home that might have been involved?'

'No, I don't think I saw another car after Buttercrambe bridge. You know what it's like round here.'

'And what about Jim? Where's he? Does he know what's happened?'

'No, he's out drilling. He hardly ever checks his phone, unless he's expecting a call. Can't hear it anyway if he's in the tractor. Even then he most likely won't get a signal.'

'Well, try him anyway.' I was already out of the office and hurrying across the car park. 'OK,' I said, 'you sit tight and I'll be with you as quick as I can.'

I got in the car, put on the blue lights and sped away through town, calling control and getting them to circulate the details, the descriptions, and to coordinate any units that were available to search for the Audi. Given the route the Land Rover took last time, and the probability that this was the same outfit, the message would also go out to York and Humberside. There was surely a chance that the vehicle would still be out on the road. With a bit of luck and a following wind . . .

I kept my eyes skinned all the way, just in case the Audi happened to be heading my way, but there was nothing. It was dead calm and the countryside seemed devoid of movement, just the odd tractor spraying for weeds. I couldn't believe that Helen and Jim had been targeted again. I just hoped that they hadn't managed to get into the house this time. Maybe they'd been spooked by Helen's arrival, but it didn't sound good. I hurried along the unmade road that led up to the farm, right past the spot where Jim had been digging the footings for the gate he planned to install. He'd be gutted when he heard what had happened.

I found Helen just where she said she'd be, sitting in her car barely a stone's throw from the house. Her eyes were red and she had a scrunched-up tissue in her hand. As soon as she saw me in her mirror she was out of the car and walking towards me.

'They've broken in. You can see the door from here, Mike. It's open, look. You – you don't think there's someone still in there, do you?'

'I doubt it very much, but we'll soon get it checked out.' I was peering at the door. 'Looks like it's been forced again. You sure there's no other vehicles about?'

'Don't think so – unless there's one round the back out of sight.'

'Right, I'm going to drive into the yard. You follow me, but don't get out of the car till I say so, OK?'

I drove in, slowly, with her close up behind. In my rear-view mirror I caught sight of Fordy coming up the lane in his car. I put him in the picture then sent him to check the yard behind the house.

Helen was still in her car, sitting there with the window rolled down. 'Right,' I said, 'do you mind staying outside for the moment while we go in?'

'What – you don't think . . .?' She cast a worried look at the house.

'Just in case,' I said. 'And the less disturbance there is the easier it'll be for our scene of crime man to piece things together.'

Fordy had driven around and come back. 'Anything?' I asked.

'Nah,' he said, 'Nobody round there. No vehicle anyway.'

'Right, let's have a look in here shall we?' The door to the house was half open, and I could see the gouge in the jamb where something had been used to force it. Inside, a stout log-splitting axe lay on the tiled floor of the kitchen. A glance at the dresser suggested that this was the work of professionals, not casual criminals. Each drawer had been pulled out to its full extent. The pro always does that: starts with the bottom one. It's faster, more efficient. Start at the top and you have to close each one before you can open the next – or pull it all the way out and dump it on the floor. No, this was a neat job, and had probably been executed by people well practised in the art.

Helen was at the door, peering in. I still didn't want her on the premises. Apart from anything else she would be upset by what she saw.

'I hope they haven't taken my mother's rings,' she said. 'I hid them somewhere safe after last time. I doubt they're worth a lot – just irreplaceable of course . . .' She tailed off and dabbed at her eyes.

'Why don't you try Jim again?' I waited while she dialled his number. This time he answered and she told him to get himself up to the house right away. Then she turned to me. 'We should've done what you said, shouldn't we?'

'What's that then?'

'Installed CCTV and so on.'

'Don't punish yourself,' I said. 'There's no saying it would've deterred these people. You haven't exactly had long to get it sorted anyway. Hello, who's this?'

The sound I'd heard was Jim, pulling into the yard in his tractor. I left Helen to tell him the news, then explained that Fordy and I were going to do our best to preserve the scene until the SOCO arrived – which, according to control, would be any time now. It seemed we'd caught him in between appointments.

'Can't believe it,' Jim said, looking at the splintered doorjamb. 'And I was halfway through getting the gate up. The bastards.'

By the time I'd filled him in on the situation Stuart had arrived. He went to work right away and was soon on his hands and knees looking for footprints. It's easy to assume that footprints mean neat depressions in the earth, or the imprints of a boot-sole on a tiled floor. In fact, it's much more complicated than that. Even when they're completely invisible to the naked eye, they can now be recovered from carpets by using ultraviolet light and certain chemicals. If someone has even walked through a layer of dust it'll leave some sort of imprint, however light, on the next surface they land on.

With Stuart on the job I was now able to let Jim and Helen into the house. They were of course devastated. It's a horrible feeling to know that complete strangers have been in your home, not once but twice, and in such a short period of time, rummaging through your possessions, helping themselves to the things you hold most valuable or precious. It could have been worse, though; sometimes they'll help themselves to food or drink, or deliberately foul the place. It's a disgusting business, but in my experience, the more mess they make the more chance you have of obtaining some forensics – not that that's much consolation to the poor householder. Some people sell up and leave. Some become ill. It's a traumatic business, to say the least. But whoever had been in here, they were at least efficient and, I have to say, pretty tidy. There hadn't been any throwing things around. They'd gone straight to all the likely places where valuables or keys might be hidden. The question was, what were these people after? It wasn't as if the house was loaded up with antiques. And if this was the same gang as before, they would know that. So why had they come back? When I asked Helen and Jim to show me where their valuables were kept, such as they were, they found nothing missing. Not in the bedrooms, nor in the sideboard in the living room – even though all of its drawers had been opened.

Then Jim went into the hallway. He'd barely been gone a couple of seconds when he called out, 'Oh hell, Mike you'd better come and look at this.'

My heart sank as he showed me back into the recess under the stairs. He was standing there looking at the gun cabinet. The door was open, and it was empty.

'Oh, shit. What've they taken, Jim?'

'All three – and one's, well, it's a classic. You saw it when you came before.' He stood there shaking his head. 'William Powell and Son. Must be worth two to three thousand, minimum. It was a gift to me dad from a titled gentleman. Goes back to his days as a farm manager, down in Warwickshire.'

'Bloody hell. What about the other two?'

'Two side-by-side Berettas. Not worth much.'

'Cartridges?'

Jim looked me in the eye. 'They've all gone – must've been about a hundred. Christ, what the hell they going to do with that lot?'

I didn't answer. 'I need to get this circulated straight away.' I said. 'Don't touch any of it. We'll get Stuart in here, now.'

This was deadly serious. I needed to put the information out to all units, including all neighbouring forces, that we had three suspected burglars at large, possibly in possession of shotguns plus ammunition. Control would also alert the armed response units. It had been over half an hour since the suspects made off, which meant they could be thirty miles away or even back at home by now. I just hoped that some poor unsuspecting cop didn't try to stop the vehicle. It's happened before, sometimes with tragic consequences. That's why I needed to get this information out, immediately.

While Helen was distraught about the break-in, Jim kept apologising. 'I'm sorry, mate. So bloody stupid of me.'

'Look, Jim, it's not your fault. What could you have done?'

'That's the whole point, Mike.' He shook his head. 'The keys, you see . . .'

'Where were they?'

He led me back into the kitchen. 'I was out with me gun only yesterday, doing a bit of rabbiting. Normally I hide them out of the way, but it was late and I was knackered.'

'So you . . . what?'

'I slung 'em in here.' He went to the top drawer of the dresser, which was still open. There was nothing inside but a small stack of neatly folded tea towels. Jim stood there shaking his head.

'No good worrying,' I said. 'What's done is done.'

I was starting to piece together a possible scenario in my

mind, linking this to the earlier break-in. Had the perpetrators spotted the cabinet on their first visit and decided to come back for the guns? It all underlined how absolutely crucial it is for licence-holders to make sure they properly secure their weapons – and the keys to their gun safes.

Right now we had a full-scale operation on our hands. Control came back to say that an extensive search of the area was being undertaken, but there was no trace of the Audi. With such scant details of the vehicle there was not a lot to go on, which was very frustrating. It left a lot of questions hanging. Who were these people, what were their reasons for stealing the guns, and where and when would they strike next?

Before Fordy and I left we got Jim to dig out his shotgun licence, so that we could record the makes and models and the serial numbers of the missing pieces. In fact, after turning his office upside down he was able to supply a photograph of the antique weapon, which was a real bonus. And I made a point of thanking Helen for her detailed description of the occupants of the car – two of them, at least.

Back at the station Fordy started to write up the report, keeping an ear open for any updates. But there was nothing. It was one of those jobs where, despite there being no result straight away, you just hope for a lucky break, or for forensics to give you a result. Until we made that breakthrough, though, we had a major problem on our hands. Whoever these people were, they'd most likely got back to wherever they came from by now, leaving us with an ongoing headache. No, more than that: a potential nightmare.

It was late when I finally got away, but I stopped outside the Jolly Farmers on the way back. I'd had it in mind to book a table for the Friday night, for me and Ann to celebrate my exam results. This was a good, good moment, and I wanted to milk it. It was only when the landlord got his desk diary out that I realised it was Soapy's wedding coming up on Saturday. 'Whoa,'

I said, 'hang about. Let's leave it for now, eh? Maybe book us in for a couple of weeks' time.'

He actually seemed relieved. 'Got enough on just now,' he said. 'That party up at your mate's place Saturday night, for a start – and half me staff reckon they're invited.'

'Oh, you mean at Algy's? After the wedding?'

'Aye. I'm fetching all the drinks up – well, the beer anyway; he has his own wine-cellar, doesn't he? And some of the grub. Gonna be quite a do – and me short-handed.'

'It'll have to go some to outshine the wedding. Poor old Soapy, he's been fretting over that for a year and more. Just hope it stays fair for 'em.'

Some people are just born lucky. I have no idea what Soapy had done to deserve it, but when the big day came it could not have been nicer. It was one of those sparkling, perfect spring days, the sun blazing down, just a few puffy white clouds in the sky, and a soothing breeze blowing in from the southwest. It reminded me of the day we all went point-to-pointing at Whitwell.

Burythorpe is a strange little church, a proper old stone job with a squat tower that stands well away from the village, all on its own in the middle of the fields. It's on a slight hill, so you get fantastic views of the countryside, across to the wold tops in the distance. There's no proper vehicular access, apart from a rough track that hearses and suchlike can just about negotiate, and at the end of that there's a parking area that takes two or three cars. So we parked in the village with everyone else, stuck our heads into the Bay Horse, and there they were – the rest of the guests, warming up for the big occasion. After a quick pint we walked up to the church, with Walter for company. He was in high spirits, and had gone so far as to pin a sprig of yellow blossom to the lapel of his tweed jacket. 'Aye, have a smell,' he said, thrusting his chest towards us. 'Go on. Right nice scent, that is.'

I leaned forward and took a good sniff. 'You're not wrong, Walter. It's lovely, is that. What do they call it?'

'Mahonia japonica, lad. Got it fresh from the garden this morning.'

'Oh,' Ann said. 'No expense spared, eh?' Ann looked pretty special, all done up in her best wedding frock. Not to be outdone, I'd unearthed my one and only suit and had it dry-cleaned. You do things like that for a mate.

'By the way, Walt' – I held the gate open to let him and Ann into the churchyard – 'did you get those doves arranged in the end? Cos old Soapy was getting proper anxious about them, last time I bumped into him.'

Walt brushed past me and headed for the church door. 'Don't you worry, lad, it's all in hand,' he muttered as he disappeared inside.

We followed him in and sat down beside him. 'You been in here before?' I asked, looking around the place. Ann's aunt had done a fantastic job with the flowers.

'Me? I was a regular, once over.' He nudged me with his elbow. 'Used to be a choirboy,' he said. 'When they had a choir, that is.'

'Right.' I was trying to summon up an image of the old boy in a ruff and a white robe. 'This is my first time,' I said. 'I mean in this church. We used to go regularly to the one in Huntington. Got shunted off to Sunday school every week, right after our Sunday dinner. I reckon Mum and Dad wanted us out the way on an afternoon. But I've not been in here before – apart from a funeral one time.'

I don't think they have regular services at Burythorpe now; maybe once a month, which seems a pity. I don't suppose I've the right to an opinion, not being much of a churchgoer, but whenever I attend a service at those old places I always find myself hoping they stay open. You turn up for a funeral or a christening, or a wedding – hatches, matches and dispatches as they say – and, well, you want a proper church, don't you? Stained glass windows, a big old organ with pipes, an antique lectern in oak or polished brass, a few stone slabs to read along the walls, and the whole place nice and chilly so that you don't fall asleep.

Not that there was much chance of that happening with Soapy involved. He announced his arrival with a good rattle of the handle and what sounded suspiciously like a kick as the door swung open. I turned to see him shoving a hip flask in his jacket pocket, wiping his mouth with the back of his hand, then buttoning up his vermilion waistcoat.

I gave Ann a nudge and she turned to survey the spectacle that was our pal Soapy, washed and brushed up with his hair all trimmed and his face gleaming.

'Look at him,' I said. 'Looks every inch the guilty schoolboy, doesn't he? I'd never have recognised him in that suit.'

'I think you'd have made a shrewd guess, Mike. I'd say velvet suits – in aubergine, or is it burgundy? – either way, they went out with the three-day week, didn't they? I bet Becky'll show up in something stunning. And *what* has he got on his feet?'

Soapy was clip-clopping up the aisle, his steel tips ringing on the stone flags. 'They'll be his Cuban-heeled cowboy boots, love. Didn't recognise 'em all shiny like that, did you?'

Soapy winked at us as he walked past and approached the front row of pews. He did look a sight. He'd even polished up his glasses. He had his best man with him, fidgeting and chewing his lip, checking his watch, casting anxious glances over his shoulder as he fingered his waistcoat pocket to check that he hadn't lost the ring. But, contrary to everybody's worst fears, Becky appeared on time, sweeping into the church bang on two o'clock in a dazzling white dress that oozed expense – and with two beautiful little bridesmaids holding her train.

There were several sharp intakes of breath and a low whistle from one of Soapy's mates, huddled together in the pews across the aisle from us. I turned around and saw one of them tuck half a cigarette behind his ear. Becky certainly did look a picture. 'Far too classy for Soapy,' I whispered in Ann's ear. 'Michael!' she hissed. 'Will you behave.'

The service was brisk and to the point. 'Looks like the vicar's got another appointment after this, the rate he's going,' I said to Ann as he galloped through the preamble and got to the vows.

'Wants to get it over with, I reckon, and get that shower over there out of his precious church. Before they start carving their names on the pews.'

'Do you, Andrew Miles Slater . . .?'

'Miles!' I said, nudging Ann as she stifled a giggle. 'Where'd he get that from?'

'Shush! You'll have us thrown out.'

Soapy stood, raptly attentive, as the vicar continued his solemn delivery. 'To have and to hold, in sickness and in health, from this day forth, till death do you part?'

Soapy threw out his chest, shoved his shoulders back and said, clear as a bell, 'Why, I reckon I do, cock-bod.'

Well, that relaxed the tension, and set the tone for the rest of the affair. I'd never heard a congregation laugh like we did – and even the vicar cracked his face. 'We'll take that as a yes, I think,' was his response, before he straightened himself up and carried on with the remainder of the proceedings. Soapy had done his piece, and didn't have long to wait before he could kiss his bride. Then the pair of them marched down the aisle, smiling and nodding to everyone in turn.

Outside, as we gathered for the photographer, I was all on edge to see what Walt's mate had come up with in the way of white doves. Walt was calmness personified. 'Well, where is he?' I said. 'Where's your man Gideon?'

'He'll be about the place,' Walt said, straightening his tie and adjusting his trilby as we shuffled into place for the group photo. 'Blending into t'background, like.'

'He blooming well wants to be, cos the crucial moment's approaching.'

'There's an old saying, lad . . .'

'Aye, I somehow thought there would be.'

'Cometh the hour, cometh the man.'

'Well, let's hope the old codger doesn't strain his hernia as he cometh up from the village. It's a bit of a pull for a ninety-year-old. Hasn't been in the Bay Hoss, has he?'

'Good turnout,' Ann said, casting an eye over the assembled multitude and tactfully changing the subject. 'Must be seventy or eighty of us. Where did they all come from? I barely recognise a handful of them.'

'Tell you what,' I said, 'I've already spotted two lads I've had the pleasure of arresting – and a suspected poacher over there. Anyway, we're off duty – and hey, it looks like we're away . . .'

Becky and Soapy headed down the church path to the gates leading to the car-parking area. They got stuck at the gate, of course. It's a tradition in these parts for the local kids to tie it shut, but it was clearly a tradition that Soapy had forgotten about. He rattled the gate, then bent over it to see what the trouble was. The trouble was several feet of skipping rope tied round and round the latch. He was all set to clamber over it – much to the amusement of a gaggle of little boys who were gathered on the other side – when Walter broke the bad news.

'Tha needs to pay 'em to let you out, lad.'

'How much are we talking, Walt? Cos I've got my penknife in me pocket. I'll soon cut through this little lot.'

'Penknife! By, don't do that. They reckon it's seven years' bad luck if you break the string. It's tradition lad, you need to throw 'em a few coins. To 'em, not at 'em!' he shouted as Soapy started hurling fifty-pence pieces and the lads ducked for cover. But Soapy was only having fun. Algy joined in as well, and one or two others, and by the time the children had opened the gate their pockets were bulging.

While all this was going on I spotted a grizzled, stooped old fellow wearing a faded grey raincoat, tied around the middle with a length of blue baling twine. He was standing just inside the stone wall, behind a tilting, centuries-old headstone. His head was bare, and almost bald; just a few strands of grey hair flickered in the breeze. He grinned a toothless grin as Soapy shouted out, 'You're on next, Gideon lad!', then bent down behind the gravestone.

There was a fluttering sound, a strange sort of cackle and a flurry of movement as a dozen or so off-white doves took to the air, followed for a few feet by a large black and gold cockerel.

'They doves or pigeons?'

'Search me, Ann, but Becky approves – look.'

The bride was beside Algy's Frazer Nash, popping away with her phone camera, before reaching across and giving Soapy a big hug. There was a shout of 'Hey, Soapy lad, reckon you've pulled!' as the birds soared and circled over the church, then swooped over the crowd before heading away to the south. The cockerel, meanwhile, was scuttling around the churchyard pursued by a surprisingly agile Gideon.

'What the bloody hell's that bird doing in with them?' I said.

'Aye well,' Walt said, 'he has what you'd call miscellaneous fowl in that yard of his, and he reckoned he had a job on rounding 'em up – doves, like. Any road, he managed to get the cockerel tangled up with them – and a couple of guineafowl – and by the time he'd separated them out his hernia was playing up. Rang me this morning to say what had happened.'

'And you said it's only old Soapy, eh? So grab the lot and get yourself to the church.'

'No bugger's complaining, are they?'

'Oh no, Walt. They're loving it.'

'That's what I told Gideon. It'll add a touch o' colour, I said.'

'I'm just relieved the lad hasn't had to fork out for it

– otherwise he might see it differently. Anyway, looks like it's time for confetti.'

Soapy and his bride were already climbing into the Frazer Nash, which stood right up beside the little gate that led into the churchyard. Algy himself was at the wheel, sporting a peaked cap, a pair of tinted goggles, and the same gauntlets he'd worn the time he rode Lord Nelson round to our place on New Year's Eve. The car roared into life and Algy manoeuvred it down the narrow track, waving and tooting the horn, before disappearing towards the village. I turned to Ann. 'Right, we'd best be getting back to the car and on to the reception, hadn't we? Before those mates of Soapy's get amongst the canapés.'

We piled into our car and made our way to Algy's place, with Walt in the back complaining about his sciatica. 'Never mind that,' I said. 'What about the delights in store? And think about this, Walt: all of it free!'

He didn't say anything. We'd just turned into Algy's drive. On the front lawn was the largest marquee I'd ever seen, apart from maybe the hospitality tents at York races. It was – colossal.

'Well, I'll eat hay wi' a donkey,' Walt said. 'It's bigger than my house. It's even got a wooden door, look!'

'Wow. A double one,' Ann said. 'He has pushed the boat out, hasn't he? Wonder what sort of spread he's put out for us.'

Inside the marquee Algy had set out two rows of tables for eight. Each chair had a large ribbon tied to the back, and every place setting had its own ornate floral display with a single candle flickering. From the ceiling hung great muslin nets of some sort, dotted with sparkling lights that flickered on and off at erratic intervals. In one corner a man in a dark suit was strumming on an acoustic guitar. In front of him guests were already sitting on a range of leather settees, sipping champagne, which was being handed round by waiters in tuxedos and white bow ties.

As we made our way towards the bar I spotted a noticeboard with a series of photographs pinned to it: Soapy and Becky as babies and toddlers, right through their school years, and a few taken in recent times. There was one of Soapy in his Scout uniform, blinking at the camera through his thick-lensed glasses and looking just like the Milky Bar Kid. When Ann wasn't looking I whipped out my pen and wrote underneath it, 'Should've gone to Specsavers.'

I'd managed to lose Walter, but just as I was starting to worry about him he reappeared to give Ann and me a rundown of the posh toilets. 'Why,' he said, 'it's like going to the owd picture palace.'

'How d'you mean?' I asked.

'They've all films playing on t'walls. Meks it hard to keep yer mind on t'job in hand, like.'

'Ye-es, I think that's probably enough information,' Ann said, and got a passing waitress to hand us each a glass of bubbly.

We'd barely finished that when Algy banged the gong and called us to our tables. Refreshment, he said, was about to be served. He meant food. Tons of it. Over the three hours or so that we sat there I counted six courses, and nearly fell out with Ann, who insisted there were seven. I think she was including the lemon sorbet they served between the fish and the meat, but Walt and I decided it was a drink, seeing as ours had melted by the time we got round to it – and as it was well laced with some sort of spirit. After the grub we had the speeches and the toasts. Soapy's best man embarrassed him by recalling some of their teenage escapades around the villages, and when it was time for the lad himself to address us he raised a few eyebrows by turning to Becky, raising his glass and telling us all to drink to his 'newly dead wife' before correcting himself. When that was over there was a bit of a kerfuffle as Soapy's family went round the tables demanding to know who'd defaced the picture of their darling boy in his Scout uniform. I put on my best choirboy smile and told them, 'I was just saying to my friend Walter here, I don't reckon anything's sacred these days.'

Somehow – despite all the food and drink – we managed to follow the happy couple onto the dancefloor for a few numbers, and then as the light faded it was time for one of Algy's firework displays, although this time the cannon stayed in the house. This was the cue for Soapy and Becky to depart for Manchester airport and a flight next morning to Mauritius. As their taxi went down the drive they looked around just in time to see a huge white rose explode in the sky, illuminating the house and garden.

'Well, that was quite a do, wasn't it?' I looked at Ann, who was gazing at the sky. It occurred to me that if I ever got wed I'd have something to live up to.

Chapter 4

Acting Sergeant

Now that I was acting sergeant I was having to learn a lot of aspects of police work that were more or less new to me. One of my new duties involved booking in prisoners as and when they were brought into the station, and for that I had to be quite sure of the procedures laid down under PACE, or the Police and Criminal Evidence Act. I'd brought plenty of prisoners into the station in my time – both here in Malton and down in London – but I'd generally left it to the custody sergeant to book them in and ensure that everything was documented in accordance with the legal requirements. Now I needed to get to grips with that aspect of the job myself. I was in charge. I was responsible. If something went wrong the buck stopped with me.

Malton is a small country nick. It's not like the main custody stations at York, Scarborough and Harrogate, and as such it only had two cells for male prisoners. They were very much the traditional type, with big metal doors, painted grey, like something from Victorian times. The doors were so heavy and old that you sometimes had a struggle to swing them. The sound of one slamming shut, and the key turning in the lock, would send a shiver down anybody's spine. Set into the door was a little wicket that you would pull down to open when you wanted to look inside and check that your prisoners were OK, or to speak to them or pass them food and drinks. Malton also had accommodation for one female prisoner, a cell in a separate wing. And there was a juvenile detention room – secure, but it had a wooden door, not a metal one, and wasn't as forbidding as a cell. But by and large we didn't detain a great many prisoners, certainly not for more than a few hours. If it was an overnight stay to let someone sober up, we'd keep them at Malton, but otherwise we'd most likely hand them on to York or Scarborough, where they were far better equipped to deal with them over a longer period.

Scarborough, for example, had up to two full-time custody sergeants for busy periods. Their full-time role was to book in prisoners and see to their needs for as long as they were held. There were civilian staff there as well, what we call detention officers. They would take meals down to the prisoners, bring them out when they needed to make phone calls, for interviews with solicitors or doctors, or to have a wash. York, with twenty or more cells, was even better equipped. They had two custody officers and a number of civilian detention officers – and, trust me, they needed them, especially at New Year, or when the racegoers ventured into the city after the big meetings. There was also the danger of visiting football supporters causing trouble; people tend to associate football-crowd violence with bigger teams, but it can happen anywhere. An away match at York is a very attractive fixture for a lot of supporters in our league, and it occasionally draws in a few troublemakers.

York and Scarborough also have a comprehensive system of video cameras and sound recording equipment installed. From the moment a van carrying prisoners is driven into the yard, the cameras are on them. At Scarborough there's a big rolling security door that opens up mechanically to let you into the parking bay, then closes as soon as you're inside. It's quite intimidating the first time you hear that door clang shut behind you, a bit like going into one of HM Prisons. And then, from the moment you're in the custody suites, as they're called, you're being filmed and recorded, both for the obvious legal reasons and to ensure the safety of all parties – arresting officers and prisoners alike. You're even videoed as you take them into the cells. Only when they're safely under lock and key does that stop.

But, as I said before, we did detain some prisoners at Malton if they were arrested for a minor offence – shoplifting, being drunk and disorderly or using foul and abusive language in a public place, for example. In these cases, taking them all the way to the coast simply wouldn't be worthwhile. They would most likely be released within six hours, and we wouldn't want to lose an officer for the two or three hours it would take to get them over there and back.

I'm not saying we weren't equipped at Malton. We were – after a fashion. There were a couple of video cameras around the custody area, but no sound recording facilities. In both of the interview rooms for male prisoners we had 14-inch televisions for playing back any CCTV footage we might have of someone who'd been caught on camera. It saved a lot of arguments about who did what; very few prisoners would deny an accusation if they'd been caught on film. The tape decks took three recordings simultaneously. One copy was for the suspect and his representatives, the second for the arresting officer, and the third constituted the actual evidence that would be submitted to the courts if charges were made. Ryedale always felt slightly behind the times in a quaint sort of way. When the senior officers moved into the wendy house next to the station we felt as though we were being dragged screaming and kicking into the twenty-first century. Thommo always said that the North Yorkshire Police badge should carry a strapline: 'Modern policing – the old-fashioned way.'

So, having passed my Part 1 exam I was officially deemed

qualified to book prisoners in. I was pretty confident that I was capable of remembering the routine. You start off by hearing the evidence of the arrest and deciding whether there are sufficient grounds to detain the suspect. You then go on to explain this to the suspect, read them their rights, and remind them that they are entitled to legal representation. If we were dealing with a non-native English speaker, one of the Polish people who worked at the bacon factory for example, you might need to do this through an interpreter.

When you receive a prisoner you need to consider a number of welfare questions. You ask them, have they drunk any alcohol, or taken any drugs? Are they on any medication, carrying any injuries, or suffering from any illness, physical or mental? Have they ever self-harmed? Depending on the answers they give, you may then need to call a doctor to assess their fitness to be detained or interviewed. It's not a simple matter.

When you've covered all that you get down to the business end of things. Before a prisoner is taken down to the cells they have to be searched for anything that might cause harm to themselves, a member of staff, or police property. We're talking about needles and other sharp objects, knives, lighters, belts, shoelaces and so on. The extent of the search depends on their perceived risk. If they're carrying any money, it will be taken, counted out in front of the prisoner, and sealed in a plastic property bag right in front of them. Cigarettes have to be taken off him too. Or her – and it goes without saying that if we're dealing with a female, then a female officer has to conduct the search. At Malton, that poses a problem since we haven't many female officers. On our shift, if Jayne's on her day off, we might need to get a female officer from York or Scarborough to travel through and assist.

Going through all of this, step by step, recording each question, answer and decision on a custody sheet and logging the property item by item, could take a good twenty to thirty minutes for an experienced custody officer. For me, new to the job and feeling my way, it could take even longer. In addition, we have to write down a description of the prisoner, recording any distinguishing marks, tattoos, scars, and so on. Where there are reasonable grounds for suspicion that they might be concealing items, then a strip-search will be necessary. This requires two officers of the same gender as the suspect. We're talking here about a thorough search, which takes place in the cell out of public view. Clothing is removed item by item so that you can check it. And you have to examine the person: their hair, under their armpits and down to their toes. This is not to be confused with an intimate search; that has to be carried out by a medical practitioner, and is not a job for the squeamish. You'd be surprised what some people try to conceal in their back passage, for example.

Once all those formalities are completed, we take the prisoner down to the cells and lock them in. The arresting officer will then set about writing up their arrest notes and obtaining witness statements. When that's done, the prisoner is ready for interview. If they want a solicitor we will arrange that, and the suspect will have a private consultation with them. They'll also receive disclosure of the evidence against them. The suspect can then be booked out of the duty sergeant's care to that of the officer who will be conducting the interview in the dedicated interview rooms. Depending on the nature of the offence and what, if anything, the suspect has to say, this usually takes between thirty minutes and an hour. At the main custody stations there is often a queue to use the interview rooms. So you can see how an officer could lose a whole shift to processing just one arrest.

After the interview, it's back to the cell for the prisoner while the custody sergeant decides what to do next. A prisoner can now be further detained; released on police bail pending further enquiries, released with no further action, or formally charged. In this last case we have to set a date for a court appearance.

Alternatively, a caution might be issued if the prisoner admits to the offence and is prepared to accept it. As a rule you try to delve a little deeper into a prisoner's past. Was this a more minor offence? Is there any record on the Police National Computer of previous convictions or cautions? Is it a first offence? If not, what kind of trouble has he or she been in before?

If the outcome is a charge or a caution you now have the right to take fingerprints, to photograph the prisoner, and take a DNA sample, usually by swab from the mouth. Sometimes, however, if for example the prisoner has been particularly obstreperous and seems likely to bite you – and some certainly would – you can pluck a hair out of their head. As to charging and putting a suspect before a magistrate, that might not happen for four to six weeks, depending on how busy the courts are in York and Scarborough.

Of course, what I've outlined here is the procedure for a standard, straightforward adult prisoner with no aggravating issues. In other circumstances things could be considerably more complex or time-consuming. Even if things go smoothly, it's pretty long-winded. And people look around the streets and wonder where all the cops are!

What I've outlined is the theory. How it's meant to go. Then there's the actual practice, the bit where you really start to learn. I'd been standing in for Cocksy for a week or so and was starting to feel that I was getting the hang of things. This particular day, I was on an early turn when young Fordy and Ed were called out to a domestic disturbance in Norton – unusual in the middle of a weekday morning. At least, we assumed it was a domestic. A neighbour had called in to say that she'd heard noises. Banging, shouting, swearing, doors slamming. You always wonder whether it's going to turn out to be someone watching a DVD with the sound turned up too high, but every time you get a call you have to check it out, and so over the river they went. As usual, I monitored their progress on the radio.

'Mike, we're at the address. We've got a domestic. The wife's saying the husband has assaulted her.'

'Any apparent injuries, over?'

'Looks like a common assault. Red marks on her face and neck. Says he grabbed her by the arms and has shown me marks there too.'

'Right, Ed. I'll get Jayne to come over and speak to the woman. She's only in town; should be with you in about five or ten minutes. I take it you're bringing the husband in. Is it all in hand, over?'

'Yes, he's very vocal but me and Fordy should be OK with him.'

It's always best to take positive action in these situations, and anyway policy dictates that you do so. You want to break the cycle of events. In a case like this, when I could clearly hear the husband shouting the odds over the radio, and making what sounded like threats, it was best to remove him from the scene as soon as possible. Ed arrested him on suspicion of assault, handcuffed him and kept him in the back of the car while they waited for Jayne to show up.

Within a few minutes Jayne was with the man's wife, taking a statement, while Fordy and Ed brought the husband in. This looked like a textbook case of ongoing domestic violence, which we know can be triggered at any time by anything. Before the lads had even showed up at the station, Jayne was on the radio confirming that the wife wanted to press charges. That's not often the case, strange as it may seem, and it frustrates us at times. Domestic violence is one of those really tricky areas, and when people won't press charges it makes it harder for the police to prosecute, or to try and make a difference.

When they brought the guy in I recognised him right away. He'd never been under arrest, as far as I was aware, but I'd seen him around town more than once, generally at night, outside one of the pubs, throwing his weight around and mouthing off. With people like that you always think it's only a matter of time before they land on your doorstep, so to speak. At this stage it looked as though he was going to be a difficult customer to deal with – his attitude and demeanour suggested trouble – but I hoped nonetheless that we could get him processed without too much aggravation. All he had to do was behave himself.

'Now then,' I said, as Ed, the arresting officer, brought him to the desk. 'What's the trouble?'

He was a big fellow, maybe six foot tall, and what you'd call well made. Muscular, not fat. He looked about twenty-five. He was wearing dark blue tracksuit bottoms and a red football top. He didn't answer at first, so I repeated the question.

'I'm saying f*** all,' he said. 'Except – whatever she's told you, she's a lying bitch. And I'll tell you what else, I ain't taking any crap off you lot, so don't be trying it, yeah?'

'Listen,' I said. 'Let's just keep calm, shall we? If you'll just stay nice and calm we'll get this sorted out as quickly as we can, but that means you are going to have to cool it.' Then I looked him right in the eye. 'Now, listen to what I'm saying. You start acting up and we'll have no choice but to send you off to Scarborough – and I'm telling you now they can keep you waiting all day, the queue of people they have to deal with. So, let's see if we can get this sorted here and now, eh?'

I thought I was being Mr Reasonable, but he wasn't having it. 'I ain't done owt wrong, so you can piss off, the lot of you.' He stood there, legs apart, hands held out in front of him, bristling with anger.

I was not in the mood for this. 'Right,' I said. 'You need to cool off. You either cooperate now or you will get searched and put in the cell until you do.'

I managed to book him in, but it was far from straightforward.

He questioned everything we did. He certainly didn't take kindly to Fordy searching him and did his best to put him under pressure. 'Do you like touching blokes then? You f****ing gay or what?' Fordy, to his credit, played a straight bat and kept quiet, then took him down to cell number 2. Meanwhile, I got on the radio and called Jayne, who was still with the prisoner's wife.

'How's she looking?' I asked.

'*Not bad. She's swearing vengeance on him – and men in general. I'm just sorting out the medical evidence and photographs.*'

'Thanks Jayne.'

I left her to take the woman's statement, which she would do at the house. As for me-laddo, he seemed to have quietened down, as they generally do once they're on their own in a cell. It tends to have a sobering effect. I looked in on him a couple of times, but there was nothing out of the ordinary. You have a duty to check on a prisoner at least every hour, more frequently than that if they're deemed to be at risk, or if they've been drinking or are under the influence of drugs. But he seemed pretty well settled. He was pacing the cell, but that's not unusual, and if it burns up excess energy that's all right with me. At about three o'clock I took him a cup of tea down. That sort of thing generally pacifies a prisoner, makes them see that if they stay nice and quiet they'll have an easier time of it. I was some yards from the cell door when I smelled burning. Never a good sign in the cell block. I opened the wicket to look inside.

'I don't bloody believe this,' I said to myself. There he was, sitting on the bed, cool as you like, puffing away on a cigarette. And on the floor beside him was a smouldering pile of scrunched-up toilet paper.

He looked up, saw the wicket was open, and grabbed a handful of the bed blanket with one hand. 'Aye, and this lot'll go up next if you don't let me out of here.' In his other hand he held a lighter, which he flicked into life.

I had to think fast. The first thing was to get him out unharmed. But he was a big lad, and it would take more than just me.

Your heart sinks when you face a situation like this, but you have no choice other than to get on with what needs doing. I got on the radio and called Fordy and Ed to come and join me in custody straight away. I'd no sooner called the control room to let them know what was going on than the other two appeared.

'Come on. We've got to get that lad out of there before he does any more damage. Bloody idiot's set fire to a ball of paper. Bloody fire alarms will be going off next. Never mind the mess in the cell. Birdie'll just love this if we don't get on top of it.'

Fordy was looking shocked. 'God, Sarge, how the hell has he set that on fire?'

'Lighter. We obviously missed it,' I said.

'Hell, that was my search. I'm sure he never had anything.'

'Look, let's not worry about it now. We need to get Guy Fawkes out of that cell and do a thorough search – before he burns the place down. Fordy, you monitor him through the wicket. I'll get the troops together and we'll do a proper cell extraction.'

As soon as Fordy showed his face the prisoner really started playing up. 'You come in here,' he shouted, 'and I'll take your frigging head off, pal. So come on, who's first? Eh?' There were several dull thumps as he kicked the cell door. He could do that all night as far as I was concerned: the only person to suffer would be him.

As Ed nipped across the corridor to fetch the shields, I heard a familiar voice shout out from up the stairs. 'What's going on now? Can I no leave the place for five minutes?'

'Thommo!' I shouted, grabbing a paper cup at the drinks dispenser and filling it with water. 'Just the fellow we need. Looks like we're gonna have to do a cell extraction, my friend.

We've got a big lad kicking off and trying to set fire to the place. Should be right up your alley.'

'Indeed.' Thommo grabbed a shield and followed us back to the cells. 'No finer way to start a shift. Gets the blood coursing through the old veins.'

A cell extraction is a technique we practised at our use-of-force training sessions. It's all about getting a violent prisoner under control and out of the cell without causing harm or damage to people or property. With the heavy door and the confined space inside the cell, dealing with violent individuals is no easy matter. When I was on the TSG, the Met's riot police, in London we used to train every month, and we'd be called in to deal with the most violent and vicious offenders. One thing I'd learnt is that when you go into a cell under such circumstances, you do not mess about. If you do, people get hurt. Speed, aggression and the shock factor wins the day.

'What's he up to now?'

Fordy still had his face against the wicket. 'I think we need to get in there, Mike. He's daubing the walls with ashes and he's melted the plastic mattress cover. Oh shit – now he's taken his top off. He's trying to set fire to that too.'

'Great. What a bloody carry-on.'

I explained to the team what we would do and who would take what position in the procedure. We gathered outside the cell door: me, Thommo, Ed and Fordy. I slid the wicket open and addressed the prisoner directly.

'Right', I said, 'you've got two options. Either pass me the lighter and sit down on the floor or we come and take you out.'

'You can f*** right off.'

I turned to the team. 'OK, lads. You know what to do, and listen: no messing about, right?'

While we'd been getting ourselves organised the prisoner had set fire to another ball of toilet paper and retreated to the back of the cell. He was standing there waving the fresh cloud of smoke away from his face. He knew we were about to come in, but he wasn't sure how many of us there were, nor how we would approach him. All the same, he'd made up his mind to tough it out. His fists were clenched and he'd adopted a determined sort of stance, half crouching with his hands raised in a kind of kung-fu gesture. 'F***ing wankers' he snarled.

'Ready?' I said. Fordy gave a nervy nod of his head. Thommo stretched his mouth into a sort of grin. Ed adjusted his grip on his shield. 'Yeah,' he said, 'let's get on with it.'

As I opened the door Fordy and Thommo moved quickly and held the shields locked together a yard inside the door. I moved up alongside them, my right arm on Ed's left shoulder just in case. 'I want you to get down on your knees,' I shouted. '*Now*! Knees! Facing the wall!'

There was never a cat in hell's chance that he was going to comply. He was spoiling for a fight.

'F*** off!' he shouted, crouching lower and raising a cracked sort of laugh.

But just as it looked as though he was going to launch himself at us I reached out my hand, showing him the paper cup. It had precisely the effect I wanted; it seemed to raise a momentary doubt in his mind. And just as his mouth shaped the question, 'Wha—?' I dropped it, right at his feet, splashing water on the floor. In that brief moment when he was distracted, we pounced, pinning him against the wall with the shields. I moved in quickly to kick his legs away from under him, at which point he felt the full weight of Thommo pinning him to the floor. Fordy and Ed secured his arms and handcuffed him. Job done.

We got him to his feet, securing his head in a downward position to stop him butting, spitting or kicking out. We then took him next door to cell number 1 and conducted a thorough search. The lighter was in his underpants.

Despite what he'd gone through the prisoner was still full of what he was going to do to us, and hadn't calmed down a great deal, so I made the decision that he was too big a risk for us to house and manage at Malton. While we had him cuffed and secure we would take him to the van and transfer him to Scarborough. As we slammed the door on him, Ed said, 'Well, Mike, that's you off the Scarborough custody sergeants' Christmas card list, don't you reckon?'

'I can live with that, bud.'

Ed and Fordy drove off and I went back inside. Maybe now I'd get a bit of peace, I was thinking. I'd not even had time to wash my hands, though, when Jayne was on the radio.

'*Guess what, Mike?*'

Her tone of voice told me everything I needed to know. 'Go on,' I said. 'Let's have it.'

'*You know, don't you?*'

'I've been down this road before, Jayne. Many times.'

'*Right, well, she's changed her mind, hasn't she? Doesn't want him charged after all.*'

'You couldn't make it up, could you? He really is a nasty piece of work. We've had all sorts of problems with him in the cells. He's on his way to Scarborough as we speak. And she doesn't want to charge him.'

'*Sorry, Mike. I've tried my best. I don't think it's the first time he's hit her either. I've offered her all the advice and support, but she's made her mind up. What else can I do?*'

'Just make quite sure she understands that she doesn't have to put up with it. Have you talked to her about an escape plan?'

'*Yeah.*'

'Given her contact details for the refuge and helplines?'

'*Yeah, all done Mike. I'm just about to get the withdrawal statement.*' I could hear the frustration in Jayne's voice. '*It just doesn't seem right.*'

'That's just how it is sometimes, Jayne. It's sad, but nothing we can do about it. That said, you need to let her know he'll be charged with criminal damage to the cell. So she may need to be prepared for the consequences. You'd better cover the fact that she's been told that – I mean in the withdrawal statement. And we need to make sure the address is flagged up for an urgent response if anything else comes in.'

'*Yeah, understood. Will do, Mike.*'

After the morning's excitement my desk was piled high with paperwork that wanted sorting, but no sooner had I mashed myself a cup of tea and started sifting through it than the phone rang. It was a farmer. His name seemed familiar but I just couldn't place him, not until he described where he lived, high up on the wold tops above Thixendale. Then I remembered. 'Didn't I come out to you about a year ago?' I said.

'Aye, you did. I was being bothered with lampers.'

'I thought so. What can I do for you this time?'

'I reckon I may have disturbed a burglar last night,' he said. 'Somebody was around the place, anyway.'

'Anything taken?'

'No. But I bet there would've been if I hadn't gone out there.'

I decided I'd better go and talk to the guy. His was one of those farms you wouldn't know was there unless you went looking, and even then you'd have a job locating it. It was tucked away in a little dip, behind a stand of mature sycamore trees, well off the road. It was a modest sized house, white painted, only you could see it hadn't had a fresh coat in years. There were dark streaks down the front, a green patch where the gutter was leaking, and one of the windowsills was plainly rotting. As I pulled up in the yard the farmer emerged from a low barn, turning to lift the old wooden door and drag it shut behind him – well, part-way shut. It was more propped in position.

He told me that he'd woken in the middle of the night, heard a noise, and gone out to investigate. All he'd heard was a vehicle driving off.

'So you've had a good look round, have you? I mean, you're sure there's nothing missing?'

The corners of his mouth turned down as he gave a slight shake of the head. 'Not a lot worth having,' he said. 'Tractor's about knackered, and we've no livestock now. Unless they were after that.' He pointed to an ageing Range Rover that was parked up against the side of the barn.

I glanced over at the diesel tank, half hidden by an elder tree. 'What about that?'

'Hardly anything in it at the moment. I mean, the price they want for diesel these days.'

'You on your own here?' I asked.

He looked towards the house. 'No, t'wife's here with me. Kids have left home now. Working in town. I run t'place on me own, like.'

I gave him the usual pep talk on the subject of security. I warned him about the recent spate of burglaries, about securing anything valuable behind locked doors, but to judge by the state of his outbuildings, and his general demeanour, I wondered whether I was wasting my time. It might well have been that whoever he'd disturbed had been having a look around to see if there was anything worth stealing. They would've gone away disappointed in this case.

'Listen,' I said, 'if anything like this happens again, try and phone us right away, will you? That time of night, especially if my Country Watch people are out, there's often a chance we could spot a suspect vehicle.' I added that I'd make sure the incident was mentioned at briefing so that the night crew would keep an eye out. Trouble is – not that I said as much – these places are so remote that they can sometimes get over-looked when you're out on patrol. 'Bad enough trying to make a go of it as things are,' he said, as I made to get back in the car. 'We get squeezed from both ends. When you get a better price for your produce the cost of fertilisers goes through the roof. It's a bloody monopoly. And don't set me off on the supermarkets.'

'Aye,' I said, 'that's what I'm hearing all over.' I had a degree of sympathy with the guy, of course I did, but to be honest I sort of dismissed what he was saying as a typical farmer's moan. I'd heard it all before, sometimes from farmers who I knew were millionaires, on paper at least. But when times are tough, it's the small outfits that get hit the hardest.

I left him to it and hurried back to town. It was getting on for five o'clock, and I was already late off. I did a quick handover to Pete the late sergeant and was just about to leg it upstairs to the locker room when Jayne appeared in the corridor.

'You OK?' I said. 'Thought you'd gone ages ago.'

'Mike, I need a word.' She seemed nervous, which was unlike Jayne. 'I know you're late off duty, but would you mind?'

'Sounds like a cup of tea and a quiet room job.'

'Please.'

While I was making the tea all sorts of things were going through my mind. Had she done something wrong? Had someone else – or me – done something wrong? We sat down in the quietest, most private place we could find – one of the interview rooms.

'Right, here you go Jayne.' I handed her a mug. 'Tell me what's up.' I genuinely had no idea what to expect.

'Mike, I'm pregnant.'

I managed not to say anything at first. I tried to appear calm while I worked out how I should react. Was this good news, or bad? I wasn't sure. 'OK Jayne. Congratulations.' I took a sip of my tea. 'It is good news, right?'

'Well, the timing's not great. But now I've got my head around it, yeah, it is. I'm just concerned about my career. I'd have been happy to start a family with Rob, but – maybe in a couple more years, that's all.'

'Well, the good news is that the police have now dragged

themselves into the twenty-first century, so you don't have to worry about your job.' I sighed. 'It's just . . . how to manage it all.'

'Yeah, I know. Daunting, innit?'

'Yeah, good word, Jayne. Daunting. I suppose it is. I never really thought about the practicalities of shifts and children before. Never had to.'

'Well, I have and I can tell you I've been fretting about this for weeks. Rob's got this job in York now so at least I'm not alone. But what about my promotion? This is gonna set me back, isn't it?'

'Well, yes, but only temporarily I suppose. They can't sack you for being pregnant these days, girl. Course, you'll have to come off the front line.' I managed a smile. 'Can't have you rucking on a Saturday night like you do and getting hurt. Hang on,' I said, 'how far gone are you? I mean, what about when we were dealing with that lad in the flat, when we thought he was trying to blow us up. You didn't know then, did you?'

'No, well I didn't know for sure. I'm just coming up to three months now. I didn't want to say anything in case . . . well, you know: things can go wrong, can't they?'

'Right. But let's face it, the last thing you want to be dealing with is headbangers. Or druggies infected with hepatitis. God, when you think about it there's all sorts of things you don't want to expose the baby to.'

'Yeah, you're right.' She put her mug down and shrugged. 'So . . . there goes the acting job at Pickering. I just hope they can find something useful for me to do. You know what, I'd really like to be around you lot somehow. I mean, whatever duties they give me.'

'Jayne, I think I can speak for the rest of the shift when I say we don't want to lose you either. But listen, you need to speak to Birdie first thing tomorrow and get this all sorted out. You realise that, don't you?'

'Yeah, you're right. Listen, Mike, thanks. Thanks for taking the time. I appreciate it. I feel better already, just having it out in the open.'

'Are you going to tell the rest of the shift or do you want me to?'

'No, don't worry. I'll do it. Can't wait to see the look on their faces at briefing. Hey, Thommo'll be jealous, won't he?'

'How's that?'

'Well, I'll have the one excuse he's never been able to use to get out of a shift I don't fancy.'

It was good to feel that I'd put Jayne's mind at rest. As I drove home I wondered what Ann would make of her news. I found her sitting on the log enjoying the last of the sun, with Henry occupying my seat.

'Busy day, love?'

'I tell you what,' I said, 'this acting lark is a right bloody carry-on. You think you're on top of the job and then some idiot tries to set fire to the cells.'

'My God, you're joking.'

'No, I'm not. But that's not the big news of the day.'

'It gets more shocking? Let me guess. Thommo volunteered an extra shift.'

'Get real, Ann. No, it's Jayne. Came to see me and told me she's pregnant.'

'That's great news.' She paused. 'Isn't it?'

'That was my first reaction: is it? But yes, she's happy enough. Just worried about her job.'

'I hope you handled it properly. Didn't put your foot in it and say the wrong thing, did you?'

'No, I don't think so. Come on, let's take Henry for his walk and blow some cobwebs away, shall we?'

Chapter 5

Have You Seen A Couple of Dogs?

Summer was starting to look like a real let-down. The bright greens of spring were already giving way to the darker shades of July, and out in the fields the barley was rippled by every breeze. The weather had turned chilly and damp. When I was out walking Henry at the end of the day I'd occasionally catch sight of a farmer standing at some gate-hole, watching the sky, doubtless speculating as to when the crops would ever start to ripen, and when the harvest would get under way. This particular evening I'd just come to the end of a long weekend, three days off in a row. And guess what? I hadn't set eyes on the sun. Well, just for a few minutes as it was setting one evening. Each day was worse than the one before: colder, wetter and more windy.

And then of course, once I was back at work, it faired up. It was a Saturday, and I was on a late turn. Normally I might have had a bit of a lie-in, but as I heard Ann drive off for the early shift I peered through the curtains and saw the sun shining brightly. Right, I thought, I'll get stuck into the garden, give her a nice surprise when she gets home, seeing that she's been on my case about the state of the grass the last few weeks. I was out with the strimmer by seven o'clock, and still hard at work five hours later, sweating like a pig and having burned my shoulders. But by the time I left for work, even if I say so myself,

85

the grounds of Keeper's Cottage looked an absolute picture. I'd got the nettles cut back, the hedge that borders the field trimmed, and the grass – well, it looked a little bit like a tennis court, the way I'd mowed it in neat diagonals.

I got into work to find we had a lot on; so much that I'd hardly been in half an hour before the place emptied out. There had been an accident on the A170 at Thornton-le-Dale, meaning I had to send Thommo to attend. Then I had to send Fordy and Ed to ferry a couple of teenage shoplifters to Scarborough custody. I'd barely got that lot sorted when we heard that a number of vehicles had been broken into somewhere out on the moors – not a proper car park as such, but one of those spots from which hikers and mountain bikers like to take off for the day. So that took care of all my officers in one fell swoop, and I had the place to myself till they started drifting back to eat, about seven o'clock time.

Thommo, who was first in, grabbed the sports section of my paper and was studying the racing results. I'd been idly flipping through the rest of it, not really finding much to interest me. I slung it onto the table. 'Aye,' I said, 'looks like the silly season is upon us once more. Once those politicians go on their holidays it'll be nowt but celebrity weddings, crop circles and . . .'

'Sightings of Lord Lucan,' Ed said, sitting down and opening his pack-up. 'Or have they given up on him? Or how about the return of the Ryedale Panther?' he added, grabbing the rest of the paper just as Thommo reached out for it.

'Don't even go there, bud.' I took a chocolate digestive from the packet in front of me. 'That case is closed, for good. You have my word on that. And the next time somebody calls in to tell me they've spotted it, I'll—' I wasn't sure what I had in mind, to tell the truth, but in any case Thommo was onto me right away.

'So. In between spitting crumbs all over the table I just wiped, ye're saying there is no panther, is that it, laddie?'

'Well Thommo, as far as I'm concerned we should look at

the facts. There's been that many rumours, and alleged sight-ings, I've lost count. But that's all we've had. No hard evidence at all; not one scrap of conclusive proof. For me, my friend, it's one of your urban myths. Simple as that.'

'D'ye fancy putting your money where your mouth is?' Thommo clenched his jaw and narrowed his eyes, as if to emphasise the importance of what he was about to say. 'I mean, listening to you, a man wouldnae think it possible that ye'd reported a UFO as recently as last year.' He reached into his hip pocket and pulled out his wallet.

'Christ, I wish you wouldn't do that!' I coughed loudly, and covered up my mouth with my hand. 'Every time you drag that wallet out – all that dust and cobwebs gets right up my nose. I shall start sneezing in a minute, and then you'll be sorry.' I leaned forward and swept the crumbs off the table with my forearm. 'Listen, Thommo lad, until I see the Ryedale Panther with my own eyes, I'll have serious doubts – despite all the speculation fuelled by rags like you're reading.'

'No, hang on. Let's be reasonable about this.' Ed popped the lid on his sandwich box and leaned back in his chair. 'I reckon we should keep an open mind. I mean, not everything has a rational explanation, does it? Isn't that the conclusion you and I came to that time on Golden Hill?'

'Nah, I was just trying to stop you from – I mean, you were on the brink there, mate. Right on the very borderline of insanity. If it hadn't been for my calming influence . . .'

'Yeah yeah yeah. Don't listen to him, Thommo. It was a different story at the time, and he knows it. Quaking in his boots, he was. You go and investigate, Ed; I'll stay here and radio for help.'

'Hey,' I said. 'Only joking, Ed, only joking. Anyway, Thommo. Now that you've found your long-lost wallet, let's have that little wager, shall we? You and me. Ten quid that we find proof positive.'

'Proof positive? Of what, laddie?'

'Oi!' Ed said. 'Respect where it's due, eh? Acting sergeant, if you don't mind.'

Thommo sighed. 'Just what kind of proof are you after, *Sarge*?'

'Let's say I come up with something to show that it's all a lot of fuss about nothing.'

'Ye cannae do it, mon. You can prove that one particular report is a load of nonsense, sure ye can. But you can never prove there *is* no panther out there. It's like – it's like trying to prove there's no God up there.'

'This is going nowhere,' Ed said. 'How about . . . how about, the bet is . . . right, when the next reported sighting comes in – which it will – Mike has to prove it's *not* a panther.'

'Yeah,' I said. 'That'll do it. I prove that the next call that comes in is just another false alarm.'

Thommo thought for a moment. If money was at stake, he wanted the ground rules spelled out quite clearly. 'We need a time limit on this, mon. A statute of limitations. Let's say we give it a month? A month on from the next supposed sighting, you provide evidence that it's a false alarm.'

'A month it is, PC Thompson. Unless I'm on holiday, in which case we deduct that time from . . .'

'Aye, I ken what you mean. I'm a fair man. Hard but fair.'

'But just hang about a minute,' I said. 'How do I stop you calling in under an assumed name with a load of bollocks about a big cat rampaging down by the river? Answer me that.'

'Ye'll just have to accept my word as a gentleman, won't you?'

'Yeah, I suppose I will. OK then, so let's make this official. Let's both put our tenners on the table, right now, to be held by Ed here.'

It's a funny thing. The minute you start talking about daft things like that, you can more or less be sure that something out of the ordinary is going to pop up. Which is not what you want when you're short-handed. And that we certainly were. After her conversation with me, Jayne had relayed her good news to the rest of the shift at the first opportunity. There was what Thommo later referred to as a pregnant pause while the news sank in, then she was greeted with congratulations and hugs all round. An hour later we were in with Birdie while he sorted out a job for Jayne in the sergeants' office, handling some of the phone enquiries, backing up the front office staff and assisting the supervisors with the admin side of things.

Two days after losing Jayne from frontline duties we had Thommo grimacing and feeling the small of his back – a sure sign that he was going to conjure up a sicknote any time soon. I suggested it was psychosomatic, all due to the pain incurred when he handed over that tenner to Ed's safe keeping, and prepared for a prolonged absence. So it was a pleasant surprise a few days later when Thommo came in and announced that he'd just been to see a miracle-worker, some kind of chiropractor who'd put his back right in ten minutes. We were on the early turn again. Ed had got called out to somewhere up Bilsdale way – another farmhouse break-in. I had one of the lads off another shift covering for Jayne, but he was busy dealing with a couple of drunk and disorderlies from the night before. Thommo was booked in to do property marking at a local village hall drop-in that had been arranged by the Neighbourhood Watch, so I only had Fordy covering around town. We were, as you might say, thin on the ground.

It was around nine thirty. The post had just been delivered and I was going through the usual pile of court returns, licensing applications and CPS advice notes when I came across one of those brown padded envelopes. You have to be very wary of packages arriving through the post these days. In Ryedale you're unlikely to get an anthrax scare or an incendiary device, but you will get just about anything else – from war relics and live ammunition to cakes and biscuits. This particular parcel came first class, and bore a Helmsley postmark. It was addressed to 'The Duty Sergeant, Malton Police Station'.

Always expect the unexpected. I've been quoting that so long I can't remember who first said it to me, but I suspect it was one of our trainers at Hendon. I held the envelope in my hands a few moments, felt the weight of it, determined that whatever was in it was solid – meaning that it was unlikely to be excrement – and non-metallic. It was too light for that. Then, using a sharp knife, I slit it open along one edge, very carefully.

The contents, wrapped in tissue paper, were what looked like a round piece of bone, about the size of a bar of soap. Well weathered, I should add. With it was a note, written in a very steady, neat hand on lined paper that looked as though it had been torn from an exercise book.

'Dear Sir (or Madam),' it read.

'Last weekend I was digging at the bottom end of my garden. It hasn't been turned over for long enough. I found the enclosed bone, which could be a human kneecap. Yours sincerely, George Dixon.'

My first impulse was to laugh. This bore all the hallmarks of someone playing a practical joke – it was verging on wasting police time. And signed by George Dixon? Who was he kidding? I checked the address, which was written on the back of the note: no, it wasn't Dock Green. I was almost disappointed.

I reread the note, picked up the supposed bone, had a good look at it and put it down again. Next thing, I found myself reaching down to feel my own kneecap, and measure it against the object lying on my desk on its bed of tissue paper. It was exactly the same size. In fact I had rolled up my trouser leg and was comparing the one with the other when Birdie walked in.

'Thinking of going for a paddle, are we, sergeant?'

'Er – not exactly, sir. Someone dug this up in his vegetable patch. Reckons it could be human.' I held it up for him to see, at the same time rolling my trouser leg back down.

Birdie took it from me, turned it over a couple of times and frowned. 'Hmm. Hard to tell. I'd hand it over to the CID if I were you.'

'Just what I was thinking, sir.'

'Very good.'

Birdie went on his way. He clearly had other things on his mind. I keyed in Des's number, but the CID man was away from his desk. Then I sat and had another look at the supposed kneecap. Putting aside my prejudices, and trying to think rationally, was there any reason why this shouldn't be treated as a possible murder enquiry? It's a peculiar feeling when you first allow a thought like that to form in your head. Murder? In Helmsley? And the victim buried at the bottom of the garden? This was straight out of Miss Marple.

The sender had put two phone numbers under his signature. I tried the landline first. No reply. Then the mobile.

'Hello?'

'Ah, hello, Mr Dixon?'

'That's me, aye.'

So, it most probably was his real name after all. 'Ah – Sergeant Mike Pannett here from Malton police station. I've received the package you sent – the possible kneecap?'

'Aye . . . now, that is a coincidence. D'you know, I was just about to call you.'

'Oh, why was that?'

'I was starting to fret. I've been down to the bottom of the garden again over the weekend. I'm double-digging, you know, to get a bit better drainage. It's awfully heavy down that bottom end . . .'

'Yes, and . . .?' The way this old guy was going on I could be here all morning.

'And I've dug up several more.'

'What, bones?'

'Aye. I mean, I'm no expert but – well, I have to say they look like human remains to me.'

'Stop digging,' I said.

'I beg pardon?'

'I said, stop digging. Right now. This needs to be investigated.'

'But there's more.'

'Which is why I'm telling you to stop digging. I don't want you to disturb any more evidence.'

'No. I don't suppose you do.'

'Listen, I'm coming right over. Put your tools away and do not touch anything, is that clear? I'll be there as soon as I can. Within the hour, OK?'

'So, have I to stop them archaeologists?'

'I beg your pardon?'

'The archaeologists. There's a party working at Helmsley Castle and soon as I mentioned my find they wanted to come round, poking and prodding, as you might say. They're all down there now with their trowels.'

'Tell them, police orders, they're to stop right now. Have you got that?'

Just as I put the phone down Fordy came in off patrol and put the kettle on. 'No time for that,' I said.

'Oh, Mike. I mean, sarge. I'm gagging. Haven't had time for me grub yet, either.'

'Sorry, mate. You might have time for a glass of water – if you hurry. You're off with me, pronto.'

He was about to argue, until I added, 'Possible murder enquiry.'

'Blimey.'

'Yes, blimey indeed. We need to get our skates on.'

While Fordy downed a bottle of something red and fizzy, I got on to control. Where the hell was our CID man? All I got was a promise that as soon as they tracked him down they'd send him across to assist me.

We didn't actually go directly to Helmsley. Instead I took a short detour to call on a vet who'd helped me out in the past with wildlife cases. I showed him the bone. To be honest, what I was hoping was that he'd tell me there was no way it could be a human kneecap, because a murder investigation was the last thing I wanted on my patch right now. Fordy, of course, would've loved it, but he didn't know how damned time-consuming they can be. It would mean drafting in the CID, setting up a murder squad, calling in Uncle Tom Cobley – and all at colossal expense. As I said to him, we couldn't afford a murder investigation, not this quarter anyway. 'Besides,' I added, 'the CID and all those other glory-seekers would monopolise the interesting jobs. Trust me, us lot at Malton, we'd be reduced to making tea and running errands. I've seen it before, lad, many a time.'

However. What was to say this had anything to do with any human remains, past or present? My good mate the vet scratched his head, got out a couple of heavyweight textbooks, turned the bone over and over in his hand, examined it under a magnifying glass, then said, 'I don't know, Mike. They could be right. It could be human. I'm afraid I couldn't say for sure.'

'Oh.'

'Let's put it this way, there's no way I'm going to stand here and tell you it isn't a knee-cap.' And with that he handed it back to me, adding, 'Sorry, old chum.'

So Fordy and I took our bone and made our way to the address in Helmsley. It was an old stone cottage, an end of terrace. There was a van parked outside, and a couple of blokes in baggy shorts, with long hair, hiking boots and T-shirts, were deep in conversation with a woman holding a camera in one hand and what looked like a brickie's trowel in the other.

'Now then,' I said, 'is Mr Dixon here?'

A slightly stooped man, about seventy and dressed in brown corduroy trousers, stepped forward. 'That's me,' he said. 'George Dixon.'

'Sergeant Mike Pannett.' We shook hands. 'We talked earlier. And this here's PC Gary Ford. Let's have a look at your garden, shall we?'

As he led me and Fordy through his front gate and round the side of the house I paused. The archaeologists were hard on my heels. 'I'm afraid I shall have to ask you to wait at the front if you don't mind. The fewer bodies we have trampling around the site the better.'

'But we've started to excavate,' one of them said. 'We don't want anything disturbed.'

'That makes two of us,' I said. 'Look, this might be an archaeological find to you, but to me it's a possible murder enquiry, and I've a number of matters to attend to.' I forced a grin. 'So I'd appreciate it if you and the rest of the Time Team could stay here.'

Even as I spoke I was aware that one or two locals had gathered at the front gate and were talking to a woman I assumed to be Mrs Dixon. 'Seems to be attracting a bit of attention,' I said to our man as he led us down the garden.

'Aye well, word got out – I mean, it wasn't as if we had anything to hide. We showed the bones to quite a few people and they all had an opinion.'

'I bet they did,' I said.

We were at the patch where he'd been digging. His spade was still in the ground and a cock robin was hopping about looking for worms. 'Now,' he said, 'there's a couple of bones right there, d'you see, at the side of me trench. That's where I'd got to when you told me to stop.'

I stooped down and there, sticking out of the soil, was what might easily have been a thigh bone, with a bulbous sort of end, and right beside it something altogether sharper and thinner.

'We reckoned that'd be a shoulder-blade,' Dixon said.

'Yeah, does kind of look like it.' Fordy leaned forward and was peering into the trench.

'Well, we can stand here all morning guessing, or we can get the scene taped off,' I said. Fordy took the cue and went back to the car. I followed him with Dixon.

'Any of those archaeologist types offer an opinion as to the age of the bones?' I asked.

He shook his head.

'Well, might as well find out.' I introduced myself to a woman who looked like the senior hand. She had white hair and spectacles. 'I was just wondering,' I said. 'Any thoughts on how old the bones might be?'

She didn't say anything for a moment. 'Well, you understand we've only had time for a cursory examination . . .'

'Of course. Before I stopped the job, you mean?'

'Well, you have your procedures, it's only to be understood. But from what I've seen they do look very well weathered. They're certainly not recent.'

'I see. And any thoughts on whether they're human or not?'

'Oh, as far as I've seen they certainly could be.'

Fordy brushed past me, the tape in his hands. 'Yeah,' I said, 'go ahead. Seal it all off, the whole plot.'

A lot of things were going through my mind at this stage. With the bones scattered the way they were, did it mean that the body had been dismembered? Or were we looking at the remains of more than one individual? And then there was their age: how old did they have to be in order that we might declare we had no interest? A hundred years? Two hundred? Or was there in any case a simpler explanation? Might we have stumbled upon a burial site of some sort?

It was clearly a case for the experts. After Fordy had got the garden taped off I told the man Dixon that this was now a crime scene, and that nobody was to enter it. I then got him to show me the collection of bones that he'd unearthed. There were the two in the ground, the kneecap he'd sent me, plus a couple more he had in the house. Just as I was noting all this down he said, 'Oh, and I nearly forgot. There were the others that went to the tip.'

'What others?' I said, pen poised.

'Why, there was one little patch where I dug up several all at once. All in the space of a couple of feet they were. I slung them in the trailer with all my other garden rubbish and we took it to the tip. This was before I found the one I sent you. Up till then, why, I thought they were something some dog had buried.'

I looked at Fordy and he looked back at me. It didn't take more than a glance to know we were both thinking the same thing. 'Would you direct us to this tip, Mr Dixon. I think it would be an idea to check it out.'

We were just about to set off when my mobile rang. It was Des from the CID. I gave him a brief rundown on what we had so far. 'Course,' I added, 'it could be they turn out not to be human remains at all.'

'That's why we need an osteologist,' Des said.

'A what?'

'Well, some sort of ologist. Bone specialist. We've got one on the contact list for cases like this. Listen, can you get all the bones that's been uncovered and bag them up, then we'll whisk 'em off to her. Leave the rest in situ.'

I got Fordy on the case while I drove over to where Dixon said he'd dumped the rest of the bones. How to make yourself popular: turn up at a recycling place on a Saturday morning and announce to everyone that they can't use the garden-waste skip until a decision had been made as to whether we needed to sift through it – a job, I hoped, for the search team rather than us.

Still, if the local gardeners were ticked off, the Dixons'

neighbours were in seventh heaven. The entire community seemed to be gripped by the excitement. Locals joined the press in speculating as to whether we'd unearthed evidence of a historical massacre, a multiple murder, or a sacred site where human sacrifices had taken place; or, as some bright spark suggested, an old cemetery, in which case the ground would have to be reconsecrated before matey could get his winter greens in.

Fordy soon had the various finds collected in individual evidence bags and was ready to dispatch them to the bones lady. We'd got the garden sealed off, and the CID had decided that, given the doubt as to the age of our finds, we could afford not to mount an overnight scene guard.

'So there you go, Thommo,' I said when we got back to the station at the end of my shift. 'Bang goes your chance of a cushy eight hours' overtime standing watch over a vegetable patch.'

'It's no loss,' he said, wincing as he stooped forward and clutched at the small of his back. 'That bloody chiropractor and his miracle cures. Twenty-four hours and I reckon I've done the lumbar vertebrae again.'

'Why, it's no wonder, the size of that wallet you carry around in your back pocket,' Ed said. 'Get it spent, lad, get it spent.'

The next day and Ann and I were both on a late turn, so we spent the morning doing a few jobs around the garden. Well, I say jobs; what we did was pick the gooseberries, of which there was quite a decent crop. Then we got carried away and started marking out a possible vegetable patch for the following year. When Ann went off to work I drove over to my mum's place and helped her with some decorating. By that I mean mixing up the paste and holding the steps while she hung the wallpaper. There was no way she was going to trust me with a job like that; it's not my strong point. I haven't the patience.

I got away about six o'clock. On the way home I realised it

was a while since I'd seen Walter. In fact, when I thought about it it was a couple of weeks ago now, maybe more. I had something for him, and I couldn't wait to see his face when I handed it over, so as soon as I'd had my tea I put Henry on the lead and walked up the hill.

'What would you say if I told you I was going to treat you to a pint?' I said, when he appeared at the gate, all sweaty in his tweed jacket and turned-down wellington boots. 'You look thirsty enough.'

'I'd say thank you very much, lad.' He took out a grubby old handkerchief and wiped his forehead. 'Been planting out brassicas all afternoon. Cabbage, cauli, broccoli. Hard work. Thirsty work.' He wiped his hands on his brown corduroy trousers and peered over my shoulder. 'On your own, eh? I mean, have I to change?'

'No, Ann's working late. And you don't need to dress up for me, mate. But you don't want to be walking down in your boots, do you?'

'Walking? I thought you might have the car.'

'Nah, a walk'll do you good, Walt. Loosen you up after all that bending and crouching.'

'I don't want to be late back, that's all. Me sister reckons to call me on a Sunday evening and I need to stand by t'phone.'

'Oh,' I said, 'is that right?' I turned away. I didn't want him to see me grinning.

Walt went to the back door, kicked off his wellies and put on his battered old brogues. 'Let's be off, then,' he said, and we set off down the hill at a gallop.

'At least they match,' I said, glancing down at his shoes.

'Course they match, lad. I've only the one pair.'

'I mean your laces. First time I met you, why, you had two different colours.'

'That was me working boots. These are me stepping-out shoes, lad. Come on, speed up, before you forget what you said about treating me.'

We were soon down the hill and into the pub. Walt grabbed a seat in the little bar where the locals like to gather and lie in wait for innocent hikers who call in for a quiet drink. Even as I ordered our pints he was explaining to a young couple about the Ryedale Panther and how it had eluded the best efforts of the police for three years now. I left him to it while the landlord filled our glasses, and popped through to the back room where people sit to eat, or to find a bit of seclusion.

'You hiding from someone, or are you wanting to be left alone?'

It was Soapy I was asking, but it was Becky who answered. 'It's our anniversary, Mike.' As she spoke she shuffled the chair round so that it was closer to Soapy's. He was giving me the sheepish look.

'But it's only—' I began.

'I know,' she said. 'Only three months but that's all the excuse a couple of soppy old lovebirds like us need.' She shuffled up even closer.

I glanced at Soapy. 'That's going to cost you a few bob, lad. Four anniversaries a year? You'll be wanting a few more roof jobs if you carry on like that.'

Soapy grimaced. 'I've enough on without clambering about on scaffolding, Mike. Has Algy boy been onto you yet, about the fete?'

'What fete's that?'

'Good question. All I know is he's volunteered to do one of them stunts where everyone gets to lob coconuts and you end up in a tub of cold water.'

'You mean an Aunt Sally,' I said.

Becky corrected me. 'No, ducking-stool.'

'Aye, that's the one. Anyway,' Soapy continued, 'he's put me down to rig it up. As if I ain't busy enough.' He leaned forward. 'Fact is, Mike, I haven't a clue. Done a few jobs in me time, like, but . . .'

Walt had appeared, walking steadily towards us with a pint in each hand. 'So this is where you're hiding, is it? What d'you reckon, Soapy, to a feller who walks off and leaves you to pay? And that after he's dragged you away from your gardening on a promise.'

'Promise? Of what?' Soapy asked.

'Just a free pint,' I said. 'Nowt to get excited over. Sorry, Walt. Here.' I dug in my pocket for some change.

'Never mind,' he said. 'You'll just have to get t'next one in.' He gave Becky the hard stare. 'Now then, what you been doing to this poor old lad? He looks as though he's lost a pound and found a tanner.'

'Well, maybe you're the man to put a smile on his face, Walter.'

Walt poised, his pint halfway to his lips, and frowned.

'What she means—' I began, but Soapy interrupted me.

'I need someone to show me how to build one of them ducking-stools,' he said.

Walt spluttered a mouthful of foam back into his beer. 'By heck, that's a bit harsh isn't it? Three months wed and you're chastising her already. What you been doing to him, Becky lass?'

I had to hand it to the girl, she took it on the chin and laughed along with him. 'Nice try, Walter. No, it's one of Algy's hobby horses. Wants to show everyone he's "a good sport". You know how he talks. Told us he's willing to make "a complete and utter fool of himself". He cracks me up, that man.'

'Shouldn't be too hard,' Walt sniffed. 'He's been a blooming laughing stock since he got that there hoss of his.'

Becky laughed. 'Anyway,' she said, 'we thought you might have some idea.'

'Aye,' Soapy said, 'seeing as it's a medieval type of contraption – more your era.'

'Wouldn't do any harm to bring it back, if you're asking me,' Walt muttered. But he agreed to put his mind to it, and I agreed to help out if I could. 'Any opportunity to get Algy boy in the drink,' I said.

'Talking of which.' Walt had already drained his glass and was licking his lips.

'Blimey,' I said. 'That never touched the sides, did it? Come on then, Walt, let's leave these lovebirds to it, shall we? Besides,' I added as he followed me to the bar, 'I've something to give you, remember?'

He resumed his seat at the front of the pub. The hikers had gone. Drank up in a hurry, according to our landlord.

'Come on then, lad, let's have it. What you got for me?' Walt took his pint, held it up to the light and nodded approvingly.

'Here.' I reached into my pocket and pulled out a mobile phone. 'Ann treated me to a new one and I thought, rather than sling this, I'd pass it on. It's all charged up and ready to go.'

Walt put his pint down on the table in front of us, and took the phone from me. 'Why, what would I want with this? I already have one at home.'

'But not a mobile,' I said. I dipped my hand in my other pocket. 'And here's a charger for you. See how I look after you?'

'But what do I want with one of them? I just told you, I already have a phone.'

'Security, Walt. Just think, if you were out walking that dog of yours, and you took a tumble.'

'I've never taken a tumble yet.'

'No, but there's always a first time, matey. And you aren't getting any younger.'

He held it up to his ear. 'Where do I speak into it, anyway?' he asked, but before I could answer he was off on another tack. 'And what about the expense? They reckon they're dear to run, these.'

'Not if you're careful. Besides, it's got a tenner's worth of credit in it already. And if you learn to text, that's really cheap. Ten pence a go or thereabouts.'

'Aye, I've seen the kids do that, down in Malton town centre. Never look where they're going either. But who'm I going to text, eh? Tell me that.'

'Why, you could send one to Muriel now and then. Tell her how much you think of her. Look, Walt, it'd put my mind to rest if you took it. You're on your own, out in the middle of nowhere. Even if you just keep it charged up and have it ready for an emergency. Should one arise, that is.'

Walt turned the phone over in his hand. 'How much credit did you say it has?'

'Ten quid, maybe a bit more.'

'A tenner, eh? So if I decided not to use it, can I . . .?'

'No, you cannot cash it in. This is a gift, from me and Ann, and it's for your personal safety. Now, I'm going to show you how to call, how to receive. That's all you need for now.'

I took him through the basics, showed him where my number was stored and left him to it. I'd no doubt that it would end up in a drawer somewhere, but, as I said to Ann when she got home that night, at least I'd tried.

Back at work, a couple of days passed and I was starting to wonder when we might hear from the bone specialist. So was our man at Helmsley, George Dixon. Three times he rang me in a single shift.

'I'm sure they're doing their best,' I told him.

'Aye, but I want to get my winter cabbages in, and them caulis and broccoli.'

I looked up at the rain spattering against the window. 'Look on the bright side,' I said. 'It's not a day to be down that garden, is it now?'

I put the phone down, and settled to my paperwork. The place was deadly quiet. More life in the chapel of rest, as Soapy would say. I'd been working ten or fifteen minutes when the phone rang once more.

'Good evening, Malton police station, Sergeant Mike Pannett

speaking. How may I help you?' Not the standard greeting; more appropriate to a call centre, but hey – the rain was lashing down and I was snug and warm in my office.

'I've found a couple of stray dogs.'

'Oh yes, sir. And whereabouts is this?'

'Just outside Eden Camp, right beside the Pickering road.'

'And the dogs are running loose, you say? Are they in amongst traffic?'

'No. They were loose, but not any more. I've collared them.' He sounded quite a cheery fellow.

'I see. Well, that's good.'

'Yes, they're quite placid. They're a pair of golden Labradors, fully matured. Well looked after, I'd say, just a bit muddy. The thing is, they were both trailing leads.'

As soon as he said that my mood changed. If they were trailing leads it suggested that they'd been out with their owner. Full-grown Labradors aren't normally the sort to run off. So what had happened to whoever was walking them? If this guy had picked them up by Eden Camp, that was a fair way from the nearest houses.

'Any identification tags on them?'

'No. Nothing that I can see.'

'Look,' I said, 'are you in a position to wait there while I come and meet you? I'm only down the road. Less than a mile.'

'No problem. I'm not in a hurry. And I've got a big brolly.'

I threw on a waterproof, went outside, grabbed the van and within two minutes was negotiating the roundabout above the bypass. And there, just where the lane turns off for Eden Camp, was my man.

'Lovely pair of dogs,' I said as I got out of the van and hurriedly put on my cap. He was all togged up in waterproofs and a wide-brimmed hat.

'Yes, haven't given me a moment's worry.'

'But definitely no identifying tags on 'em?' I asked, reaching down to feel their collars.

He shook his head. 'Could be chipped of course.'

'Could be, aye.'

My concern was very much for the owner. The dogs didn't have the look of excited runaways. So had the owner had an accident, or fallen ill – a heart attack, maybe – or was it some elderly person who'd got lost, or confused?

I put the dogs into the back of the van, where they settled quite happily. It was obvious that they were well looked after and well trained. Probably grateful to be brought in out of the wet too. Next thing, I got on to control. My assessment of the situation was that we needed officers down here right away to start a search. I thanked the man for his assistance, and took his details in case we needed to contact him again, then got on with calling in my available officers. I was lucky. Fordy was in town, and Thommo was only in Norton. There's an awful lot of open country north of the bypass and it's very popular with dog walkers. There are a number of lanes and it would take the three of us some time to cover them all. If we drew a blank there we might have to think about searching the actual countryside – and I was not looking forward to that. The fact is, I had a bad feeling about this.

We spent the next hour or so combing every lane and footpath on either side of the dual carriageway. As we went we knocked on the door of every house in the immediate area, but nobody had any information or knowledge about the dogs. What was more worrying was that, all this time after our man had found the dogs, nobody had contacted the station to report them missing. Meanwhile Fordy had come out and was ferrying the dogs back to town, where he would get a vet to scan them for any identifying chip they might be carrying.

It was starting to get properly gloomy now. The rain was still coming down in sheets and there was a stiff wind out of the southwest. I'd called the specials in and I had Will MacDonald with me, searching to either side of the lane that runs north from Eden Camp, parallel with the Pickering road. We'd been looking in the hedge bottoms and were approaching a patch of woods. 'Is it worth climbing over the fence and looking around?' Will asked.

'Might be,' I said, 'but what would a dog walker be doing there?' We stood for a moment in silence. 'Sod this,' I said. 'We need to rustle up some more support. It's a good hour and a half since those dogs were picked up. Whoever they belong to, if they've fallen sick they could be in real trouble now – especially in this lot.'

'*Control to 1015, over.*'

'Go ahead, over.'

'*Yeah, Mike, we've had word from the vet. He's run his scanner over your dogs. Neither of them are microchipped, over.*'

'Right, well . . . this is serious now. I reckon it's time we called out the Scarborough search and rescue team. We could do with their expertise, not to mention manpower.

'*Will do Mike.*'

'Also, can you get onto the local media and see if they'll put out a few details on the radio? Might get us something.'

'*Received Mike, will do.*'

I put the radio away and turned to Will. He'd come out without a hat, and his hair was plastered to his scalp, the drips running down his neck. 'I know what I want,' I said.

'What's that?' Will asked. 'A nice drop of Scotch?'

'That'd do nicely,' I said. 'No, I want to call out the helicopter.'

'You've got a thing about that, haven't you?'

'You might say I have, Will. And I'll tell you what my thing is. It's costing the taxpayer a small fortune, it's a bloody fancy bit of kit and we rarely get to use it out here. I tell you what though, it could be invaluable.' I pulled the radio back out and called control again.

North Yorkshire don't have a helicopter and rely on the surrounding forces to supply the service, which comes at quite a cost. The Humberside helicopter was based at Pocklington, fifteen miles south and east of York. Yes, I was told, it would be available shortly, and if I really needed it . . . It arrived at nine thirty, just as the light started to go. At ten the search and rescue team arrived. At ten thirty the helicopter was called away to pursue a stolen car on the A1079. The crew had managed to do a heat-seeking search of an area about a couple of miles square. Every little helps and all that, but we were now left to cover the rest on foot.

It wasn't until two thirty in the morning, by which time we were wet through, starving hungry and half frozen, that we made the decision to call off the search. We had covered what we felt was the relevant area. We took into consideration that the dogs, when they were first found, weren't muddy, which suggested that they'd been on defined paths rather than walking cross-country. We had now covered every track, footpath and roadside and felt that that was as much as we could do. The search team, as ever, were keen to stay and work for as long as needed. But to be honest we were baffled as to what had happened, and I couldn't really see any point in their continuing, at least, not until it got light.

Back at the station we revived ourselves with hot chocolate and biscuits and prepared for home. I was the last to go. I was not happy, not happy at all, to have something like this left unresolved on my watch. It was an odd feeling, and an unpleasant one, to know that there's nothing else you could've done, yet to feel that you'd somehow failed.

I grabbed a few hours' sleep and was back in at eight thirty next morning. I wasn't actually due on duty until lunchtime, but in cases like this you can't help yourself: you're involved; you feel responsible.

When I walked into the station it was like the *Marie Celeste*.

Everybody off the early turn was out searching, although I hadn't been there very long when the odd officer started coming back in for a bite to eat. It may have been high summer, but the weather out there was more like autumn. Overnight the wind had strengthened, and we'd had reports of whole branches being ripped off trees and blocking minor roads. But the constant rain, had, at least, turned more intermittent and the clouds had lifted somewhat.

'Have the press been called in to photograph these dogs?' I asked, when Birdie came to see how things were going.

'I don't believe they have,' he said. 'Yes, somebody ought to have done that by now.'

I was just picking up the phone to call the *Gazette* when I was summoned to the front counter. Standing there was an elderly couple, both wrapped up in waterproof coats and dripping all over the floor.

'Now then,' I said. 'What brings you out on a wild morning like this? You want to be cosied up by the fire.'

'Well, chance would be a fine thing,' the lady said, leaning her brolly against the counter, 'but we waited all last night and – well, we thought we ought to come and ask you.'

'Yes?'

She leaned forward, as if about to part with a valuable secret. 'You haven't by any chance had anybody report a pair of dogs running loose, have you?'

'Ah. Wouldn't be golden Labs by any chance, would they?' I asked.

She brightened visibly. 'Yes. You mean . . .?'

'We've got them in safe keeping. Have had for' – I looked at my watch – 'I'd say fifteen hours, getting on for. I take it they're yours?'

'Oh yes.' It was the man who spoke. The lady was almost hugging herself with delight. 'We would've reported it earlier, of course, but we went out looking yesterday evening and we realised you had some sort of . . . well, we assumed it was a major operation on. There seemed to be officers everywhere we went. And then – well, when we saw the helicopter I said to my wife here, I said, it must be something serious to be fetching that out.'

He looked at his wife. 'Yes,' she said, 'a manhunt perhaps. So we decided to wait until this morning, see whether the dogs got home on their own.'

'Do they – er, do they often go missing?' I said.

'No,' the lady said. 'This is only the second time. We'd been out for a walk, came home and took them straight into their run. Didn't even take their leads off, which was rather lax, I suppose, but we were both absolutely drenched, and so were they.' She turned to her husband. 'I wonder whether the wind could've blown that gate open?'

'I suppose it must have done.'

Then, as I gathered my thoughts, she asked, 'So did you catch whoever it was you were after?'

'Well, this may come as a bit of a shock to you, but all of those people out searching last night – ah, they were looking for you two.'

At first they looked perplexed, then worried. 'But what do you mean? Why were you looking for us?' She answered.

'Well, when you find dogs running loose with their leads on, you naturally wonder what happened to the owners. My concern was that you might have been injured or taken ill while you were out walking them. I may as well tell you I was very worried.'

'Oh dear,' they said, almost in unison. 'So we've caused you rather a lot of trouble.'

'Don't worry,' I said. 'It's what we're here for. I'm just glad and relieved that you're both all right. By the way, have you ever thought about having your dogs chipped?'

While they digested what had happened I called Jayne through. She started on the paperwork and would return the dogs to the couple. Meanwhile I shot into the parade room where Ed and Fordy were putting their dripping outer garments onto hangers and mashing a pot of tea.

'Right lads,' I said. 'The search is officially over. We have located the missing persons, and I can report that they are safe and well.' Nobody spoke. 'So that's it,' I added, 'it's over. Case closed.'

Fordy was looking at me, his mouth half open. 'Blimey, sarge. I mean – where did you find 'em? And how?'

'You're not going to believe this but they've just this minute turned up at the front office.'

'You what!'

'Yep. Didn't want to bother us earlier – because they could see we were so busy.'

That wasn't quite the end of the matter. It rarely is these days. A day or so later I found myself in Birdie's office, listening to him read a memo from on high about the Malton station's cavalier eagerness to call in the helicopter at considerable expense.

'Look, I'm sorry, sir,' I said, 'but my assessment at the time was that whoever the dogs belonged to might well be in danger.'

Birdie looked at the sheet of paper in his hand. 'Yes,' he said, 'I'm inclined to agree with you on that one. Don't worry, Mike, I'll stand up for you. But here' – he handed me the note – 'better take this. Always useful to have a copy in case it comes up again.'

Indeed it is, I thought, as I hurried my way back across the car park, holding the note above my head to keep the rain off.

I'd only been back a few minutes when my mood brightened. The lads had made a fresh brew and Ed had brought out a tin of excellent chocolate-chip cookies his missus had baked for us. I was just about to get stuck in when a fax came through from our bone specialist. She'd made a thorough examination of the finds from Helmsley and here were her findings. 'Listen up,' I said, flourishing the document in front of them all. 'You'll be pleased to hear that what we had was – and I quote – "a miscellaneous collection of very old *cattle* bones, mostly from the legs . . ." blah blah blah . . . ah yes, here we are . . . "somewhere in the region of a hundred years old". Right,' I said, 'I think you ought to nip over to Helmsley, Fordy, and convey the glad tidings. Tell matey he can get on with his double digging, eh?'

The postscript to all this was a note from our Mr Dixon a week or two later, telling us that he'd indeed done some digging – not in his vegetable patch, but in the library – and had found out that until about 1900 his cottage had been a butcher's shop.

Chapter 6

Prison Camp Break In

It was August, and at last we were getting some proper summer weather. Ann and I were spending most of our spare time in the garden at Keeper's Cottage, pottering about, drawing up grandiose plans – and retiring to the log to sit and sip a cool beer and decide that, yes, a productive plot with a pond like Walter's would be a great idea. One day. When we had more time, and energy.

'Anyway,' I said, looking around at the tall trees that surrounded our grounds, as we liked to call them, and Henry lolling in the long grass with his tongue hanging out, too lazy even to chase after the odd wasp, 'the way I see it we've worked hard at making this place our home. We've earned the right to sit and enjoy it for a while. And besides, Walter says we shouldn't start digging till after Christmas.'

'Oh. That right?' Ann was only half listening, and I couldn't blame her. For the first time since last summer we'd actually got the sunloungers out and done the job right: shorts, T-shirts, cooler full of drinks, and the makings of a barbecue all stacked up in the kitchen for when the sun went down.

'Yeah, you want a frost on it, that's the thing. That's what he reckons, anyway. Break up the clods. Boxing Day, he says. That's when you want to get digging.'

'Mmm . . . right'. I heard the clink of ice as Ann picked up her glass. She took a sip and said, 'We going where on Boxing Day?' I glanced across at her. She'd had her head buried in some piece of chick-lit. Her favourite way of relaxing. I don't think she'd heard a word I'd said.

'We don't go anywhere, love. We stay home and get our wellies on. Boxing Day morning: it's when you're supposed to get the spade out and start digging.'

Ann put her book to one side and reached for the suncream. 'Digging for what? Lugworms? Buried treasure?' Then she looked at me and laughed. 'Do you know, Mike, you sound more and more like Walter every day.'

'Hey, you carry on with your reading, love.' I lay back down, luxuriating in the warm sunshine. 'I'm quite happy talking to myself. At least no bugger interrupts me. And as Algy would doubtless say' – I cracked open another bottle of beer and took a long pull on it – 'it's a matter of no real consequence.'

When you work shifts a simple thing like being able to spend a Sunday afternoon together in the garden, doing absolutely nothing, is a proper treat. Comes round about once every six weeks if you're lucky; and then it's a pound to a pinch of you-know-what that it'll rain. But not today. No, today was looking good. Nice and quiet and relaxing, the way a Sunday ought to be, the way I seemed to remember it was when I was a lad. And by a miracle, it lasted all day. No unexpected showers, no visitors calling in unannounced, not even a phone call. Wonderful. As afternoon faded into evening we fired up the charcoal, brought out the burgers and bangers, lit a couple of those insecticide candles – and then, just as we were about to get stuck in, who should come rattling up the drive in a clapped-out Datsun pick-up but Soapy.

'Why, you don't reckon to be scoffing that lot on your own, do you?' he said, making a beeline for the sausages. 'I mean, there's enough there to feed—'

'Excuse me . . .' Ann was shaking her head. 'Have you ever seen Mike when he's confronted by a mound of sizzling flesh?'

'Only on t'beach at Scarborough, lass. And he told me not to tell you 'bout that.'

'Come on,' I said, before Ann could respond. 'There's plenty for all. Help yourself, Soapy.'

'As it happens,' he said, grabbing a burger and stuffing half of it in his mouth, 'I'm not that hungry. Me and Becks have just had our tea. Popped round to remind you about the old fete job.'

'What's that you say?'

'You know: you, me and Algy, and that there ducking-stool. Remember? When we was in t'pub?'

'Oh hell. That. I'd clean forgotten. When did you say it is?'

'Sooner than you think, my friend. Two o'clock Saturday. I hope you've kept it free.'

'Could be a problem there, matey. I'm on a late shift. Have to be at work by then.'

Soapy took a fat pork and leek sausage, nicely blackened on one side, and smothered it with French mustard. 'By, these are all right,' he said, rolling his eyes as he wrapped it in a bread bun and popped it in his mouth. 'Oh well, that can't be helped. But you and me put ourselves down to rig it up, remember?'

'Oh dear. So we did. You ever made a ducking-stool, Soapy?'

He laughed, and wiped a dribble of grease off his chin. 'Hey, they was mekking 'em back in t'Middle Ages, cock-bod. How hard can it be, eh?'

I had to remind Soapy what he'd said later in the week when we sat in Algy's yard surrounded by assorted lengths of timber, several coils of rope, a collection of miscellaneous nails and screws, and a plastic paddling pool. But, fortunately for us, Algy was on hand.

'The original contrivance,' he said, 'was a simple pivot. Load times load arm equals effort times effort arm and all that tosh.'

'Er, one more time, but slowly?' I said.

'O-level Physics, old chap. The basic principle of the lever.' He picked up a plank and balanced it on a wooden stump to demonstrate. 'The operator's at this end, like so, and your termagant wife is tied to the seat at the other. The chap simply leans on this end whenever he wearies of her yapping – and dunks her in the pool. Divinely simple, don't you agree?'

Soapy was unimpressed. 'Aye,' he said, 'but this is the age of automation. Your modern-day punter wants to lob a half-brick, trigger sommat clever and – ker-splosh. Get the picture, do you?'

'Quite so, quite so.' Algy scratched his head, and I kept schtum. I knew what Soapy meant, but couldn't see how we were going to get there.

There was a bit of humming and ha-ing, before Algy slapped his thigh and said, 'Do you know, I think I have the very thing in my other workshop. I'm sure a pal of mine rigged something up for an event at Castle Howard some years ago, and if I'm not mistaken . . . Only thing is, I seem to recall it was rather sensitive. Sort of a hair-trigger affair, if you know what I mean.'

An hour later Algy had fetched his 'contrivance', and we'd cobbled the rig together, agreeing that it was perhaps 'a trifle sensitive,' in Algy's words. Soapy, our City and Guilds tradesman extraordinaire, explained that this could be easily rectified by a sharp wallop with the lump hammer. All was well and we dismantled the structure ready for transporting. Soapy would bring it down to the fairground on the big day and I'd just have time to set it up with him before I went in to work.

Back at the station, things had been relatively quiet for a few days. That lasted until our briefing, when Birdie put on his serious face and told us the bad news. We'd had another outbreak of burglaries, and to emphasise the fact, he waved a sheaf of papers at us and started thumbing through them. 'The one at Stockton-on-the-Forest,' he began, 'is York's to worry about; but it bears all the hallmarks of the one you dealt with, Mike.' He glanced over at me and I nodded as he shuffled the pile. 'First a reconnaissance, then they come back to take everything of value, although in your case it was a 'two in one' with the Land Rover and then the shotguns, wasn't it?'

'Yes sir,', I said, 'and one of them was antique; worth a lot of money if they can find a buyer.'

'Right. And now, this last weekend, for those of you who haven't heard, a large house over at Sledmere – just on Humberside's ground – was broken into in daylight. Various artefacts, a number of paintings, a substantial amount of jewellery and antique furniture taken. No unusual vehicles seen in the vicinity – either on Sunday or in the lead-up. They'd done their homework. The owners were away for a week, abroad, and the burglars had the run of the place. Parked up inside the grounds, nice high wall between them and the neighbours. Nobody saw a thing. So, if this is the same lot we ran up against earlier in the year, be aware that they're active again.'

He paused before going on. 'And if it's another lot, well, we've something else to worry about, haven't we? Amanda, the crime analyst, is liaising with York. She'll be fully up to speed on this and any associated activity. So, anything you hear of, any queries, speak to her. It's what she's here for.'

Some of us thought he'd finished, and were shuffling out of our seats. But he hadn't.

'There's more,' he said. 'When I say there's been an outbreak I could've said epidemic. There was a third break-in at Helmsley, also in the daytime. Private house, small estate on the edge of town, owners away for the weekend. Now, one thing Amanda has come up with is that they seem to be targeting places with no alarm system, and also houses with patio doors. You might say it makes sense – they're softer targets – but the thing to bear in mind is that they're obviously reconnoitring these places, and others, gathering information. These are not amateurs, not opportunists. They are serious players, and we need to put them out of business. Meanwhile, and I hope I don't need to be telling you this, you should be advising people on your beats about target hardening, making it as difficult as possible for the thieves to gain entry. I would also suggest that you stress the need for increased vigilance.'

'Tell you what sir, I'll make contact with the *Gazette* and get them to put a piece in.'

'Good idea, Mike. The more public awareness, the better the chances of beating this.'

I'd already made a note to pull another newsletter together for my Country Watch people, and I would try and get around to visit as many as I could on my rounds – although I was now scrabbling for time to do that sort of thing, what with my extra duties as acting sergeant. So much for my plans. As ever I was thrown off-course by the unexpected. Fresh from briefing, I got a call from my old friend Gerald, the naturist up at Howsham Woods.

'Now then, sir, what can I do for you?'

'Well, to be perfectly frank with you, Constable Pannett . . .' I was tempted to interrupt him and put him right as to my rank, but I let it go. It wouldn't cut much ice where he was concerned. 'To be honest,' he continued, 'I could recite you a list. But what's on my mind just now is these travellers.'

'Oh yes?' I said. I'm always wary when people start talking about 'these travellers'. It's a bit like talking about 'these young people' or 'those football supporters' – as if you can count them as a job lot, each one indistinguishable from the rest. And it just isn't that simple. 'Tell me more,' I said. 'Have you been falling out with them?'

'As a matter of fact I haven't, but I very soon shall do if things go on like this. I've had a disagreement with them, and if you want my opinion it's in danger of escalating.'

'I see. Well listen, Mr . . .' I realised I'd forgotten his second name, but he took the cue.

'Rodgers. With a "d".'

'Ah yes, Mr Whitaker. Look, why don't I pop over and see you later this morning – providing nothing else comes up. It might help if we talk this through face to face. Will you be about?'

'I don't go very far, Constable Pannett, especially this time of year. I prefer to be in the woods. It's an awful lot safer there.'

'OK then. And by the way, where are you calling from?'

'From just near my place – about a hundred yards up the hill. I get good reception there.'

'Oh, you've got a mobile have you?'

'Mobile?'

'As in mobile phone.'

'Ah yes. I see. Yes, my daughter brought it over. Insisted I should have one. I was dead against it, I have to say. But do you know, I find it rather useful. Because the nearest public phone to here – well, it's further than I care to go some days. Anyway, it keeps my daughter happy. She worries about me.'

I was going to say that it didn't surprise me, but I let it go. Normally I would have tasked one of the team with this job, but everyone was tied up just now. Besides, I wasn't sure that young Fordy or Thommo would appreciate sharing a cup of tea with our man Gerald. He was an acquired taste.

It was some hours later, getting on for noon, when I caught up with him. I parked on the track that makes a circuit through the woods. It's used by dog walkers, hikers and joggers, but I doubt that more than a handful of them ever get off into the trees. Once you do, you're in another world: enclosed, quiet, isolated. There's no doubt about it, places like this have a definite atmosphere – in this case an almost magical one. I ended up fighting my way through a thicket of hazel saplings, rank grasses and low branches before I stumbled, quite suddenly, upon the little clearing, by which time I was breathing heavily. And, with the good weather having kept up, I was sweating. As for my pal the naturist, well, even as I called out 'Anybody home?' I knew what to expect.

I wasn't disappointed. Mr Gerald Rodgers, with a 'd', emerged from his hut, caravan, shelter – I'd never really worked out what it was, what with all the bits he'd nailed on or draped over it – wearing a skinny little rag of a towel. Nothing too outrageous about that, you might say, were it not for the fact that it was slung over his shoulder. Other than that – and a single, yellow rubber glove on his right hand – he was as naked as they day he was born, but a lot browner.

'Just catching up on some domestic chores,' he said, flour-ishing one of those old-fashioned dish-mops. He had a sturdy wooden stool set up outside the shed, with a white enamelled bowl perched on top of it. Scattered about the grass, all upside down, were his assorted pots and pans. To one side of the hut he'd got a little plot fenced off with chicken wire and was growing tomatoes, lettuce and one or two other things.

As I stood there waiting for him to find me a seat it occurred to me that you can think what you like about a man like that, but you have to admit it: he was living out some sort of dream there in the woods. On a day like this a little part of me – well, I wouldn't say I envied him, but with the sun streaming down between the overhanging branches and his old paint pots full of geraniums and nasturtiums in full bloom, I could see there was a certain charm to his existence. If only he'd learn to cover himself up when people came calling . . .

He unfolded a deckchair, the sort that you only see these days in seaside postcards, dusted a couple of spiders off the faded, striped canvas and set it down. 'Have a pew,' he said.

I sank into it and took out my notebook. 'Now then, tell me what's troubling you. You said something about a disagreement with—' I tell you what, interviewing a stark naked man is no laughing matter. You sort of find yourself on edge, hoping he keeps his legs crossed and his hands in his lap – which, for the moment, our man Gerald was doing.

'With travellers. Yes, you may as well say it.' He'd put his washing-up bowl on the ground and was perched on the wooden stool. 'You'll remember that I occasionally deal in scrap items. Just dabbling, really, but it brings in a few coppers.' And then he laughed, exposing a set of very regular white teeth. 'Pun unintended, you understand.'

'Eh? Oh, coppers. Yes . . .' I said. 'Yes, last time I was here you were burning off old electric cables.' I glanced around me. 'You don't seem to be doing that any more.'

'Ah, but I am,' he said. 'And that's the root of the problem.'

'I see.' Actually I didn't. I was just waiting for him to carry on – at his own pace. Because that's the thing about a bloke like Gerald. He was absolutely his own man – to the point where nothing you could say would hurry him on. He'd got me on his territory and he was set on playing the game by his rules, and in time with his own leisurely beat.

'I used to load up my scrap across the handlebars and cycle down to that yard at Norton. You'll know the one I mean. And one day I bumped into some of these travelling types. They said they could deal with me direct, cut out the middle man. And I'll tell you what happened – because I didn't like it one little bit.'

He was silent for a moment, half cocking his ear as a woodpecker hammered away somewhere in the woods. 'Lovely sound,' he said, before continuing. 'But yes, as I was saying, these people found out where I live.'

'What, they came here?' I asked.

'Yes, looked over my pile of scrap, made me an offer, which I felt obliged to accept, and were off. Well, I need hardly tell you, Constable Pannett, that I no longer feel entirely safe – especially when I paid a visit to the scrapyard and found that metals, particularly copper, are rocketing in price and they . . .' He tailed off.

'They got it off you for a knock-down price, is that it?'

'I believe the saying is, they ripped me off. Anyway, they were there that day when I went back to the yard, and I challenged them about it. Told them they had a moral obligation to share some of their profits with me.'

'And?'

'Oh, things nearly got quite ugly. Let's say they were confrontational. Menacing.'

'Well, what did they do? Did they make threats?' I asked. 'Were they aggressive towards you?'

He shook his head. 'They didn't threaten me verbally. It was their – their demeanour. I found it rather frightening, I have to say. But I can tell you here and now that if they ever show their faces around here again, well, I shall challenge them all over again. Oh yes, you can count on that.'

'Be very careful what you do,' I said. 'My advice to you would be not to go provoking people unnecessarily. If you think you have a case against them, talk to us and we'll make sure it's handled the right way. Anyway, you haven't said – that is, I don't suppose you can give me a name for any of these people, can you?'

He shook his head. 'No. I can't.'

'Well, how many were there?'

He thought for a moment, uncrossed his legs, then crossed them again. I wondered for a moment whether he was doing it deliberately, although to be honest I don't think he was conscious of his own nakedness any more. A bit like Adam before the Fall, you might say. But before I could pursue the thought any further he was answering my question.

'There were two of them came here, but I think there was another one waiting further back in the woods, on the track there – in a vehicle, I should imagine. That's what frightened me. And the second meeting, at the scrapyard, there were three of them. They had a small truck. With a white cab. It was all full of old washing machines, prams, odds and ends of guttering. The usual kind of thing.'

'Well, that's a start,' I said, noting it down. 'Did you get a number?'

He shook his head. 'I wish I had now, but I didn't.'

'And can you describe the men?'

'That's not easy. I'm afraid that to my unskilled eye they looked like – well, like travellers. Short, dark. One had a black waistcoat on, I do remember that, but no, I wouldn't like to . . . They were all of an age. Fortyish, I would say. But no – I'm afraid my mind was elsewhere by this time. I was very, very angry, and, if I'm perfectly honest, quite frightened.'

I closed my notebook. 'It's not a lot to go on,' I said. 'To be honest, Mr Whitaker, this is a civil dispute between you and them about the price of the metal. However, if they turn up again or you get any more intimidation then that's a different ballgame.' I tapped the notebook. 'But the information you've given is useful. As you've just pointed out, the price of certain metals has risen sharply and we've seen a huge increase in thefts. So it's a help.'

'Glad to be of assistance, Constable. I must say, I feel rather vulnerable now that they know where I live. I'm very much on my own out here.'

'Yes, but thanks to that lass of yours you're in touch with the outside world.' I got out of my seat and prepared to go. I told him that he was to contact the station straight away if he had any further visits – and I gave him my mobile number, although I had to key it into his new phone for him, just as I had with Walter. I was about to take my leave when I stopped to ask him about his little dwelling. 'So what exactly do you call this,' I said, 'is it a chalet or what?'

'Well,' he said, suddenly breaking into a smile, 'what people don't realise is that it is in fact a caravan.' He pulled back a sort of plywood skirting to reveal a white painted wheel with a fully inflated, if half perished, rubber tyre. 'And there's another on the other side, of course. So in theory,' he said, 'I could take to the open road – if the fancy took me. And I had a car to pull it.'

'Yes,' I replied, 'or maybe a pair of shire horses. But you'd have a job on to find another spot as good as this, eh?'

'Precisely.'

It was, as always, an odd encounter. I realised as I drove back to town that I was smiling. The thing with Gerald was that, yes, he was a bit of a challenge, but he was – what's the phrase? – comfortable in his own skin. Especially when the weather was fair.

However, the weather didn't stay fair for long that week. On the Friday, when I was on nights, it was back to the wet and windy pattern we'd had so much of that summer. Just getting from my car into the station I got half drenched. I remember thinking it would be a good night to stay indoors, and as I said to Ed when he followed me in, let's hope our local villains feel the same.

What we heard at briefing, however, reminded me that there was plenty to think about, whatever the night threw up. Further to the break-ins at Helmsley and Sledmere it emerged that we'd received a potentially handy piece of intelligence. One of my Country Watch people – a farmer's wife, as it happened, who lived on the edge of the Sledmere estate – had called in to say that she'd spotted a hire van cruising around the lanes on a couple of occasions the previous week. She'd thought nothing of it until she heard about the burglaries. And that tallied with something we'd had from another source, that a similar van had been seen parked up at Stockton-on-the-Forest in the days before that incident.

'Well,' I said to Jayne, as she joined us for a brew before

going off duty, 'it all helps to build up a picture, bit by bit – and then we'll have the buggers.'

'Pity I'm not in on it with you,' she said. Jayne was no longer working nights – just the busier day or late shifts – but she was finding plenty to occupy her and was starting to spend a little time with Amanda in crime analysis when she had a few moments to spare.

'Don't worry,' I said. 'You'll get back to this sort of thing soon enough. Right now though, I reckon you need to be watching out for your bump.'

It was, as I'd hoped, a quiet night. The news from town was that the pubs were more or less deserted. One or two of them had even closed their doors early, for lack of custom. The only thing of note was when I had to send Fordy out to see about a beech tree that had shed a huge branch right across the Castle Howard road. It got to about three o'clock. Fordy and I had finished eating and were about to head back out. Thommo and Ed had just landed for their break. Ed and I were speculating about York City's chances of promotion in the season that was just starting when control came on to say that the Eden Camp alarms had been activated. They had one of those systems that sends an alert to the alarm company several minutes before it activates the alarms on site, meaning that we had time to get there before the intruders, if there were any, realised they'd triggered it.

There was the usual scramble as everyone grabbed their gear and ran to the vehicles.

'*Control to 1015.*'

'Go ahead, over.'

'*Mike just to let you know we have a dog unit in the vicinity, will be with you in a few minutes.*'

'That's a piece of luck, all received.'

We were up at the camp within two or three minutes, and we'd no sooner arrived than we were wishing we hadn't been so keen. Above the sound of the wind whistling through the power lines, the alarms had already started and were making a hideous row.

'Fit to wake the dead,' Thommo said. 'And I suppose we have to stand and listen to this racket until the keyholder turns out.'

'Well,' I said, looking at the fence that surrounded the place, topped with three strands of barbed wire, 'we'd best get the place boxed off as best we can. Ed and Thommo, can you two take the far side? Fordy and me will cover the front. I'll let you know when the keyholder and the dogs arrive.'

'They can take their time for me, laddie,' Thommo said, climbing back into the car. 'I could do without a drenching. Hello, is this your man?'

A vehicle was approaching us from the roundabout. As it turned towards us the headlights illuminated the Spitfire that stands guard over the main gates and the wooden lookout tower behind it.

'Blimey,' Fordy said. 'Looks like Stalag Luft whatsit.'

'Used to be a prisoner of war camp. Haven't you learnt any local history since you've been here, Gary?'

But before he could answer the keyholder had driven alongside us and was winding down his window. 'Got here as quick as I could,' he shouted. 'Figured I could afford to break the speed limit down the Beverley road, eh? You lot all being out here.'

I let the remark pass and told to him to lead on. Behind him I could see the blue lights of the dog van approaching along the A169. We followed our man to the main gates, waited as he unlocked them, and drove into the grounds. Opening a little wooden sentry-box sort of affair, the keyholder threw the switch that put on the security lights, then finally – to our huge relief – silenced the alarms.

'Bloody hell,' Fordy said. 'That's better. So where we gonna start?'

'Where indeed?' We had no idea where the intruders had got

in – if indeed there were any. And if they were inside, well, there was an absolute labyrinth of paths between the various huts.

I spoke to the dog handler and we decided that the best course of action was to let the dog do its search first. I warned Ed and Thommo that it was about to be released, and sent Fordy with the handler to back him up and gain a bit of experience while I waited with the keyholder, well out of harm's way. You don't want to be getting in the way of a working police dog when it's looking for suspects, especially in the dark.

We stood there getting colder and wetter. Nobody said much. We were waiting for some sort of response from the dog, and after five or ten minutes we heard, from somewhere in among the rows of wooden huts, a deep, loud, insistent barking.

'Eh up,' I said. 'That sounds promising.'

The next minute Fordy was on the radio, his voice all but drowned out by the dog and by the handler shouting instructions.

'*Two detained in the canteen, Mike. Just young lads. No problems – he's bringing them out now.*'

'Excellent,' I said. You don't often get a positive result like that. Suddenly it didn't matter that the rain was getting down my collar and my trousers were sticking to my shins.

It wasn't long before Fordy emerged from the main gates with two juveniles, both of whom looked terrified after their encounter with the dog.

'Well done, Fordy lad. Let's have those two searched and in the van, eh?'

The dog handler completed searching the grounds but found nothing more. It was now our turn to go in and find out where exactly the lads had been and what was missing. Fordy had recovered a couple of Coke cans and pockets full of loose change from the prisoners. We just needed to tie it all together.

The keyholder pulled a great jangling mass of keys from his pocket. 'Where d'you wanna start, sergeant?'

'Probably at the beginning,' I said.

There must be twenty, maybe thirty, Nissen type huts at Eden Camp, each one of them housing a display to illustrate a different aspect of the war. We decided to take them one by one, Ed, Fordy, Thommo and me, leaving the dog man to watch over the prisoners. As we set off he was rewarding the dog for its good work – not with a rare treat, but with its favourite chewy toy.

I'd hardly set foot in the first hut – the U-Boat Menace – when I received the first hint of what we were in for.

'*Mike, I've got someone else!*' It was Fordy, half whispering but highly excited. Dashing through the passageway towards the door at the far end of my hut, I was brought to a sudden standstill. My heart almost stopped as my torch illuminated a mannequin dressed up as a drowning submariner.

'Yeah, but what bloody hut are you in?' I shouted into the radio as I regained my composure, emerged into the rain – and ran round the corner and smack into Thommo.

'And where are you going, laddie?' He threw his arms around me and squeezed hard.

'Thommo, for f***'s sake!'

'Oh. Sorry sarge. Thought you were Fordy's—'

But Fordy was back on the radio, sounding sheepish. '*Sorry everyone. It was a just a dummy. Bloody realistic though . . . Sorry.*'

'We're going to have this problem in every blinking hut, aren't we?' I said. 'I've been round this place before. Took my mum round for a Mother's Day treat. They've got life-size models all over the place.'

Half an hour later we'd more or less done all the huts apart from the canteen, and had come up with nothing more. I'd just emerged from a very spooky five minutes in Hut 6, The Blitz – dead bodies galore, and a nasty smell of burning – when I crashed into Thommo once more. 'Looks like it's just the canteen and the shop, sarge. They've forced a door.'

I followed him down between an anti-aircraft gun and a half-track to the old NAAFI building. The door was ajar and the lock was hanging loose. We entered the building with our torches. The keyholder squeezed past us and flipped the lights on, then made his way to the cash register. 'Well, they've not touched this,' he said.

'That's odd,' I said. 'With all that loose change in their pockets I thought this was a dead cert.'

Then he looked around the counter. 'Why, the evil little bastards!'

'What is it?'

'I bet it's the charity box they've done. For the Royal Air Force Association.' He had another look around the counter area, then searched underneath it. 'Yep, that's where they got their money.' He shook his head and showed me the empty box. 'Kind of people that rob churches.'

'Well, that makes sense,' Ed said. 'Don't suppose you've any idea what was in it?'

'Not a fortune, but for a charity box, well, there'd be a fair bit. I usually empty it every couple of weeks and the last time will have been – ooh, a week last Wednesday. Took sixty quid out of it. But we're into peak holiday time now. You could be talking a hundred. All in coins, of course.'

'Well, we'll soon find out,' I said. 'Just tot up what those two herberts are carrying.' I looked around. 'So, any damage apart from the door and that box?'

He had another look around the place and shook his head. 'Don't think so.'

It seemed we'd covered all the angles, and no serious damage had been done. I looked at my watch. It was five thirty. Fordy and Ed took the prisoners through to Scarborough with a view to handing them over to the early shift. Thommo stayed on site to take the keyholder's statement. I hitched a lift back to the station with the dog man, who couldn't believe his luck. 'I was en route from a job in York when I heard the call,' he told me. 'Doesn't often fall in your lap like that, does it? This'll look good on my end-of-month review, won't it?'

'And ours,' I added.

By the time we got back to Old Maltongate the early shift were just arriving and making a brew. It was gone seven by the time I stopped in the Castlegate newsagents for a paper, almost half past by the time I got home. The skies had cleared and the sun was streaming through the trees. I was feeling more wide awake than I had most of the night. I got Henry out of his run, slipped his lead on and set off for a walk across the fields. The grass was soaked with dew and the hawthorn hedges were full of red berries amongst the skeins of gossamer. Down in the Vale of York there was a thin veil of mist. No doubt about it, autumn would soon be on its way.

Chapter 7

Things Always Happen In Threes

'Soapy,' I said, 'between you and me, I'm glad it's Algy boy who's gonna be sitting on this ducking-stool contraption. I'm not sure how safe it is.'

Soapy pulled on the rope that was attached to one of the several poles we'd erected, and looped it around the iron spike we'd driven into the wet, roughly mown grass. 'Why,' he said, 'what's the worst that can happen?'

I shivered and glanced up at the sky, which was full of low clouds. There was an autumnal feel to the air and everything was damp. 'You mean, apart from him catching pneumonia?'

'Should've taken up Walt's offer, shouldn't he?' He stood back a few yards and surveyed the arrangement of poles, planks and rigging, the old tractor seat and Heath Robinson triggering device that Algy had dug out for us.

'What offer was that, mate?'

'Didn't you hear? He said he'd lather him in goose-grease, like they did in the old days. Makes you waterproof, he reckons.'

'And fragrant too, I suppose.'

Soapy laughed. 'Nah, he'll be fine. Plenty lard on the old bugger. He can stand it.'

I tugged on a rope. 'Wish I had your confidence,' I said as the timbers shivered and the fixings creaked.

'Relax.' Soapy took half a cigarette out from behind his ear and lit up. 'Anyway, 'tisn't your actual structure you wanna worry about. These timbers' – he whacked one with the flat of his hand – 'these are solid as a rock. It's that there release effort he's rigged up. That's your Achilles tendon, cock-bod.'

'Heel,' I said.

'He'll what?'

'No, Achilles heel.'

'Aye, like I said. Weak spot.'

'Whatever.' I looked at my watch. 'Anyway, I'm afraid this is where you're going to have to excuse me. Duty calls.'

'You what?'

'Soapy, I told you last week. I have to be at work, mate.'

'Oh, so you did. So I'm on me own, am I?'

'Till Algy shows up, yeah. Sorry, sunshine. I'd like to help you, but . . . Maybe catch you in the Farmers afterwards. About ten thirty? If I can get away on time, that is.'

I left him to it, got in the car and headed towards town.

Despite that bit of fun on the village green I'd had a gloomy sort of feeling all morning, for no reason I could think of. I would never describe myself as a superstitious person, but there have been moments in my life when I've started to wonder – just enough for me to say I've got an open mind. I mean, is everything as it seems on the surface? I was thinking of my dad. He reckoned to have had the odd premonition. Nothing of any great significance, no Grand National winners or anything like that, but I do remember him saying, more than once, that he wondered whether he didn't have some sort of ability to see into the future. One time, when I was quite a young lad, maybe thirteen or fourteen, he said, 'You know, Michael, I've a funny feeling that you're going to end up as a police officer.' At the time I was still dreaming about becoming a footballer, so I took no real notice. It was years later, after I'd done my training, that my mum reminded me what he'd said. She wondered whether he really did have some sort of gift – and I've wondered, in turn, whether I might have inherited it. Because I have, from time to time, had an odd feeling, a general sense that something good, or bad, was about to happen.

Driving into town that afternoon I noticed that although it wasn't actually raining, the roads were sort of . . . slick. Maybe it had rained in the early morning and never quite dried out. It was that kind of day. Everything was a bit clammy. What with that, and the poor light and the still air, I had this sort of sombre feeling, like you get when you wake up knowing you've had one of those dreams that you can't quite remember anything about, except that it's left a lingering unease in your mind.

I'd only been at the station five minutes, barely had time to wipe the steam off my glasses and stick my bait-tin in my locker, when I remembered the job I'd conveniently shoved to the back burner a day or two earlier: PDRs, or performance development reviews. They're basically end-of-term reports on your officers – or used to be. When they first started we had to score everyone on their general attitude to work, their arrest record, performance in dealing with the public, and so on; even how they handled paperwork. And although it was a bit of a chore, well, it was only once a year. That was until 'they' decided it would be really useful if we could update the scores monthly, and that officers would have to provide evidence of their performance on a regular basis. Whoever made this decision, it seemed they were intent on creating more paperwork for the frontline troops, leaving them less time actually out on patrol. The only good news was that things would probably change again soon. They always do. I've lost count how many different methods we've had to employ to work out whether someone is performing to a satisfactory standard. And with each new scheme comes a more complicated form we have to fill in. It could make you weep, it really could. Or smile knowingly. Whatever helps keep you sane.

I clearly remember looking at the clock. Quarter to two. I was just about to start the briefing. Three of the previous shift had been involved in taking a couple of prisoners over to Scarborough and wouldn't be back for another half-hour. So the place was pretty quiet, with none of the normal change-over banter. Just as the early-turn shift sergeant was getting ready for home he took one last call from the control room – and I think that's when that uncomfortable feeling worked its way back into my head. I could only just make out what he was saying, but I could read the tone in his voice as clear as day.

'Oh hell,' he said. 'Yeah, right away. OK then, will do.' He put down the phone and looked at me. 'Sounds like a nasty one, Mike. HGV, North Grimston. On its side, driver trapped, road blocked.'

'D'you know, I had a bad feeling when I was driving in.' I sighed. 'You get off, mate. I'll get it sorted.'

This sounded like an all-hands-on-deck job, so I collared Fordy, Thommo and Ed. We grabbed our gear and our fluorescent jackets, and piled into our vehicles, me and Ed in one, the other two taking a car apiece. It's always a good idea to take a spare car, just in case you have to deal with another call. We shot down Castlegate, blue lights flashing, and swung over the bridge, making for the Beverley road. Over the radio we heard that an ambulance was on its way from town, and that a York traffic officer who'd been in Scarborough was also on his way. He'd be approaching on the Duggleby road. He had with him a Ryedale officer on attachment over there, so that was another pair of hands. There were no updates from the scene. Everything we'd got so far had come from a villager who'd called it in, and control had relayed the message.

'1015 to control.'

Brian came straight back. '*Afternoon, Mike. Go ahead, over.*'

'Brian, just confirm fire brigade are en route.'

'*That's a yes, Mike. Put the call in as soon as I heard the driver was trapped.*'

'All received, thanks.'

As a shift you rely on your control-room staff to take care of what's going on. Having people like Brian and Julie was hugely reassuring: with all their years of experience they know what you need before you even ask for it.

The roads were more or less deserted, and I was able to get my foot down. Barely ten minutes after leaving Old Maltongate we were crossing the low bridge and taking the sharp double bend that brings you into North Grimston village. There's not much of it: a church, a rather grand pub, a few stone cottages, and on this particular dingy afternoon a 38-tonne lorry slewed across the road displaying its grimy underside and neatly aligned wheels, all twelve of them.

'Christ!' Ed was already unfastening his seatbelt, reaching for the door handle.

Approaching the stricken vehicle, I took a few seconds to register that something seemed to be missing from it. The cab. That was half buried in what looked like the ruins of a small house, reduced to a jumbled pile of pale yellow stones. On either side of the wreck doors were half open, and people were standing in little knots, looking at the scene. One or two were in the road, circling the lorry.

'Right, let's see what condition the driver's in and keep people back until we make it safe,' I said, as we pulled up. Glancing in the rear-view mirror I could see Fordy and Thommo, right on my tail. I'd just opened my door when I caught sight of another set of blue lights, partly hidden by the overturned lorry. It was the traffic car.

'That's good,' I heard Ed say as we got out of the car. 'Least we got a specialist on the job.'

Approaching the rubble I could now see the HGV driver, in the cab and clearly trapped by the roof, which had buckled under the weight of stones, and his door, which was twisted and stoved in. He let out a sharp cry, and his face contorted into a grimace as he struggled to free his right arm. But there was no way he'd be moving till the fire brigade came with their cutting gear. The traffic officer was bent over him, trying to keep him calm. All I heard was 'Try to keep still, mate. We've an ambulance on its way. Should be with us in a couple of minutes.'

I got on the radio. 'Yeah, we're on scene. Driver is conscious, talking to traffic, but we'll need to wait for the fire brigade to cut him out of his cab.' I shot a glance at Fordy, who was staring at the trapped man. He looked concerned. It's never good to see or hear someone suffering, especially when you know there's not much you can do. 'Don't worry,' I said. 'He may be hurting but the good news is he's letting us know. It's the ones that go all quiet you need to worry about.'

I looked around and saw now that the pile of rubble wasn't a house, but the remains of a shed or barn. The handles of a ride-on mower were sticking out from the stones, along with an upside-down wheelbarrow. Beyond the lorry, just around the corner from the pub, I could see a couple of locals stopping a car. They looked to be telling the driver he'd have to turn round.

'Right,' I said. 'Thommo, can you go and deal with traffic coming from town. I guess you'll have to turn it around and send it . . .' I paused to think. 'Through Birdsall and onto the 166?'

'Aye, I reckon that's the simplest. Apart from any locals who want to go Wharram Percy way.'

'Up to you,' I said. 'You know what you're doing.'

I edged past the cab and along the length of the trailer with Ed. I heard him draw in his breath, sharply. On the road was what looked like a naked body, but as we got a bit closer we saw that it was actually a side of beef. I heard myself let out a sigh of relief. When a lorry goes over you never know whether someone might have been caught under it. Beyond it were three or four more slabs of meat, and as we got to the rear end of the trailer we could see that the doors had been forced open by the impact. Inside was a wall of pink and white carcasses piled up on each other.

'That's our house right there.' One of the bystanders was introducing himself. His front gate was barely ten feet from the trailer end. 'I was having ten minutes in the recliner, like, just heard an almighty bang, but my lad here—'

'Aye, I heard his brakes.' The younger man next to him pointed up the hill. 'You can see the skid marks. Must've been travellin'. We've been up there turning t'traffic around.'

'Well, thank you for your help. You've done the right thing. Just give me a minute and I'll send one of my officers to take over. Where you been sending 'em? Back through Duggleby?'

'Aye.'

'Good man.' At that moment a flickering blue light lit up his face. I turned to see the ambulance pulling up, and behind it, through the trees, the fire tender. Ed and I walked back to meet the ambulance crew. You're always glad to see those people arrive; it leaves you to get on with the work you're trained to do, rather than trying to do their job. The paramedics were already reassuring the trapped driver, and the station officer was inspecting the wrecked cab.

It's brilliant to watch how different emergency services work so well together. It's as if they choreograph every move. Once the paramedics had made their assessment and tended to the driver, they gave the nod to the fire crew.

'We'll leave the door as is,' the officer said. 'Just prop it up. Then it should be a case of taking the roof off and we're in.'

His men were already bringing the cutting gear over. They had what looked like a large pair of tree-loppers, hydraulically powered, connected to the tender by long flexible hoses. They snipped through the crumpled metal in moments, it seemed, and the paramedics were soon inside, preparing to manoeuvre the driver free. It's no simple operation. It needs to be done very carefully, minimising the risk of further injury to the patient. Everyone, including our traffic officers, operated under the command of the paramedics, who issued very precise instructions. At this stage we didn't know what damage the driver might have sustained, but there was no blood on him, and he was much quieter now, murmuring his thanks as he was lowered gently onto the spinal board.

While that was going on one of the firemen had been checking around the vehicle for spilled fuel. 'Looks like we got lucky there,' he said. 'Tanks are unharmed.'

'Thank God for that,' someone said. That's one of your worst fears at a crash site, fuel leaking out and being ignited. I hadn't smelt anything when we arrived, but you never can be sure.

A villager came out with a tray of tea in mugs. Biscuits too. A bit of a breeze had got up now, and the clouds seemed to be lifting, along with my own mood. This could've been a very nasty incident, but . . . touch wood.

I now had Thommo and Fordy stationed at either end of the village turning the traffic round. The traffic officer was already at work with his camera and tape measure, trying to work out the path the vehicle had taken and establishing its exact position. To me, the black marks smeared along the road and back up the hill seemed to tell the story, as the young villager had suggested: yet another driver who'd underestimated just how steep that incline is and failed to take into account the slippery conditions. People are always coming to grief there, and with it being such a narrow road, as well as a busy one, it's always likely to cause a problem. Ed had already gathered names and addresses from witnesses, but the few statements he'd got were going to be brief. Some had heard a bang; some hadn't. All anybody had seen was the end result of the accident. The good news was that the traffic officer was on the ball. He had got on to control to get them to organise recovery of the lorry, which would take a bit of shifting. It also meant the hauliers sending out a second wagon to recover the meat. All this would take time, and tie up some of the team for a couple of hours at least. I got control to call the council out to set up diversions. Once that was done my guys could leave the scene.

'Right,' I said. 'I reckon you and me may as well get back to the station, Ed. Everything here's in good hands. Tell you what, though, we're bloody lucky it wasn't worse than it is. Lorry like that, careering down that hill . . .'

'Oh hell aye. Could've had fatalities, fire, you name it.'

We were en route back to Malton when Ed was allocated a call to deal with a case in Pickering, someone causing damage to the play equipment at the park. Once he'd dropped me off at the station I checked the box – the computer, that is – to see if any lower graded calls had come in that needed allocation. Sometimes they can stack up when everyone is tied up, as we had been, and I was well aware that for the next couple of hours, perhaps more, there would be just the two of us to cover 600 square miles. Or so I thought. As I was taking stock Will MacDonald, one of our specials, turned up. That was a surprise, but a welcome one. Most of the specials try to get in for a late shift on a weekend, or if there's an operation or event on, but you never know which of them is going to show. So seeing Will was a real bonus.

'Excellent,' I said. 'We can use another pair of hands. Pity we can't send you out in a car, though.'

'Ah, but you can,' he said, pouring himself a mug of tea. 'The powers that be have decided we can now take vehicles out as a basic driver. Mainly to get from A to B.'

'They have? When was that?'

'A month ago. Maybe six weeks. Not sure, I've been on holiday.'

'First I knew of it.'

'Mind you, we can't respond to emergency calls, or use the blue lights when we're driving,' he added. 'One day, maybe . . .'

'OK then,' I told him, 'out you go. Town and around, then the top end: Pickering, Kirkbymoorside, Helmsley.'

'OK, no problem sarge. Any particular vehicle?'

'Grab the keys for the Focus and go and wave the flag.'

I've always been a big supporter of specials, and it made sense for them to be able to make use of the cars. Given the size of the Ryedale beat, they needed that freedom – and it gave us far more flexibility in deploying the officers available. It was one of the changes we welcomed.

It was now four thirty. I was on my own again, about to get stuck into those PDRs. I'd barely sat down and opened the first file, though, when I heard the call over the radio. *'Serious RTA on the A170 at Allerston. Motorbike versus HGV, head-on.'*

Oh, Christ. Again? I grabbed my stuff and ran to the car. This did not sound good. A motorcyclist in collision with a lorry? Fifteen times more likely to be killed than a car driver. It's an established fact.

I put on the blue lights and two-tones, sped out towards the bypass and onto the A169. Allerston is maybe five miles east of Pickering, so it was going to take me a good fifteen minutes to get to the scene. At least the weekend traffic heading for the coast would've died down by now, but there would soon be a steady stream heading back. Ed should be there well before me. In fact, he was already on the radio saying he was just about to arrive on scene, and, to be honest, I was glad. This sounded very serious and, as I've said before, me and dead bodies are not a good mix. I got on the radio and called for Will to make his way over to the crash site too. I needed him there, but I had to remind him that he was to drive from A to B, B being the crash site, within the speed limit and with no blue lights. Yes, it was bending the rules, but sometimes you have to make the job work and this sounded like a life or death situation.

As ever, control were getting a lot of calls from the public. Some useful information, of course, but a lot of repeats. The road, we were hearing, was blocked, and the motorcyclist was lying on the side, some way from his machine. An ambulance was en route from Scarborough. Yet again, the realisation that I was in charge here made my pulse race and my hands sweat on the steering wheel.

'1015 to control, any chance we could get a traffic car, over?'

'*We've got one coming, Mike, but it'll be twenty minutes yet, over.*'

Before I could digest that, Ed came on. '*Mike, I'm on the scene. It's not good.*' There was a substantial pause, then, '*The rider looks like he's proved. We've got traffic backed up both directions. We're gonna need more officers.*'

'All received Ed, will be with you as soon as we can. You're just going to have to hold the fort.' I didn't wait for his reply. '1015 to control.'

'*That was all monitored, Mike. Trying to get another unit to assist from Scarborough.*'

'Received, thank you.'

Several minutes later I knew I was approaching the scene. A couple of members of the public were standing in the road, slowing down the oncoming traffic. The cars were backed up, right up the hill on the approach to the village. I pulled out and passed them in the offside lane, driving as fast as I dared, then parked up a hundred yards or so short of the crash site, and left the car with the engine running and blue lights on. Ed was walking towards me, shaking his head.

'No,' he was saying, 'no use at all, Mike.'

We walked towards the motorcyclist, who was slumped against the wall of a terraced cottage, his right leg bent under his torso at an impossible angle. He wasn't moving. He had a black and red leather jacket, blue jeans and a helmet still in place. His bike was on its side about thirty yards from him. A man and a woman were standing at the door of a neighbouring cottage. As I walked towards them she covered her face with her hands and turned away. Further away was a small knot of people, and beyond them the head of the queue of cars from the other direction.

'Must've been killed outright,' Ed said. 'Initial impact. Either that or when he hit the wall. I checked for a pulse, but as you can see . . .'

Just looking at the motionless body, I could see he had horrific injuries, not the sort you want to describe. There was no mistake: the poor guy was dead.

The sound of the ambulance approaching broke the silence. They drove around a seven-and-a-half tonne Luton van, about the size of those things they transport racehorses in. It was standing at an odd angle across the white line in the middle of the road. The front end was stoved in. It bore the name of a local retailer.

'So what's the story?'

Ed turned and pointed at the van. 'The witnesses I've spoken to so far seem to think this fellow was trying to overtake, skidded across to the offside and . . . well, he caught him head-on. He'd no bloody chance. If they're right we could be looking at some serious offences.'

'Where's the driver?'

'One of the neighbours has taken him in.' He pointed to a house on the opposite side of the road. 'Young lad, and he's in a right state of shock. No injuries though, as far as we can tell.'

'OK, good. Once the ambulance crew have finished here, I'll send them over to check him out. Can you go and get the breath test done?'

The paramedics had knelt down beside the victim. We waited a moment while they conducted the usual checks to determine whether, in the official jargon, life was deemed to be extinct. I hurried back to the car and fetched a blanket from the boot.

As the paramedics stepped away I leaned forward to spread it over him. I needed some kind of ID, but as ever I dreaded having to reach inside his jacket. Then I spotted the outline of a wallet in his hip pocket and took that out. Oh, shit. There was a photograph of a woman, quite young, and two children, maybe ten or twelve years old. There was also a driver's licence with a Teesside address that tallied with the registration number of the bike. I thought to myself that some poor cop was about to be sent to do an awful job. I then got on to control and asked for an officer to go and deliver the death message for us.

When you're dealing with a fatality – and especially when the victim is lying a few yards away – it always seems extraordinarily cold to be getting on with the mundane business of sorting out a queue of traffic; but that's your job, serving the public. You go onto autopilot, or I do at any rate. The casualty was being dealt with; I now had a crime scene to protect. It meant closing the road completely, turning the traffic around and setting up diversions.

Looking at all those people in their cars, some of them standing out on the road, checking their watches and trying to calm down their fractious kids, you know very well that, yes, they'd be sorry for the guy who got killed but, meanwhile, they want to get moving. Can we carry on with our day out, officer? Life, as they say, goes on.

As well as the traffic issue I was thinking of the broader situation. This scene needed investigating and would take time. There would probably be an arrest – of the van driver – which would take another officer. Then we would need an officer to perform the coroner's officer duty; to provide the continuity of evidence when the undertakers eventually removed the deceased. Finally, I would need staff on the road closures until the highways division could get the diversions in place. Then I had to think about what would happen if another urgent job came in. I began to think. How long before I could ask for the night shift to come in – or anyway, those that could be contacted? I decided I'd give it an hour, see how the lads were getting on with the meat lorry at Grimston.

Right now I had Will speaking to those drivers who were heading to the coast to get them to turn round and follow an alternative route. I didn't need to worry about him. I had a whole list of other things to see to. First off I got on to Brian in control to call in the collision investigation team from Tadcaster, the SOCO, and the highways team. I also asked him to keep the duty inspector at Scarborough, my next in line, informed of what we were doing. And would he contact local radio stations so that they could put out an alert, advising travellers of what was happening? Then I checked on what was happening at Grimston.

The news from there was good. The hauliers had got through with a forklift and were transferring the load from the wrecked lorry to its replacement. The highways people were in the process of setting up diversions and would be making their way over to us as soon as they were done. All that was needed was the specialist recovery unit, to right and remove the lorry. Here at Allerston the traffic officer had showed up, double crewed. They were taking witness details and first-account statements. They'd also arrested the driver of the Luton van on suspicion of causing death by dangerous driving. He would no doubt point to the slippery conditions. That clamminess I'd felt when I left home was still in the atmosphere, and the roads did still seem greasy. Having said that, it was no excuse and he had some serious questions to answer.

While we waited for the highways team to turn up and sort the diversions out, I helped Ed and Will get on top of the traffic issues. 'AIU should be here any time now,' I said. The accident investigation unit were based at Tadcaster, forty-five minutes away, maybe a little longer. As soon as they showed up Ed and I drove back to Malton.

At the station he slumped in a chair in the parade room while I mashed some tea, and piled the sugar into his mug. 'Here,' I said, 'get that down you.' Thank God all that's over, I was thinking as I went into the sergeants' office to get a further update from Fordy.

He reported that he and Thommo would soon be done at Grimston. That was good news, because if the phone went now it was down to me and Ed again, as Will was still helping with traffic at the fatal. As it happened, there was a call, but it was from York District Hospital, reporting on the driver of the wrecked meat wagon. As I'd suspected, there was nothing life-threatening: he'd sustained a broken collarbone and a couple of cracked ribs. There were a couple of calls from the newspapers too, wanting details of both accidents, the where-who-when-how, and whether anyone had been arrested. We have a great relationship with the local press, so we try to give as much information as possible, but you need to be careful not to pass on any personal information before relatives have been informed.

After I'd done all that I stepped outside for a moment and lit a cigarette. I stood there for a minute or two enjoying the fresh air. The weather was clearing and the sun was shining through the leaves and making the grass sparkle. I gave a long sigh and felt my shoulders relax. That was one crisis I'd come through unscathed.

Back inside I poured myself another mug of tea, then went and sat down with Ed. I was debating whether to ask him how he was feeling when control came on the radio.

'*Any officers to deal? Serious RTA Coneysthorpe crossroads. Car versus car.*'

'What? I don't bloody well believe this.' I looked at Ed. 'Come on mate, I'll drive.' I took a last mouthful of tea, grabbed the radio to confirm that we were en route, and headed for the door. What the hell were we going to find this time? I didn't have a good feeling about it. They do 60mph down that Castle

Howard road, and anybody coming out from Coneysthorpe direction and trying to cross – well, once you decide to go you need to get your foot down. Hard. There's that little time.

Town was busy now, with considerable traffic both ways. The sun was out and so was half the North Yorkshire public, it seemed. I was weaving my way through the traffic on Yorkersgate, blue lights on, two-tones as well, while Ed was talking to control. 'From 1015, can you get Fordy and Thommo to make their way from Grimston, over?'

'*Will do. We're getting calls coming in; sounds like it's a serious accident, several injured. We've two ambulances en route, Mike, both from York and the fire brigade from Malton. Trying to get hold of a traffic unit from York too. Looks as though you're going to be first on scene, over.*'

Even as Brian said that last bit I could feel my stomach muscles tightening up. I was racing over the bypass now, just three or four miles to go, and thank goodness this road was more or less empty, just a couple of farm vehicles to pass and a group of cyclists to slow down for.

As soon as I got to Coneysthorpe I knew I had a serious problem on my hands. There was a line of twenty cars, maybe more, backed up towards me. Some of the occupants were in the road walking towards the crossroads; others were heading back towards their cars. You could see the concern on their faces. Up ahead of me were several people sitting on the grass where the two roads met. I drove slowly past them and there, as I got to the crossing, were the two vehicles.

The Astra had been hit on the side. Completely T-boned, with massive impact damage. One of its wing mirrors and a wheel was lying on the edge of the road. The Mondeo had taken the impact with its front. It was a mess. The bonnet was buckled and sticking up in the air, one of the front wheels was misaligned and the tyre had more or less been ripped off the wheel rim. Two people were walking away from the Astra, one of them shaking his head. I got out of the car and made my way towards it. In the car was a woman. Her face was barely recognisable as a face. She'd got massive head and upper-body injuries and there was a lot of blood. The injuries were simply too horrific to describe in detail. I was in no doubt that she was dead, but I had to be sure. I put my hand in through the broken window and put my fingers tentatively to the side of her neck. The blood on her skin was tacky and she was cold to the touch. I could feel myself wobbling, probably going into slight shock at what I was seeing, but I knew I had to stay calm, or at least appear calm, because I was the one people would assume was in control. There was no pulse. I backed away, tried to compose myself and looked around. All these people – the walking wounded, the drivers lined up from four different directions – they were all looking to me to make things right.

'She just pulled out right in front of us. We couldn't stop. Hadn't a cat in hell's chance.' It was a middle-aged man. He was holding his left arm awkwardly to his chest as if it was injured. In his right hand he was holding a coat.

'Are you the driver of that car?' I pointed to the Mondeo.

'No,' he said, his voice faint and shaky. 'Me wife were driving. She's over there.'

I could see her, hunched on the grass with her head over her knees, staring at the ground.

'Is she hurt?'

'She's complaining of a pain in her chest. We couldn't do a thing, officer, she just—' He stopped, and held up the coat. 'I'll go and make her comfortable, shall I?'

I walked over to her while Ed spoke to a group of people who had gathered some distance away. As I did so, I updated the control room with the situation report, and requested that the usual teams be called. I asked them to make contact with the night shift to see whether they could get one or two of them in early. Another incident now and we would have nobody to send out. Nobody at all.

While I was on the radio I could see Thommo pull up, get out of his car and hurry towards me. Further back, Fordy was weaving his way past the backed-up cars. I turned to the man who'd been talking to me. I carried out a quick examination of his wife before asking Thommo to grab the blanket out of his car boot. 'Yes, if you could sit with her a while and keep her warm,' I said to the husband, 'we'll sort this lot out. There'll be an ambulance here in a few minutes and they'll take care of you.' From what I could see both of them were in shock, and had sustained some injuries from their seatbelts, which is what usually happens in a collision. I got Fordy to stay with them, and keep them both calm and talking. We didn't want them passing out on us. Thommo was looking at the line of cars on the Castle Howard road, then at the crushed Astra. 'Right,' I said, 'let's get on, shall we? I'm afraid there's nowt to be done for the lass in there.'

'Thought not. Ye'll want me to turn this lot around then?'

Thommo knew what to do, and so did I. I had to somehow preserve yet another crime scene. With so few staff it was going to be a challenge. Until diversions were set up all we could do was get the traffic turned round and on its way.

We were joined a few minutes later by a traffic officer from York. He got on with the witness details while I started taping off as much of the crossroads as I could to preserve the scene. The lads from Taddy would be with us as soon as they had finished at Allerston, and would do the investigation to establish how exactly the accident had happened. But that takes time and we could be a few hours away from a result yet.

I was on automatic pilot by now, thankful for the experience I'd gained over the years. Thankful for the training, too; it gives you a framework to work to, and you certainly need it. Just like with the last crash, we would be waiting for the highways people to come and put up diversion signs once they had finished at Allerston. While we waited we would do what we could manually. Thommo had got his line turned around and had gone to Bulmer crossroads to redirect the traffic from there. The ambulances had arrived and taken the couple from the Mondeo to hospital, and things more or less settled into the same routine we'd followed at Allerston, barely three hours ago. Same crews in many cases, same paramedics, same awful business of spreading a blanket over a dead body, identifying it and appointing some poor sod to take the news, in this case to the unsuspecting parents of a 24-year-old student. Absolutely dreadful.

It was some time after nine when Fordy and I, Thommo and Will, who'd also come across from the other accident, were able to regroup back at Old Maltongate. The last thing I remember seeing at the crossroads that day was the highways team with their hoses and brooms, cleaning the road of oil, glass and blood. These are the details of an accident clear-up that the average member of the public never sees, probably never thinks about. A lot of people deserve a lot of credit for doing these jobs.

In the parade room we did what we so often do after something as traumatic and shocking as that. We drank tea and ate biscuits. It had been quite a day; it had been relentless and had tested us to the limit. You don't often get such a sequence of events in such a short period of time, and it tends to knock you sideways. We talked, in fits and starts, about things we'd seen and heard, about what we were feeling. Talking things through with colleagues is like a kind of counselling session as well as a debrief, a postmortem if you like. Some cops tend to bottle things up, and often don't talk even to their loved ones at home. Perhaps they don't want to upset them. Perhaps they don't think they'll understand. I don't know.

You do what you can for your colleagues. I always made a point of thanking everyone for their hard work. It's often only after the dust has settled that you realise your officers might have been hard at it for five, six, seven hours without taking time out for a bite, a drink, even a visit to the toilet. This had been a particularly bad day at the office. I remembered to thank Will for giving up his day to help us out. People like to be thanked, because come rain or shine they'll be back next day to face whatever's thrown at them. Stray dogs, domestic disputes, thefts, fights, unlawful tipping, death. It's our job, and we handle it. So, if we had stuff to get off our chests, if we wanted to sleep that night, we'd best spit it out now, around that mess-room table, with the people who shared the experience and knew what we were talking about.

I was lucky, of course; I had Ann, who'd been through such things herself, many a time. If I needed to, I could unload on her when I got home. But for the others, this could be their best chance and I hoped they would take it. Tomorrow there'd be something else to occupy their minds. You see a lot of ugly, disturbing and distressing sights as a police officer, and you have to deal with them. I tend to be able to store them away, somewhere at the back of my mind. I never completely forget them, but they're tucked away where I don't have to think about them.

I drove home, more slowly than usual, and when I crossed the road that leads from Kirkham to Grimston, instead of just slowing down I stopped, looked both ways, and gave an involuntary shudder before making my way across. I pulled up on the other side of the crossing, checked that I had a signal and called Ann. 'Listen, love,' I said to her. 'It's been a bit rough. I'm going to call in at the Farmers, catch up with the lads. You wanna join us?'

She said she would, and I drove on towards the village. I paused outside the pub, took a deep breath and walked in, bracing myself for an exaggerated account of the day's happenings at the fete and the outbreaks of laughter that would follow. It was as if I'd flicked a switch on the TV and was changing channels, from a hard-hitting documentary to a Sunday evening sitcom.

According to Soapy, the ducking-stool was doomed from the start. But of course it was none of his fault. 'Nowt to do wi' t'structure, mate. It was bloody Algy boy here. Wouldn't sit still, would you?'

Algy was trying to stop a large sticking-plaster from peeling off his forehead. 'Guilty as charged,' he said. 'My own daft fault. I'm afraid Algernon cannot resist the temptation to give a crowd value for money.'

'Go on,' I said, 'what happened?'

'I'm afraid I found my own line of patter rather too amusing, Mike.'

'Aye, daft old bugger,' Walter added. 'Cracking jokes and laughing fit to bust. That's how he did it.'

'Did what?'

'Why, collapsing the bloody thing.' Soapy drained his pint and got out of his seat. 'First customer of the afternoon, wasn't it? Little lass from Kennythorpe. Slings her ball and—'

Becky was laughing as he spoke, but still managed to interrupt him. 'Yeah, so he dives to one side, the ball whizzes past his ear and next thing—' She doubled up then, dabbing at her eyes with a tissue.

'Next thing,' Algy said, 'yours truly is in the drink, the sling is round his neck and the timbers are groaning. Talk about "collapse of stout party". It was more a case of "collapse of not so stout mechanism".'

And so it continued. Laughter and merriment, shoving the day's events to the back of my mind for an hour or so. It wasn't until Ann and I went home that I felt that bit of guilt, about having a laugh and a joke, being at home with my loved one when other families had been torn apart. But you can't allow yourself to be drawn too far into those dark thoughts. Today's memories needed to be filed away into one of the memory boxes. Tomorrow, as we say, is another day.

Chapter 8

A Grim Business

One of the great pleasures of my job as a country copper is that I really do get to know my community. When you work in the city, yes, you're on talking terms with certain shopkeepers, pub landlords, your local schoolteachers, lollipop ladies and the like – and of course, even some of the local villains. But it's different in the country. You get to know all kinds of people, right across the social spectrum. You get to know who they are, where they live, what they do for a living, and who they're related to – all of which can come in handy. No use denying that it helps if you're aware that a third party you're talking about is actually the first party's cousin, or brother, or ex-wife. Out here you'll maybe meet someone once and the chances are you're going to recognise them the next time; because there usually is a next time. It's a small world. You might bump into them at the livestock auction on a Tuesday, at a village fete on a Saturday, along the high street, in the queue at the post office, even behind the goal at Bootham Crescent on a Saturday. You'll pass them on the road too. A lot of the country lanes I patrol, if you see another vehicle the driver will give you a wave. If you recognise the driver, or the car, you might even stop, wind your window down and have a brief natter. It maintains good relations – although not, admittedly, with the man in a van who suddenly appears in your rear-view mirror and wants to get by in a hurry – and it gets you known. Now and again, when you need cooperation or a bit of information, it'll pay off, because if someone's used to passing the time of day with you they're that bit more likely to talk to you, pass on what they know.

So much for the chance encounters. There are also the people you'll go out of your way to stay in touch with: your farmers and landowners, gamekeepers of course, people who hunt or shoot, dog walkers and hikers – because these are the people who know what's really happening out in the country. There are my Country Watch members as well, and they form a vital network. Then of course there are victims of crime. As far as I'm able to, and as much as time allows, I like to check up on them. People who've suffered break-ins, for example. If I have a spare half hour and I'm in the neighbourhood, I like to go and see how they're getting on, find out if they've any worries as a result of what happened. In a case like that of Jim and Helen, the farm couple whose house had been burgled twice recently, I was interested to see whether they'd acted on my advice and tightened up security. If they had, I'd congratulate them; if not, I'd give a little nudge. You could say it's all part of a country copper's aftercare service.

Jim and Helen were fine, they assured me. They'd put new locks on all the doors, installed a decent burglar alarm, and were even thinking of splashing out on a CCTV camera for the front of the house and the yard. After all the upset of the break-ins, everything in the garden, and on the farm, was rosy.

I'd called by early one afternoon in September. It was the kind of day that reminds you that there's still a little summer left to enjoy, even though the holidays are over and the children are all back in the classroom. The leaves on the trees were still green, apart from the odd horse chestnut, and the hedgerows were still full of berries, making me think about how nobody bothers to pick brambles these days. Around the villages the lawns were dotted with fallen apples.

When I arrived at the farm, Jim was wearing a smile to match a glorious day. His fields, he told me, had produced bumper crops and he'd managed to get them all in safely without any damage from wind or rain.

'So it's feet up and light the big cigar, is it?'

He looked at me and laughed. 'You should be on the telly, Mike, sense of humour like that. I might be smiling now, but it's all bloody go. I know I've been lucky, but let me tell you, just because the harvest's in, don't mean we're home and dry. Not by a long chalk. It's a never ending job on the farm, as you should know.'

'By heck,' I said, 'talk about conforming to the stereotype. You farmers, you're never satisfied, are you? Harvest safely gathered in, prices through the roof. You've nowt to do till next spring, surely, except count all that money.'

I was joking, of course, and he knew it. 'We can always swap jobs if you like, Mike. Tell you what, I'll have a spell riding about in that shiny car of yours, supping tea in all the farmhouses, and you take over from me. Then we'll see who begs for mercy at the end of the month, eh?'

Before I could answer he was reeling off the list of jobs he had on his slate right then. 'We can start you on t'ditches. And soon as you've cleaned them out there's all me machinery to overhaul. Then I've a leak in me barn roof, but maybe that can wait till you're done ploughing and planting. Not to mention laying bait around the yard for rats and suchlike – oh, and of course getting me books up to date. And while we're at it I've still not finished off around that gate I put in.' He grimaced, folded his arms and looked me up and down. I held my hands up. It was no contest. 'So,' he said. 'What do you reckon? Just give me the keys to the squad car, and we'll get started, shall we? Oh, and while I think of it' – he pointed to a clump of trees away to the west end of the yard – 'while you're down yonder you'll see I've a huge great stack of brash to burn.'

'Oh? You haven't been grubbing out hedges again, have you?'

'Have to, Mike. They've been giving out grants to plant mixed species now, y'know. That's the latest directive. So I've been cutting down all them hawthorns I put in twenty years back – well, they're trees near enough; now the roots want grubbing out. Aye, that's another job for the list. Then I shall order me stock and replant.'

'Got any plans for them?' I said. 'For your hawthorns, I mean?'

'Like I said, a great big fire. Why, you want to bring some burgers and sausages, make a party of it? November the fifth?'

'I'd rather have some of your beef steaks, Jim. But no, I was thinking more like a chainsaw and a trailer. Always on the lookout for firewood, me and Ann. I mean, hawthorn stumps – just the job. Make a lovely blaze.'

'They certainly do. Well, if you want to cut 'em up you just come over and help yourself, Mike. You'll be doing me a favour.'

'I might do that, Jim. Soon as I get a day or two spare. I don't know if you've ever noticed, but when you're burning free fuel it seems to warm you up that bit better. Anyway, now that we've heard all your complaints, are you in the mood for a bit of good news?' Jim gave me a long hard stare. 'No, seriously,' I said. I'd been dying to tell him this. I'd no idea how I'd managed to keep it under my hat for so long.

'Go on, let's have it,' he said.

'Right. Well, a few weeks ago there was a serious crime took place in Hull. A murder, in fact. A stabbing.'

'I think I read about that, in the *Yorkshire Post*.'

'Aye, you will have done. It was on one of the big council estates.'

'Pretty rough down there, from what I've heard.'

'Well, they vary, those estates. There's better areas and worse ones. You don't want to tar everyone with the same brush. I've met some real diamonds. And a few headbangers. Anyway, the police there have been conducting a series of house-to-house enquiries and searching various properties. And that's led to the usual thing of course: your criminal fraternity frantically disposing of materials they'd rather you didn't see. We're talking all sorts: drugs, knives, stolen goods, firearms, bootleg cigarettes, untaxed booze. You name it. And, my friend – well, guess what?'

Jim pulled a face. 'Missing cattle? Sheep rustlers?'

I couldn't help laughing. 'That'd be something, wouldn't it? No – those shotguns of yours that were stolen. The two cheap ones and the antique.'

'You're kidding!'

'No I'm not.'

'Well, what a stroke of luck that is.'

'It's how it goes. Sometimes that's all you want, that little bit of luck.'

'That's fantastic. I can't wait to tell Helen. She's never stopped fretting over those weapons. She was worried that they were in the wrong hands and someone would get hurt.'

'Well yeah, she would. But she can forget about that now. Anyway, even better from our point of view, the guns have been sent off to the lab to check for forensic evidence.'

Jim frowned, and said, 'What, you think there's a chance we might find out who it was after all?'

'I don't know, but we'll certainly try.'

'Right . . . and how long'll that be, d'you think?'

'Could be a few weeks, maybe a bit longer. I'll let you know, don't worry.'

I left Jim to reflect on his good news and made my way back to town. The station was pretty quiet, which was a good job because Thommo was away on annual leave. He always tried to book his holidays when the kids were back at school. Saved him a fortune, he reckoned. So I had Ed, Fordy and Mel, a female officer from another shift. All three were out on patrol, with one of the specials due in at six to give me a bit of extra cover. But before he arrived I got called out.

The call came from a manager at a care home for the elderly. One of her residents, an elderly woman, appeared to have gone missing. She gave me the name of a place out Helperthorpe way. 'And when was this woman last seen?' I asked.

'Oh, it'd be some time after lunch.'

'You mean she's been missing two or three hours?' I looked at my watch. It had turned four.

'No, we have a large garden here, and extensive grounds. A lot of our residents like to get out when it's fine. And to be honest, nobody missed her until half an hour ago when we served afternoon tea.'

'I see. And you've made a thorough search?'

'Everywhere we can think of, and we're still looking.'

'Inside and out?'

'Oh yes. And the old greenhouses, the stable block. We've even had someone go down to Weaverthorpe and check that she hasn't wound up in the pub. It wouldn't be the first time. I mean for one of our residents, not her in particular.'

I told the manager I'd come over, and got on the radio to control to inform them of the situation. Before I set off I gave Mel and Ed a shout to attend the scene as well. Any report of a missing person needs to be taken seriously, although at this stage I wasn't too concerned. Incidents like this are pretty common, and in nine cases out of ten the missing party will show up, announce that they've been having a nap somewhere and wonder what all the fuss is about. However, it's not our job to make assumptions. And it seemed that the people at the care home had done all that could be expected of them. The fact that this was an elderly person made it a matter of urgency. What if they'd collapsed somewhere? What if they were confused? How far might they have wandered? Might they have got hurt? All these things go through your mind, and in the circumstances calling us was the right thing to do. The last thing we wanted was to be looking for someone in the dark. I got into the car and made my way out along the A64, then turned south through Wintringham and over the top to West Lutton.

The care home sits up a quiet lane, surrounded by mature trees. I think it's an old vicarage; either that or it belonged to somebody with a lot of money. It dates back to Victorian times, and has large bay windows, a south-facing conservatory and a couple of little turret rooms. Beyond the grounds, which are mostly lawns and shrubs, there's a fringe of mature trees and after that nothing but ploughed fields and a couple of narrow wooded valleys leading up into the hills.

'She's losing her memory, you see.' The lady who met me at the front doors was quite worried now. 'I mean short-term.'

'And what sort of shape is she in, physically?'

'That's what's worrying us. She's actually very fit for an eighty-two-year-old. Used to be a keen walker. Still goes out on hikes with her son, so if she decided to wander she could have gone quite a way.'

'Any idea what she's wearing?'

'That's a point. Let me ask one of the assistants and see whether they know. It'd be her tweeds, most likely. She's a real old-fashioned, what you'd call county type.'

As soon as Mel and Ed arrived I had them make a quick missing-person report. They needed to try and get a photograph and the most up-to-date description available. Then they had to search the care home all over again, but thoroughly, with a member of staff: the lady's own room, other residents' rooms, as well as places like bathrooms, kitchens, any outbuildings she might have ventured into. I reminded both of them about the young girl we'd found a couple of years ago hiding in a laundry basket after the parents had insisted they'd searched the house from top to bottom. Different circumstances of course, but I wasn't going to leave anything to chance. As well as searching the likelier places, I reminded them, they needed to poke into the unlikely ones: the cleaning cupboards, the under-stairs places, the disused coal bunkers, etc.

While Mel and Ed were getting on with that I made a request for a dog unit, and some further assistance from officers stationed at Eastfields. Once you initiate a search the more hands on deck the better. After that I got on to the control room to ask the duty inspector to give me a ring on my mobile.

'It's a difficult one, Mike,' he concluded after I'd given him a rundown of the circumstances. 'I'll leave it to you, but let me know if we need to escalate the search.'

You need to take all sorts of things into consideration on a job like this. The time of day, the weather, the location – these are all factors that can affect the way you go about your search. At this stage I was reasonably happy with the resources I had available. I had the dog section en route. As soon as that arrived we could start searching the grounds; and once Ed and Mel were finished in the house they could link up with the two officers from Eastfields and search the roads nearby, spreading out to the adjoining villages. Control were letting the local radio stations know, and I'd rung several of my Country Watch people. Well, I'd rung the Colonel and he promised to call as many other members as he could get hold of, and ask them to keep a lookout.

While all this was going on I rang the Scarborough and Ryedale search and rescue team supervisor and alerted them that we had a situation that might result in them being called out. Forewarned is forearmed, as my old TA sergeant used to say. Beyond that I was thinking about making a request for one of my favourite pieces of police equipment: the Humberside or Cleveland helicopter. But that was very much a last resort. First, the basics. The dog section had arrived and we were just discussing the best approach when my phone went. It was control.

'Yeah, Mike, we've had a young man on the phone. Farmer's son, very distressed. He works in York, but his mother called him from the farm to say his dad's been missing for some time.'

'Right. So what's happened?'

'He drove over from York, searched the outbuildings and found him. Hanging in a barn.'

'Dead?'

'According to him, yes.'

'Oh hell. And where is this?'

'Out Thixendale way, top of the wolds.'

As soon as they said that I had an uncomfortable feeling that this was going to be the fellow I'd called on back in the early summer, the one who thought he'd scared a burglar off the premises. Then they named the actual farm. 'Oh God,' I said. 'Yeah, I know the place. I know the farmer too.'

'Anyway, the son has stated that he was definitely dead. There's an ambulance en route anyway. The family called one.'

I got straight onto the radio – first to Ed, to tell him he was taking over the search for the old lady and holding the fort there, then to Fordy, who was over Westow way. He needed to make his way to the farm and await my arrival. As of the previous month we'd had a new procedure in place for dealing with any sudden death. The new order was that a supervisor must attend every death, and if it did not appear to be from natural causes it had to be treated as suspicious until it was assessed otherwise. A possible suicide would remain suspect until all other possibilities had been excluded. Senior management had decreed that this was how we were to play it, and we had no choice in the matter. We also had to call the duty detective inspector, who had to attend the scene, as well as the crime scene manager and SOCO. It has to be said that we weren't all convinced that this was always necessary. The way we saw it, a good copper will know whether there's anything dubious, any unanswered questions, and can use their own judgement as to whether or not to call out a senior officer. That's the way we'd always done it. Still, ours is not to reason why, as the old saying goes . . .

I called Des, who was out on the road, and told him what was happening. Then I explained to the manager of the care home that I'd be leaving Ed in charge of the search for the time being, and drove out to the scene of this new incident.

The day was coming to an end now. A sheet of high, grey cloud had moved in from the west, and the air felt much cooler, more autumnal. High up on the top the leaves of the tall sycamores that towered over the farmhouse looked dry and shrivelled. Against the side of the house, behind Fordy's vehicle, the old Range Rover had been jacked up, and a rear wheel was missing. Behind it I could see a single lightbulb glowing through the kitchen window. There were a couple of other cars in the driveway, belonging to relatives of the dead man, as I discovered when I got inside. Fordy had only just arrived and was talking to the two paramedics next to their ambulance. 'We've had a look,' one of them said as I walked across.

'Yes?'

'I can confirm your man is dead. Several hours by the look of him.'

'Right, thanks. Did both of you go into the barn?'

'Yeah, we had to use a stepladder to get to the body. Found one leaning against the outside wall there. Andy here held it steady while I went up to do the checks.'

'What did you do with it after?'

'Left it next to the body.'

Well, I thought, that was one job done, even if it might have compromised the forensic evidence. I got Fordy to start a log and make a note of the time at which life was pronounced extinct, as well as the name and crew number of both para-medics. They were no longer required. They'd done their job.

Just as they were leaving another family member arrived at the farm. I quickly went over to the house and introduced myself to the son, who was standing by the door. I then collared Fordy. 'C'mon,' I said, nodding towards the barn, 'we'd better go and take a look.'

Fordy didn't say a word. I couldn't remember whether he'd done this before and I didn't feel inclined to ask him. But I knew I had to.

'No,' he said, as we walked round the back of the house. 'I've been to a few deaths. Never a suicide.'

'Suspected suicide,' I corrected him. 'Because we haven't to assume anything at this stage.'

'Yeah, I know, but . . .'

'That's OK.' We were both trying to calm our nerves. I knew that.

The barn was a ramshackle affair. The front of it was made of corrugated iron nailed onto a timber frame, with a wooden door let into it. The pale grey paint was peeling off, and it was hanging half open on one rusting hinge.

We both hesitated a moment, then I said, 'Come on, let's get it over with.'

Partly it was my own fear that I needed to overcome, but also on my mind was the fact that when somebody hangs himself it's a particularly unpleasant sight. It's not always as easy, or as quick, as people think to kill yourself by hanging. This man, however, seemed to have been determined to end it all, and he had taken pains to make sure that he did the job right.

I didn't want to enter the barn if I could avoid it. If two more of us went in, that would be two more chances of disturbing any forensic evidence as per procedure. In this case I could see perfectly well from the doorway what had happened. The man had taken a long, heavy hemp rope, dark with age, tied one frayed end to the front of a tractor and slung the other over a beam that must have been twelve feet above the litter-strewn floor. Then he'd built a stack of bales, and as far as we could tell climbed up to the top of them before jumping off.

'Oh, Christ.' Fordy had come up beside me. I could feel him shiver slightly as he looked inside. The man's eyes were open and his face was a nasty blotchy colour, his head twisted to one side. He was wearing a pair of grubby overalls. On the floor, underneath him, was a battered deerstalker hat. It's always a horrible business, but this case seemed especially gruesome, perhaps because it felt . . . close to me. Here I was, looking at the dead body of a man I'd had a conversation with, not a dozen yards from here and barely a few weeks previously.

I looked around, and saw the paint-splattered set of wooden steps the paramedics had used. A pigeon flapping its wings and darting out through an open skylight made us both jump.

'Right,' I said, stepping back. 'That's that. We'll leave him to the CID, shall we?'

'Do we still need CID? Looks like an obvious suicide to me, Mike.'

'New rules, Fordy lad. Came in the other week. Need to get the experts in to assess it.'

'Have you dealt with anything like this before, Mike?' Fordy said as we stood outside, composing ourselves.

'By hanging? Yeah,' I said. 'Well no – no, that's not true. There was one in London, years ago, when I'd only been in the job a few months. Very strange one, as it happens.' Fordy was looking at me. 'Guy had injected himself with heroin. Pile of books on a stool, rope round his neck, looped it over a beam and tied it to a little top window – to the handle thing, you know? – then kicked the books away. But I tell you what the weird thing was. He'd decided to have a last cigar, a big fat expensive one, and it was still there between his fingers. It had gone out but the ash was still on the end of it. Must've been a good inch of ash.' I shuddered. 'Could never smell a cigar, for years after, without seeing that scene in my head, all over again.'

The barn was now a crime scene and, as sergeant in charge, it was my job to protect it. Nobody else could enter now until the arrival of the D.I. Fordy was busy adding our movements to the log he was compiling in his pocketbook. I left him guarding the entrance while I went to the house to speak to the family.

The farmer's wife was seated at the kitchen table. She'd turned her chair away towards the sink and seemed to be staring at the floor. The son, the one who'd called us and who I'd just spoken to, was standing beside her, a hand on her shoulder. He was shaking his head, in either disbelief or sorrow, and trying to comfort her at the same time. I took the details of two other people who'd showed up, the woman's sister and her daughter. These are things you have to do. You feel for the family, and it's a dreadful situation. But you can't let that get in the way.

It's always hard to deal with any death. We're helped, of course, by having so many duties to perform, because it's very hard to know what's best to say at such a sad and shocking time. I knew, however, that I needed to address them all. I kept it short, just told them I was very sorry about what had happened. I was looking at the dead man's wife, who was in too great a state of shock to say anything. I suggested that maybe somebody should made her a cup of tea, but nobody responded. They were all numbed, silent. In a situation like that you find yourself standing there, knowing that they've yet to come to terms with what's happened, let alone think about the whys and wherefores. All you can do is explain to them what you are doing and why, with as much compassion as possible.

Just for a moment I wasn't quite sure what I was supposed to be doing next. Then I dug up another of those mnemonics from somewhere deep in my memory, the ones that always come to the rescue when your feelings are all over the place. CDCD. That's the one. C for CID; D – Duty Officer; C – Coroner's Officer; and D – Doctor. The CID were on their way and would be here shortly. There was no need for a doctor, as the paramedics had already attended. As to the duty officer, that was the inspector at Northallerton. After I'd called and given him a further update I stepped outside and rang Ed for a situation report on the missing lady over at Lutton. 'How's it going?' I said.

'We've finished searching the house, Mike. Negative result. The officers from Eastfields are on patrol and covering the roads around the care home. The dog section's still searching the grounds. Should be done shortly. Mel and I are heading into the village to let people know what's happened. Might get a result there; you never know.'

'Let us know when you've exhausted all avenues,' I said. 'Or if you get a result, of course.'

'Will do, Mike.'

Back in the house the tension had broken. The dead man's son had made a pot of tea. The wife was talking, fitfully, through tears. 'He never gave any sign this was going to happen. He'd been worried. We all had. Worried that we'd lose the farm. It gets to be a way of life. Fuel prices, fertiliser, feed, always on the rise. House repairs. Then the brakes going on the Range Rover. You try to take it in your stride.'

Her son put a hand on her shoulder. 'Aye, but foot and mouth. That's what really did it, wasn't it? That took a lot out of you both. Losing your milk herd, and . . .'

'It did, but we came out the other side. Thought we had, at any rate. And now—' She broke down again, and he was on his knees, putting an arm around her.

It's so hard being a bystander when someone else is going to pieces. All you can really offer is kind words, and sometimes they just sound hollow. Tea and sympathy, as someone once wrote. And there was Fordy, logging the times that everybody had showed up, taking names and addresses, making his list of who had been into the barn and when, who had seen the body.

It all sounds trivial, I suppose, but you learn that there comes a time, when the investigation of a death gets into gear, when every last detail is required, and as a supervisor your job is to make damned sure that the information is available, every last scrap of it, and that it's accurate. If you don't, you're storing up trouble further down the line.

When Des the CID man showed up he came with the on-call detective inspector from York. Also with them, to my surprise, was the superintendent who was the late-turn senior officer for the force. She had heard the call and decided to ride out to see what was what. I was aware that she'd worked as a detective in her younger days and was gratified when she took me aside and said 'Well done, Mike.' She was pleased with the way I'd secured the scene, that we'd kept out of the barn and started a running log.

After I'd thanked her for her support and briefed her on the situation she took charge. Stuart the SOCO arrived to take photographs and do the usual forensic stuff. Once again, I was struck by the awful eeriness of the scene in that barn: the dusty old timbers, the piles of bleached straw, the cobwebs, the occasional flutter of a pigeon's wings, Stuart walking stealthily about in his white suit, and of course the horrible sight of the body, still suspended in mid-air. Your gut instinct is to get it taken down, maybe even to cut the rope. It's a sight that truly offends the eye, and it seems callous to go about your business with a corpse suspended over you. But these things have to be done according to a procedure, and you have to learn to accept that. Once Stuart was finished, then the decision would be taken for the body to be lowered to the floor.

The undertakers arrived right on cue, just as Stuart was packing up his things and getting ready to leave. By this time the superintendent had talked to the dead man's wife, and the son. Now she was surveying the scene in the barn. One of the things you need to ask yourself in a case like this is, are you sure it's feasible for the individual to have taken his own life? Does the visible evidence stack up? She shared my view that this was a suicide, no doubt about it. Nailed on, to use her words. But that was just our opinion. There would of course be a postmortem examination and an inquest. So the information-gathering continued. Was there a suicide note? And when the body came down somebody had to inspect the knot in the rope, make sure it was photographed and ensure that the knot remained intact. This would all be part of the evidence in the coroner's report.

Finally the superintendent was done with me. 'Right, Mike, haven't you got a missing lady to find before it gets dark?'

'Yes, Ma'am, I have.'

'Well, if you can leave PC Ford here to assist, you'd better crack on. And keep me informed, will you?'

As I drove back down to Helperthorpe I called Ed. They'd made no further progress. Dusk was falling and the question now was, what further steps could I take? I was coming to the conclusion that it was in all probability time to think about requesting that helicopter. But even as I framed the thought, and started thinking about the possible outcome should we draw a blank, events overtook me. I was approaching the care home down a long valley road where the fields rose gently on either side. One was planted with winter barley; in the other a flock of sheep was grazing peacefully – that is, until a quad-bike appeared from over the skyline, bumping and lurching as it came down the hill at speed. Whoever it was was in a tearing hurry and appeared to be waving at me, frantically, as the sheep scattered in every direction.

I slowed the car, and as the quad-bike drew close I saw that it was in fact a passenger, perched on the rear end of the machine, who was doing the waving. The driver was a young farmer, one of my Country Watch people. The passenger seemed to be a lady, and an elderly one at that. Could it . . .?

It was. The quad-bike had come to a standstill and the farmer, Harry, was helping her to the ground. She was wearing a tweed jacket, a corduroy skirt and a pair of what my mum used to call sensible shoes – brown brogues with leather laces. She marched towards the sheep-netting that skirted the pasture, looked up at me and said 'I hope you haven't been searching for me, young man.' I opened my mouth to speak but, just for once, nothing came out. 'I'm quite capable of looking after myself, you know. I was out enjoying the lovely weather and I must have gone a little further than I intended.'

Harry was suppressing a grin and pointing back the way they'd come. 'Found her in the copse, yon side of the hill,' he said.

'Yes, I was resting there and he very kindly offered me a ride home.' She turned to me. 'And were you? Hope you weren't searching for me. I wouldn't want to be the cause of a lot of fuss. I really don't like a fuss, do you?'

Was there anything to be gained by telling her I'd had my entire complement of officers tied up for three hours, plus a dog unit, and a couple of officers from York en route, and was on the point of fetching the search and rescue team, bringing the helicopter in yet again and making a huge hole in Ryedale's annual budget? 'Not at all, madam,' I said. 'We're just glad you enjoyed your walk and had the good fortune to bump into young Harry here. But in future perhaps it would help if you let the care home know that you are going out. They were worried about you. Anyway, would you like me to take you the rest of the way home? I mean, to save you a walk.'

'Oh, that would be a real treat,' she said. 'What an afternoon. First a ride on this young man's contraption, and now a squad car. It's *years* since I had a ride in a police car – back in my demonstrating days.' She wagged a finger at me. 'I was at Greenham Common, you know. Arrested for obstruction.' Then she smiled and said, 'I don't suppose we shall need the sirens, shall we?'

'I don't think so, madam.' I held the door open for her.

'Such a shame. Still, it'll be quite a story to tell them when I get back, don't you think?'

'Absolutely,' I said. 'I'm sure they'll be all ears. In you get then.'

When a search is resolved in such amusing circumstances it's easy to dismiss it as unimportant. But the fact remains that the day could easily have had a tragic outcome for the old lady. If Harry hadn't been out counting his sheep or whatever he was doing, she could've remained lost in the woods until dark and spent a night in the open, which might have been the end of her, regardless of whether I'd brought the helicopter in. Sometimes the realisation of what might have happened only hits you after the dust has settled. You look back and realise that it's no wonder some days you arrive home feeling exhausted, wrung out. And if you live with another copper, as I do, you hope that she's had an easier day, that she has something left to give in the way of sympathy, or a willingness to listen to your story. I was fortunate. Ann had had an unusually quiet shift. For her, the hard work started when I arrived back at Keeper's Cottage and started to answer her innocent question: 'So, how was your day?'

'Hmm . . .' I said, 'where shall I start?'

Chapter 9

So, How Am I Doing?

'I've never known a run like this. I'm telling you, it beggars belief.'

We'd just had our briefing. We were on an afternoon shift, and Ed was seated at the mess-room table, flipping through his notebook.

'Wassup, mate? That team of yours giving you grief, are they? You wanna support a decent team, you do. Like Millwall.' Now that Jayne was on daytime shifts all the time and getting plenty of sleep she was constantly on the wind-up – and Ed was her favourite target.

'It's got nothing to do with football, Jayne. Nothing so trivial.' He picked up a sheaf of papers that was lying on the table in front of him, held together with a paper-clip. 'It's these daft things.' He read from the top sheet. 'Performance development review.'

'Yeah well, never mind your sex life, mate . . .'

But Ed was not amused. 'Give it a rest will you, Jayne? This is complicated stuff I'm dealing with here.'

'What, filling out your PDR?'

'Yeah, and it's not looking good for PC Cowan, let me tell you. I've hardly nicked anybody the last month or so. I mean, Halloween, Mischief Night, Guy Fawkes . . . you generally reckon to make a few arrests this time of year, don't you? But me?' He flipped through the book once more. 'Nothing. At least, nothing of note, let's put it that way.'

'I don't geddit, Ed. No arrests? What's your problem? That's good news, innit?' Jayne had left the table and was on her feet, swaying to and fro from the hip, trying to ease the backache she'd been complaining about over the past few weeks as her bump grew . . . and grew. 'Don't it suggest . . . I mean, lemme get this right. If you're not making any arrests, don't that mean we're winning the fight against crime?'

'Jayne, do us a favour.'

'Wass that?'

'Save the fairy stories for when the baby comes along.'

Jayne stopped swaying and sat down. 'Oh, so you're saying you're just a crap copper, is that it?'

'Very funny.'

'Ed, you can't have it both ways. If the crime figures go up and the press start mouthing off that we ain't doing our job right, you're the first one to get up on his high horse and call them a bunch of cop-hating whingers.' She turned to me. 'Isn't that right, sarge?'

'No comment.'

'And then if the figures go down you're complaining you've got nothing to do.'

Ed sighed. 'Jayne, I learnt a long time ago when my missus was expecting our first . . .'

'What? What did you learn, mate?'

He picked up his forms and threw them back down on the table. 'Never to argue with an expectant mother. Look, all I want is to do my proper police work. Fighting crime, bringing the bad 'uns to book, like we were trained for. Remember that? Not filling in these stupid bloody questionnaires. After all these years, if I don't know what I'm doing – well, I might as well pack up and go home. I've half a mind to whack this lot through the shredder, except knowing my luck it'd jam. Pile of . . .'

While Ed was sounding off I was keeping quiet, which required quite an effort, because I have strong feelings on this subject. I've been known to get quite hot under the collar about the subject of form-filling, and other activities that keep us in the office and off the streets. I felt exactly the same as Ed did, but I knew I mustn't get drawn into this. As acting sergeant, it was part of my job to see that everyone filled in their PDRs – and filled them in on time. Then I'd have to sit with each officer and go through them section by section, before adding my own assessment of their work. It was a proper nightmare. Worse still, as a supervisor I would in due course have to do my own PDR and sit down with Birdie while he went through it with me. As part of that review he would be assessing how well I'd marked my own teams' PDRs. God, was it any wonder I was going home with headaches? – and had I been fair in my assessment? Had I been unduly harsh, or treated them too softly? As I've probably said before, it doesn't help that the forms seemed to get more complex every year.

Still, the one positive aspect was that we were all in this together, and more or less united in our dislike of it. The one exception on our shift was Thommo. There was a section in which you were invited to write down anything that you felt would enhance your capabilities, such as courses you would like to do. Well, Thommo had a field day there, and fell on it with a glad cry, every time.

However, in the end Ed's moaning and complaining was nothing more than a ritual. He knew it, Jayne knew it and I knew it. Next day it might be her turn to sound off. We all did it from time to time, letting off steam about red tape and bureaucracy. Ed was still bellyaching when the calls started coming in. One by one everybody got ready to do what we do best, out on the streets. The next time we sat round that table we knew we'd be moaning about something else: the weather, or the cost of living, or the traffic down Commercial Street.

The station had fallen quiet. It was just me, the ticking of the clock, and an occasional message overheard on the radio. I remember glancing out of the window and being grateful that I wasn't out and about. It had been a miserable, grey day and the light was already fading. They were all out now – except for Jayne, who was in the CCTV room going through the footage from the previous few days. We'd had a couple of incidents of metal being stolen around town, and Birdie had expressed concern that this was part of a pattern. Somebody – person or persons unknown, as we say – had been nicking lead from rooftops. Not only that but copper pipe, brass fittings and the like from building sites in the area. Whoever was doing this – and we had no way yet of knowing whether it was a single gang or several – had started going into part-completed houses and ripping out the pipework as soon as it was installed. In a couple of cases they'd had the boilers too. The only sniff of any intelligence we'd had was a report of a white van leaving the site of one of these thefts out along the Beverley road, followed by a report from a late-night dog walker who'd seen a similar van heading across the river from Norton. With a bit of luck we might have caught it on film. So that was Jayne pretty well occupied for the rest of the shift. Ed had got called out to a minor road-traffic accident at Ganton; Fordy was doing a school visit to talk about road safety and visibility on dark nights, and Thommo was up at Dalby Forest, investigating the first Christmas tree thefts of the new season. Like the decorations in Wheelgate, they seemed to be starting earlier every year.

As for me, I'd managed about half an hour's work on my PDRs when I monitored a call passed to all units over the radio. There had been a serious accident at an industrial premises out along the A64. In a rural area such as ours, if you call 999 there's no guarantee that an ambulance or fire tender will reach you as quickly as you'd hope they would in a large town. The services are scattered, the roads narrow and slow. So it's often the case that the first on the scene will be a police officer, and in this case it looked as though it could very well be me. The informant had reported that a man working on a circular saw of some kind had severed his arm, so as I drove out onto the Malton bypass and sped east, blue lights flashing, I was eager to hear whether anyone else was en route. A severed arm, I was thinking. That would take some dealing with by whoever was there. It could well be life-threatening. I'd dealt with some horrific injuries over the years, but I couldn't remember anyone who'd had their arm sawn off. 'Christ,' I said out loud, as my mind conjured up a picture of what I might find. Let's just hope whoever's in charge has managed to stop the flow of blood, I thought. If you can do that you're halfway there.

'*Control to 1015, over.*'

'Go ahead, over.' I was just passing the Ham and Cheese pub at Scagglethorpe, looking for a chance to pass the dozen or so cars that were stacked up behind a tractor and muck-spreader tootling along at 25mph with its orange lights twinkling in the gloom.

'*Just to let you know, we have an ambulance en route from Scarborough, Mike. The informant called them first so you shouldn't have too long a wait.*'

'That's all received, thank you.' That was good news. I could feel my shoulders relax.

Once the cars in front of me heard the two-tones they pulled over to the side of the road; the tractor had turned into a field and I was able to speed away through Rillington and on to my destination. It's a tricky road is the A64: poorly lit, single carriageway with a lot of bends, and this evening the surface was damp and slippery, especially near the field entrances where the potato-wagons had been trailing mud in and out. So although this was an emergency I avoided the temptation to go too fast. I've never forgotten what my instructor told me when I was on the fast car course, years previously. 'Better to arrive in one piece,' he said, 'than not at all.' Or as my dad put it, 'Better ten minutes late in this world than twenty years early in the next.' Yes, sound advice, I thought, as I slowed down on the approach to the premises.

The yard wasn't the easiest to negotiate. There were two or three HGVs parked up, and one was backing its way out from a loading bay. I squeezed by, then pulled up beside a security guard. 'Can you tell me where the injured man is?' I said. 'The lad who's cut his arm?'

'He's sliced it clean off, poor bugger. That's what they reckon.' He directed me along the side of the main building, past a couple of forklifts and a stack of wooden pallets, then into the building through a wide entrance where a set of tall sliding doors had been pulled back. In the distance I thought I could hear the sound of the ambulance coming in on the main road from Scarborough direction. Fingers crossed. Ahead of me, under a sort of overhead gantry, was a group of four or five men in blue overalls and hard hats, and a woman in a white coat holding a clipboard. Two other men were kneeling on the concrete floor supporting the victim. One of them was holding a large wad of pale blue scrunched-up paper towelling against the guy's left side. You could see where the blood was seeping through. I got out of the car and approached them.

'Right,' I started, 'how we all getting on?' Before anybody answered I squatted down and spoke to the injured man. He looked pale, very pale indeed, and was obviously in a state of shock. 'And how are you doing, mate?'

'Not so good,' he said.

Well, I thought, at least you're conscious – although I could see that he was scared. Pale and shaking. I took a deep breath, tried to calm myself, and took a closer look at his injury. His arm had been detached just above the elbow, an angled cut that ran up towards his shoulder. I could see he was losing a lot of blood, so I quickly removed my belt and made a makeshift tourniquet just above the stump. I looked around and saw someone leaning over us with a large white pad. 'Here,' I said, 'press that here – over the paper towelling – but not too firmly. And let's make sure we keep this arm elevated as much as possible, OK?' You realise when you attend incidents like this that although you're no expert, you actually have far more first-aid skills than the average person – or at least you hope you have. And of course, as ever, they look to you to take the lead. They assume you know what you're about.

'What's your name?' I asked the injured man.

'Andy. It's Andy, officer.'

He must've been in his early fifties, slightly built, and shaking like a leaf. 'Right, Andy. Looks like we've stopped the bleeding, and the ambulance crew will be here any second. Listen – you can hear it coming. They'll soon get you sorted.'

He didn't answer, and one of his workmates, the lad who was holding the towel over the stump, glanced at me with a questioning look on his face. 'It's OK,' I said. In the couple of minutes since we'd put the new pad in place a red stain had appeared through the material. The guy was looking as though he might pass out at any moment. Please don't, I was thinking. My heart was thumping and my mouth was dry. God knows what the victim felt like. But at that moment the ambulance pulled in to the building, flooding the place with flashing blue light. 'Here he is, lads,' I heard myself say as the paramedics got out of the cab and hurried towards us. 'You're all right now, mate.' I stood up, and steadied myself against a steel locker before stepping back so that they could get to work.

A moment later a doctor appeared. Somebody in the factory must have called him. As he bent down to examine the patient I remembered something. I walked over to the small group of people who were standing there, watching. 'Where's the er . . . what've you done with the guy's – with the severed limb?' I asked.

The lady with the clipboard was pointing towards the workbench where the accident had taken place. Blood was still dripping slowly from the steel surface and there, lying on its own, was the man's bare arm, the hand clenched, his wristwatch still in place.

'Right, can you get me a large clean towel, anyone?'

'Here.' Somebody handed me a neatly folded old-fashioned roller towel, white with two blue stripes.

'Cheers, my friend.' Using the towel as a glove I got hold of the arm and wrapped it up carefully. It was surprisingly heavy. I carried it to the car, took out a large plastic property bag and popped the arm straight in. It was a very strange feeling carrying someone's amputated limb like that. Even stranger, it seemed to me, was looking down and realising that the guy's watch was still working. I think part of me had imagined that it would have stopped at the time of the accident.

I closed the car door. With the injured man now in capable hands, my role in the emergency was effectively over. I got on the radio and updated the control room. Then I watched the paramedics lift the injured man into the ambulance. I went back to the car and handed them the plastic bag containing his arm. 'Yeah, cheers,' someone said. Sometimes, I'd heard, it's possible to reattach a limb. I have known it done with fingers, so why not?

'What'll they do, stitch it back on?' I asked one of the paramedics as she slammed the rear doors and went to get into the cab.

'Yeah. They'll try, at any rate. You'd be amazed what they can do.' And with that she climbed into her seat, shut the door and reversed slowly towards the doorway.

Once they were out of the way I was able to get on with

sealing off the whole area around where the accident had taken place. You treat it like a crime scene, although in this situation it would be the health and safety people who would conduct the investigation.

What I had to do now was call in the health and safety executive, who would lead on the investigation. And I needed to seal the area off for that to take place. I also needed to get the SOCO to the scene, to liaise with the duty inspector and get details of the witnesses. There was also the business of making sure that the guy's relatives had been informed. After I'd seen to all that I was able to drive back to town with the tail-end of the rush-hour traffic. Passing the fish and chip shop in Sherburn and catching a whiff of hot fat, I realised I was suddenly hungry. Always the same after a shock like that.

Back at the station Ed had come in from patrol and was cracking on with his PDR. 'That sounded a nasty accident, Mike. All sorted, is it?'

'It was bloody awful, Ed, I can tell you.' I started to give him a brief account of what had happened, then changed the subject. It was too fresh in my mind. 'Anyway, you feeling any better?' I asked.

'Me? How d'you mean?'

'Well, you sounded pretty fed up earlier.'

'Oh, that was just me getting things off me chest. You know how I hate all this review caper. Anyway, at the end of the day you just have to do it.' He pushed his papers to one side and leaned back in his chair. 'No, it's not all about figures, is it Mike? I know I do a decent job, and I'd like to think the rest of the shift do too. I mean, I've just been out there helping some old lad who'd got his bike stuck in the railings outside the supermarket. Had a word with a couple of youths who were just on the point of lobbing stones at an empty house. Old-fashioned police work, Mike. If I'd been a bit quicker on me feet I could've helped an old lady across the road, I dare say. But it all goes unnoticed by them upstairs, doesn't it? It just seems all the management want these days is numbers, something the buggers can feed into a computer that'll tell 'em whether I'm good, bad or indifferent. I mean, half the stuff we do when we're out on patrol – talking to the general public, reassuring them, listening to them – none of that's on the bloody PDRs, is it?'

'True.'

'Ah well, no good bleating on to you about it, is there? You're more on their side of the fence now. And, say what you like, what you really want every now and then is a good, straightforward direct arrest. Something you can bang down on these forms. Like nabbing these metal thieves, for example. That'd do for starters.'

I knew just what Ed was talking about, and I agreed with him one hundred per cent. Being a good cop is one thing; but what we all want is to be a lucky cop, somebody who catches the villains red-handed once in a while. I left Ed to get on, mashed myself a cup of tea and picked up a packet of biscuits and a newspaper, one of the nationals. There was an article about the outbreak of metal thefts around the country. What was bothering me was that this sort of crime was becoming flavour of the month with the local villains. It seemed that the price of scrap was rocketing. There were even cases being reported of cables being ripped up from railway lines. As I read on I shuddered to think of the safety implications – and the article went on to say that somebody down south had already electrocuted himself. On our patch we'd now had two church roofs stripped but, touch wood, no reports from the railway companies. To tell the truth, though, this whole business didn't surprise me. It's one of the easier crimes to commit, even if it is one of the most dangerous. But operating on rooftops – well, I wouldn't fancy it. Hugely hazardous.

I didn't give the matter much thought until a week or two

later when we came in for the early turn to hear that someone had called in from Hovingham and reported the loss of a substantial quantity of lead from his roof. The team were all tied up with various jobs, so I said I'd go and see the guy, although it was be mid-morning before I made it out there.

He lived close by the Malt Shovel pub, on the main street. As soon as I pulled up outside the cottage he was making his way down the garden to the front gate. He walked with a stick. He must've seen me looking up at the roof of his cottage, squinting against the low autumn sun. I couldn't see any sign of damage.

'No,' he said, 'it's not here. I've another property on the edge of the village. That's where the buggers have been. Shall I drive down and show you?'

'Aye, if you wouldn't mind.'

He led the way and I followed him to an old stone barn, a very handsome building that must have housed livestock at one time. It stood alone on a patch of rough grass, fifty yards or so from the nearest dwelling, screened off to some degree by a clump of trees. He got out of his car and pointed up at the roof. 'All the flashing gone, see, plus there's a section they've stripped bare, around the back. And look at this' – he was showing me the old windows, four five six of them in a row – 'all the flashing around them too. That's a lot of lead they've taken, and they wouldn't have got it off in five minutes, would they?'

'Any idea of the total value?' I asked. 'Could you put a figure on it?'

He looked up at the roof once more. 'If you was to pin me down I'd say . . . blimey, several hundred at least.' He shook his head and flicked the head off a dead thistle with his walking stick. 'I suppose I'll find out if I get an estimate for making it good. Although you have to wonder whether it's worth it or whether the buggers'll just come back and have it off again. 'S what they do with churches and suchlike, isn't it?'

'I'm afraid so. These people don't care who they target these days.' I looked up at the roof, wondering how they'd got up there, whether there would be any clues in the mud that surrounded the building. 'So when did you find out this had happened?' I asked.

'Walking the dog, early on. Always take her out first thing, down through the village; then we call in for me paper on the way back.'

'And did you hear anything? I mean, anybody in the village see anything?'

'As a matter of fact, there was a fellow in the shop said something about a van parked up this end.'

'Who was that then?'

He gave me the name of a retired teacher who lived in the village, someone I'd met at the gamekeeper's place one time. 'Well,' I said, 'you never know. I'll go and call on him. He's round the back of the baker's shop somewhere, isn't he?'

'Yes.' He gave me the man's house number. 'Should be about the place. Always busy in his garden.'

I got a few more details, took a statement, then had a quick look around to see if I could spot anything that could be used as evidence. I then drove back into the village, and made my way up the lane to a cottage that stood overlooking the little beck. When the guy answered the door I explained to him that a crime had taken place, and asked him what exactly he'd seen. He told me he'd been coming back late from a night out. 'Gone midnight, it was. I'm not usually out that late, but I was just coming back from a Rotary do at Thirsk. I came around that bend there and spotted a van – a Transit, I think. Something like that. I mean, I only caught it in my lights for a second, and then I was past it. But I remember thinking to myself, hello, I thought, what are you doing there? You know when a thing's parked at an odd angle, how it catches your eye?'

'Yes. So did you see anybody? Was anybody in the van or hanging around the place?'

'No. Never saw a soul, but as I say, I only caught a glimpse of it as I turned the corner.'

'And it was parked where exactly?'

'Imagine you're coming in from Helmsley – Stonegrave way.'

'Yeah?'

'Well, it was on that side, close up against the building, as if they'd used the roof as a sort of platform.'

I thanked him for his help, drove back to the old barn and parked up on the far side of the road. I walked across towards the side wall of the barn. It faced north and was in full shade. Under the eaves, next to a pile of old bricks, the grass was threadbare and the soil exposed. There was a clear tyre-mark coming out of a puddle, and one or two footprints. This was looking promising. It's so often the way it goes: one piece of good observation from a passer-by can prove immensely helpful. I got straight on the radio to control. 'Can I have the SOCO out here as soon as possible? We've some nice tyre-marks, possibly made by the van used in the theft here.' I glanced up at the grey clouds that were sweeping across the sky, and the trees bending before the wind. 'So long as he arrives before the rain,' I added.

I took another look around, treading carefully so as to avoid the muddy parts. As well as the tyre-marks, there was a nice clear wheelbarrow track. Yes, I thought, that all figures. Stuart'll have a field day when he gets here. There was more, too. Back on the road you could see where the van had taken off and left a pair of muddy wheel-marks curving off the grass and onto the tarmac. I went around the back of the barn and found two or three plastic fertiliser sacks. I laid them over the tyre-marks to protect them from the rain that was already starting to fall, and weighed them down with bricks from the pile.

Just as I got in the car to make my way back to town Stuart

called me to say he was en route from his base at Pickering. It was only an hour or so later that he came back to the station to report his findings.

'What do you reckon?' I asked him.

'Yeah, excellent,' he said. 'Got a nice set of tracks, as advertised, plus' – he paused dramatically – 'a wheelbarrow. Now, how about that?'

'Stuart, I told you about that, remember?'

'Oh. So you did. Anyway, I also got a couple of shoe-prints. So all you have to do, my friend, is bring in the suspect – or suspects, plural – and we'll have 'em.'

'Yeah,' I said, 'just a matter of bringing them in, eh?' I grimaced at him. 'Now, what makes me think you'd rather have your job than mine, eh?'

He didn't answer that. Just laughed and took off.

Of course, Stuart was right. His evidence, good as it was, would be no use without a suspect; and as the days went by we were no nearer to finding one for him. Thefts of the kind I'd investigated at Hovingham continued, however. And our briefings brought home to us that the problem wasn't just within our area. It seemed that neighbouring forces were dealing with exactly the same sort of incident, and we were under pressure to get a result. I remained confident that we would, in the end. It was my old theory about criminals being like gamblers. A gambler, I'd learnt years ago, never stops till he goes bust; and a criminal won't give up until he's caught. So long as someone's getting away with it, he – or she – will continue to pull the same sort of caper. Think about it. They rip a few sheets of lead off a roof, sell it on for cash, no questions asked, and find they've made enough money to keep themselves in clover for a week or two, perhaps longer. This is working great, they say, and scout around for another building to attack. To them it makes good sense. But in repeating the crime they multiply the chances that they'll get caught. And maybe they eventually get a little too confident, a little too casual, and a bit of carelessness creeps in, they make a mistake and get themselves caught.

It must have been two or three weeks later. It was, I recall, a Sunday afternoon, some time around three o'clock, maybe three thirty. I was out in the car with Ed. We'd been around town, up and down the bypass and out to Low Hutton. It all seemed very quiet, nothing of note going on; certainly nothing to stop for. You get shifts like that now and then, and this was one of those flat calm, late-November afternoons when you start to hope that something will happen – anything that'll get you out of the car. Out in the country autumn was turning to winter. There were still one or two splashes of yellow in the thorn hedges along the side of the A64, and a handful of copper-coloured leaves drifting quietly down from the beeches along Old Maltongate, so the landscape still had an autumnal feel to it; yet it was gloomy enough to feel like winter – and pretty cold too, as afternoon turned to dusk. We had the heater full on in the car and it was making it stuffy.

'That's the trouble with having a Sunday roast before you come out,' Ed said, shifting in his seat.

I looked at him and wound the window down. 'Hey, it wasn't me, mate.'

'Yeah, very funny, acting sergeant Pannett. What I meant was that you get drowsy.'

'Oh, right.'

'So never mind the fresh air: wind that bugger back up, will you?'

'*Control to 1015, over.*'

'Yeah, A64, go ahead.'

'*Passer-by has just seen two males on the roof at . . .*' She gave us an address in Norton.

'We're on our way, Julie. Is anyone else available?'

Before she could answer Fordy cut in. '*Yeah, on my way from North Grimston. Be with you in a few minutes, sarge.*'

'All received, Gary. Me and Ed aren't far away. Make it a silent approach when you get within earshot, over.'

'*That's a yes yes, will do.*'

'No point announcing your presence,' I added, and then wished I hadn't. I was still treating Fordy like a new recruit, whereas in fact he'd been with us three years or so now. Four, according to Ed.

The premises were just over the river from Malton, behind the petrol station. As we sped down Castlegate I had my fingers crossed. 'Wait for it . . .' I said as we came over the bridge. 'You wouldn't believe the number of times I've been caught by these the last few weeks.' But this time the level-crossing gates were open and we bumped over the tracks.

The place we were heading for was some sort of clothing warehouse – or had been. It was empty now, with a large FOR SALE board on one side.

We turned off the road into what had once been the car park. Fordy came on the radio. '*Just passing the bacon factory, sarge.*' Ed and I got out of the car and set off, stealthily, around the outside of the building. I gave my CS gas canister a quick shake just in case. It wasn't quite dark yet but I had my Dragon Light with me too, in case we had to go inside. The main front entrance was heavily padlocked, the windows boarded up with corrugated sheeting. Around the side the goods delivery doors were blocked by a rusting yellow skip piled high with brick rubble and a tangle of grey electric wiring. I peered behind it, but the door was barred and padlocked.

'Here we go,' Ed murmured. We'd worked our way around to the back, and there was a battered white Transit, parked beside a narrow wooden door that had clearly been forced open and then pushed to. 'And here comes the lad himself,' he said, as Fordy drove into the yard. 'You've timed that to perfection, my friend.' Ed pointed at the door and raised his eyebrows.

Fordy pulled a face and looked at me. 'You want me to go in?' he said.

'No. Hang fire,' I said. 'We've got the van in situ. Let's make sure we've got the place secured so they don't leg it on us.' I looked along the dark brick wall that formed the side of the building. 'Seems this is the only exit, so why don't we just do the sensible thing, eh? Wait here for them to come out – right into our hands.'

We didn't have long to wait. There were two of them, young, red-faced and sweaty, their shoulders and knees covered with grey dust. They hardly had time to register their surprise before we had the handcuffs on them and were telling them they were going to be detained and searched while we established what exactly they'd been up to.

At first they didn't say a word, just stared at us, mouths open. I knew one of them straight away. He came from York. I'd had dealings with him in the past: dodgy-looking vehicles, generally suspicious behaviour, hanging out with known villains; but we'd never really pinned anything on him. He was the kind of lad you just knew would be up for this sort of thing, the type that you fully expected to be nabbing some day. But so far, we didn't actually know what they'd been doing in the old warehouse. I walked towards their van. 'Let's have a look inside here, shall we?'

'There's nowt in there,' the York lad said. I swung open the rear door. It was indeed empty, apart from . . . yes. I almost laughed. A wheelbarrow.

'Right.' I turned to Ed. 'I'm going to check inside the building.'

I didn't have to go far to find what we were after. Right beside the door were three neat stacks of lead. It was all cut into oblong strips, the edges glinting dully as I flashed my torch over them.

I had a quick look around the rest of the ground floor, but there was nothing much to see, just an old workbench covered in pigeon crap and a large puddle on the floor under a dripping overhead pipe. I went back into the fresh air and rejoined Ed and Fordy. 'Okay,' I said, 'looks like these two gentlemen have been helping themselves to a fair amount of lead. It's all piled up just inside the door there. Can you two do the honourable thing and arrest them both.'

The lads were informed that they were both under arrest for burglary and causing criminal damage. I cautioned them both, and added, 'And while we're on the subject, we'll be seizing the van, boys.'

They didn't like that. They were outraged. 'You can't take the f***ing van. 'Tisn't even ours. You've no f***ing right.'

You don't bother to answer stuff like that. It's just bluster, and they know it. We put them in the cars, one in mine, one in Fordy's van. We weren't having them cooking up a story on the way to the station. As I drove back I got my thinking cap on. There was every likelihood that we'd be dealing with other offences these two might be linked to. Given the nature of the arrests they'd most likely be in custody for more than six hours, so that ruled out detaining them at Malton. They would need to be taken to Scarborough where our CID man could interview the pair of them. I got on the phone and called Des. He was one very happy detective. He told me he'd head straight over and pick up the investigation, then asked me whether I could spare Fordy to assist. 'Good idea,' I said. 'He could use the experience. We don't get many of these.'

It wasn't until the very end of our shift that Gary landed back at Malton to fill me and Ed in on how the interviews had gone. The accused, he told us, claimed that they'd just driven by the warehouse, seen the open door, and decided to have a look around. When you hear this sort of nonsense – which you do, time after time, week after week – it's like water off a duck's back. It's old hat. Once in a while, however, you do hear some-thing new, some choice snippet, some attempt at an excuse that makes you laugh so much you can't wait to share it with the lads over a cup of tea – and Fordy had a classic for us. 'You'll never believe this next bit,' he said. 'They reckoned they were walking around the building, right, when they heard a cat mewing inside. And get this – they felt sorry for it because, the lad said, they're animal lovers. They thought it was trapped, so they went inside to see if they could rescue it.'

This was all good for a bit of fun, but when Fordy got to the serious stuff, he had some promising news for us. It seemed that the suspects' hands were grey from handling the lead, so they'd taken swabs, which gave us a nice bit of forensic to bolster the case. Then he and Des questioned them about other incidents over the past few weeks. Did they know anything about two separate church roof jobs, for example? Course not. Didn't even know where the churches were. Had they been in the Hovingham area at all? No. Why would they? Despite their denials Des was satisfied that he had enough on them to press charges, but he wanted more. It's the old belt-and-braces approach. Why settle for one conviction when you can get two? While Des did the questioning, the SOCO had been over the van and taken impressions of the tyres – and those of the wheelbarrow.

Following a break, they'd questioned the two suspects further about other possible offences, including Hovingham. Both of them had taken the 'no comment' option, and there was nothing anybody could do about that. So . . . frustration all round. The bad news for the suspects, however, was that if the results from the comparison came back in a few weeks' time and were a match for the ones at Hovingham, they would face a second set of charges. Had they confessed when under interrogation by Des, they could've had the other offences TIC'd – 'taken into consideration' – and had the magistrate or judge deal with all the crimes together. The route they had taken, however, could well lead them to more severe punishment. It was a dangerous game they were playing. They'd both been charged for offences committed at the abandoned shop premises and bailed to appear at Scarborough magistrates court the following week. We would simply have to await the forensic results to see whether further charges would be brought against them.

Either way it was a good result, no question about it. It's often the case in a rural area that a spate of thefts such as these turns out to be the work of one team, which means that one arrest can bring the crime wave to an end – at least for a while. We were all feeling pleased with ourselves, even Jayne. 'Old Birdie'll be well chuffed,' she said when she heard the news next day. 'Hey, and you Ed. You'll 'ave all sorts to write on that PDR now, mate.'

Ed didn't answer. He was busy moaning to Fordy – not about bureaucracy this time, but about York City's early-season form.

Chapter 10

All Bets Are On

'That's what I love about this job. Never a dull moment. One thing after another.' Ed had just trudged into the parade room. He shook his head and slapped a sheet of paper on the table. 'It's like my first sergeant said to me, the day I arrived from Hendon. Welcome to the force, son. You might die of exasperation, but you won't die of boredom.'

Fordy looked up from his newspaper. 'What's up with you these days? When I first came here you were Mr Chirpy. I remember thinking, blimey, I hope I'm that cheerful when I get to his age. But look at you now . . . you're always moaning about something.'

'Hey, you young whippersnapper. I've a perfect right to moan. You put in the years I've put in, son, and you'll know what I'm talking about.'

'I dunno. You don't get Thommo bellyaching all the time, and he's been here longer than anyone. I mean, it's not like he isn't a pain in the neck at times, but . . .'

'Fordy mate, there's one simple reason why you rarely hear Thommo complaining, and that's because he's never here. Think about it.'

'Yeah, all right.' Fordy threw his paper onto the table and sighed. 'Go on, then. What is it? What's on the agenda today?'

'Why, it's these new rosters; all this chopping and changing. You can hardly keep pace. First Jayne goes and gets pregnant and can't work nights. Then Pannett forgets where his true loyalties lie, decides to go for sergeant and they fetch this new lad in to cover – except he's on leave for two weeks so nobody's set eyes on him yet; and now, instead of a keen young bright-eyed recruit fresh out of college, and possibly good-looking, what do we get? We get Thommo on nights with us. I'm telling you, this nick is getting more like York City every week. It needs a settled side. A bit of consistency in the selection.'

''Scuse me butting in, but what's wrong with having Thommo on board?' I asked.

'Oh, sorry. Didn't see you there, Mike.' Ed picked up Fordy's discarded *Press* and sat down. 'No, don't get me wrong. There's nowt the matter with Thommo – when he shows up. Good man in a crisis and all that. It's just . . .'

'Hey, I know what it is,' Fordy said, grinning from ear to ear and snapping his fingers. 'Yeah – that's it. Now it makes sense. It's Jayne, isn't it? I'm sure Mike told me when I first started you had a bit of a thing for her. You're missing Jayne, aren't you? Go on, admit it.'

'Tell you what,' I said, nipping in before Ed could deny the charges, 'he ain't the only one. You can say what you like about the lass, but she's always the same, day in day out. Not like some moody buggers I could mention. Yep, for a Cockney I'd say she isn't bad at all. And I'll go on record as saying I miss her too, and her banter. Anyway lads, more to the point, all of this shuffling the pack means we're thin on the ground again. I'm out on patrol tonight, so you two are doubled up, and Thommo – hey, where is he anyway?'

'I'm right behind you, sarge. Entering stage left, bang on cue.'

'That figures. You always were a drama queen. Anyway, I've got you down for town tonight; these two'll cover the top end and rural, and I'll double up with you later on, once I've got a grip on me paperwork.'

The best laid plans of mice and men. I was busy working through a case file that was due to be submitted to the CPS by the next day, when Fordy and Ed were called out to a domestic, way over Kirkbymoorside direction, and Thommo got caught up with a couple of underage drinkers behind the library in Norton. All this on a Sunday night, I was thinking, the one time when you could hope for a quiet start to the shift. At least, that used to be the case.

I needn't have worried about the lads, however. They were all three back at the station by a little after midnight, chuntering about storms in teacups. That's the great thing with experienced officers like Ed and Thommo: they know how to get on top of a spot of minor aggro and prevent it from getting out of hand. They took a quick tea break, the way we normally do on a Sunday after we've seen all the pubs turned out and people safely back home. By the time they went back out in their cars they were confidently expecting a nice quiet shift – and most likely telling themselves they deserved it. Thommo was staying local until I'd finished in the office. It's not great to be single-crewed on nights, although in rural areas sometimes you have no choice. I've done it plenty of times myself in the past. It just means you have to be that little bit more careful and not go jumping in until you have backup in place. Anyway, I wasn't far off being done. With a bit of luck I'd be able to join up with him pretty soon.

It must have been half an hour later when I heard Fordy calling control. He and Ed were out along the A64, on Golden Hill.

'*Yeah, we've just been passed by a white Mondeo heading towards York, one headlight out, travelling at speed and being driven erratically. Registration number . . .*'

I paused at what I was doing and listened. As a sergeant, you always keep an eye, and an ear, on what's happening out there. It's a combination of things. One, you want to know what your officers are doing, and that they're safe; two, you need to keep tabs on what resources they might need at any one time. And of course with such a small force at your disposal you always have to be prepared to drop whatever you're up to and lend a hand.

'*Managed to get behind it, over. Just approaching the dual carriageway heading towards Whitwell.*'

Often in a situation like that you'll be ready to send for reinforcements, but in this instance there was no need. It wasn't many minutes before Fordy and Ed had stopped the suspect vehicle, breathalysed the driver and arrested him for drink-driving. Normally you would expect to book a prisoner into custody locally, but in a case like this, where the roadside test indicates excessive alcohol, you have to follow up with a CAMIC test. That's a breath-test device manufactured by the Car And Medical Instrument Company – hence the term CAMIC – that measures the levels of alcohol in the blood. It provides you with the kind of solid, accurate evidence you require when the defendant appears in court. It's quite a sophisticated bit of gear, and you have to be trained to use it. None of us at Malton had done the course as yet, so this youth was going to have to be taken to York – which meant that for the next couple of hours or so I would be operating with half the normal complement of staff, namely myself and Thommo. I got on to control and asked if the night duty dog section covering York might be able to make their way over to offer some support. The good news was that they would; the bad news was that they couldn't make it until they'd seen to a spot of bother outside one of the nightclubs.

I got on the radio to Thommo. 'Anything doing out there?'

'*All quiet on the eastern front just now, sarge. Has the feel of an old-fashioned Scottish Sabbath.*'

'Yeah, all received. Only six hundred square miles for you to worry about. I've managed to get the dog unit to head over from York in a bit.'

'*That's cheering news, sarge. When can we expect them?*'

'Like I said, Thommo, in a bit. Listen, I'll give you a shout to come and pick me up shortly, OK?'

'*All received. But sarge, take it from me: there's no need to be worrying. Ryedale is in safe hands tonight.*'

You have to laugh at Thommo. He loves to see himself as the central figure in some ongoing drama. Although to be fair to him, at this moment it really was him out there on his own. Still, I thought, it's Sunday night. Fingers crossed: he should be OK. I went back to my reports.

It was about two o'clock when Fordy called in to say that he and Ed were tidying up the loose ends at York custody. Their man had blown over twice the legal limit. He was being charged, and they would be through with him shortly. This was looking as though it was going to pan out nicely. I'd got my paperwork tidied up, and would shortly have all my officers available. I gave Thommo a shout to come and collect me from the station, grabbed my gear and headed into the back yard to wait for him. It was a very dark and still night. There was supposed to be a moon, but just now the sky was covered with cloud and there was very little wind. Old Maltongate was deserted, and the only noise was the distant hooting of an owl over towards the cricket club. Then I heard Thommo approaching from town. He was just pulling into the yard when Julie came on the radio.

'*Control to all units. Suspects on premises at the Half Moon public house, Acklam. Units to deal?*'

'Yeah Julie, can you show me and Thommo dealing?'

'*All received, Mike. Informant is the landlord. Reports alarm activated. Says it's a silent one, only audible in the house; triggered from the outside cellar doors, he thinks, so intruders*' *possibly on the premises. Says he has a secure door between himself and the pub itself, but he's worried for their safety.'*

'That's received. Just leaving Malton now.'

Even as I got in the car and fastened my seatbelt control came on again to say they were talking to the landlord. '*He says he can hear intruders downstairs, inside the pub. I've advised him to stay in the private quarters and keep the door to the pub locked, awaiting your arrival.'*

'Where exactly is he, Julie? And is he alone, over?'

'*He's in the upstairs bedroom with his wife. I'm keeping them on the line.'*

Thommo put the blue lights on and turned out of the station compound on to Old Maltongate.

'Julie, have we any other officers making their way, over?'

Before she could answer, Fordy came on. He and Ed were done with the drink-driver and were making their way to the outer ring road. And now we were hearing that control had spoken to the dog unit. They weren't needed at the nightclub after all, and were en route from Osbaldwick, just outside the city. Given their location, they shouldn't be long either.

'Twenty minutes and we'll have reinforcements,' I said, as Thommo took us over the river and away up Welham Road. 'Maybe less.' I rubbed my hands. You get a special kind of energy when you're on your way to a crime in progress, a huge adrenalin rush. You're ready for anything, and although you're nervous there's that sense of anticipation that all cops are familiar with, the real possibility of catching someone in the act, of halting a crime before any serious damage is done to people or property; and, of course, more or less guaranteeing a conviction. This was one of those jobs you really get a buzz out of.

As we hit eighty on the road up to Leavening I was thinking. If the landlord had a silent alarm then the burglars would have no idea it had been triggered. That could spell good news or bad. Yes, there was the possibility that we might catch them in the act, but there was also the chance that far from being rattled they might assume they were undetected, enter the house and threaten the occupants. So I wasn't sure at this stage what we would be dealing with, and how best we would play it.

Control were maintaining telephone contact with the landlord and relaying the important stuff to us. He and his wife were now in some distress; they could actually hear the sound of splintering wood. The pair of them were effectively under siege in their own home. Julie was updating them and keeping them as calm as possible, reassuring them that we'd be there very soon. We were into Leavening now, barely a mile from the scene, and Thommo was driving as fast as the conditions allowed. Thankfully it was dry, the clouds seemed to have parted, and there was nobody about on the roads.

'1015 to control, we're just approaching Acklam now. About two minutes away.'

We had already switched off the blue lights, way back; no way were we going to announce our arrival to them. We pulled up a hundred yards or so short of the pub. With luck, we could approach on foot and not be seen or heard.

In the shadow of a house just around the corner from the Half Moon, I reached into the back seat, grabbed my body armour and spoke quietly into the radio, with the volume turned right down. '1015 to control.'

'*Go ahead, over.*'

'Right, we're on scene. Any update from the informant, over?'

'*No, it's been quiet for a couple of minutes, Mike. Backup's still a good ten minutes away.*'

'That's all received.'

While I was talking, Thommo had got out and was at my side window, cracking open his Asp, his Dragon Light tucked under one arm. 'I'm ready, laddie. Let's have 'em, shall we?'

'OK, let's go.'

We walked slowly towards the pub, keeping to the shadows. We passed a dark VW Golf, ten years old. I put a hand over the radiator grille. Warm to the touch. I turned to Thommo, pointed to it and nodded. He quietly passed the details to control.

'Where's the cellar doors?' he whispered as we crept round the side of the building.

'Control says round the back, in the car park.'

As soon as we got there we could see them. They were closed, but the padlock was lying to one side. The steel plate it was fixed to had been crowbarred, or forced free with something, the screws ripped out of the door's wooden frame. Beside the doors was a large planter, one of those sawn-in-half barrels full of soil and dog-ends.

'Looks like we've two choices,' I said. 'Wait for them to come out or go in after 'em.' Thommo didn't say anything. I knew what he'd be thinking. Same as me: how many were we dealing with here? Two, three, four? And were they violent? Armed? These situations are never as easy as they might seem. My first thought was that we could wait for them at the cellar doors, but there was nothing to say they'd come back out that way. If they were working their way through the pub, they'd more likely exit through a door – and there were two of those to the rear, plus the main front entrance. I took the CS gas canister off my belt, gave it a shake and popped it back. Thommo followed suit. Julie was on the radio. With the volume turned right down I had to press it to my ear to make out what she was saying. It was a useful bit of info: the car we'd walked past belonged to a well-known criminal from the Bridlington area.

The night was colder now, or so it seemed, with patches of mist forming. Above us a full moon was peering out from between patches of mottled cloud, and out of the corner of my eye I saw a cat hop up onto one of the bins at the far side of the car park. But I don't think it was any of that that made me shiver. I think it was the sheer uncertainty. This was one of those situations where I honestly wasn't sure what to do next. The only good news was that control still had the landlord on the phone. If he and his wife came under immediate threat, we'd know right away. But as to our best course of action, there was no correct answer, no best answer. Things would of course be different when our backup arrived. Once we had sufficient officers on the scene we could go straight in.

Suddenly Thommo tensed up and cocked his head to one side. I'd heard it too, a low rumble and couple of thumps coming from inside the cellar. Someone swore, and there was a momentary flash of light through the crack between the doors.

I braced myself, tightening my grip on the Asp, then glanced at Thommo, who had moved forward a couple of paces and was assuming a half-crouched position. One of the doors opened, just a few inches at first, then someone said, 'Gerra bloody move on, will yer,' and it was flung wide open with a metallic crash. Both of us flipped our Dragon Lights on.

'Don't move!'

'Stay exactly where ye are!'

'It's the police, boys. You're under arrest.'

There were two pairs of eyes blinking at us from the open door, two lanky figures hesitating. Neither of them looked more than twenty or so. One of them muttered, 'Oh, shit.' The other one didn't say a word.

'Right, out you come – you first.' They came one at a time. I made them lie face-down on the ground. Thommo fixed the beam of his Dragon Light on them while I knelt down and applied the handcuffs.

'How many of you?' I said, as they stood up.

'What?'

'Any more inside?'

'Nah.' The youth who spoke was about six feet tall but I

doubt he weighed ten stone. He was wearing a white T-shirt, a pair of dark coloured cargo pants and a close-fitting black hat.

'You sure?'

'Look, it's just us, OK?'

'Let's hope you're right,' Thommo said. He walked over and closed the cellar doors, then he went and straddled the barrel, walked it slowly across and heaved it on top with a great thump. 'Cos they'll be trapped now, won't they? Eh?'

They didn't respond. We walked the prisoners round the side of the pub and on towards the road. There was no struggle. They didn't even look as though they had it in them to struggle. Out the front we patted them down. Both of them had their pockets absolutely stuffed full of pound coins.

We locked one youth in Thommo's car, the other in mine. Just as we'd done that the dog unit arrived, and Fordy came on to say that he and Ed were two minutes away. 'That's great,' I said to Thommo. 'They can watch the prisoners while you, me and the dog man search the pub.' I updated control and requested them to get the landlord to come down and let us in.

It took him and his wife a couple of minutes to make their way down from their flat, by which time Fordy and Ed had arrived.

'Thank God you blokes turned up when you did.' The landlord was wearing a pale grey jogging suit; his wife was wrapped up in a thick, dark dressing gown, holding it tight around her and shivering, although inside the pub it felt warm to me, with my body armour on. They both looked drawn and worried, particularly the wife. 'We've been frightened half to death,' she said. 'I mean, we could hear them downstairs banging and crashing. We didn't know what to do. Thought they'd be through into the flat any moment.'

'Listen, you did the right thing,' I said. 'Staying put and calling us. A lot of people think they're going to take these burglars on; trust me, it isn't worth the risk. Let's just get the police dog to have a quick look round, shall we? I don't think there's anyone else, but we'll just satisfy ourselves, eh?'

While the dog handler went about his business I looked around the bar. As far as I could see, things were relatively undisturbed. 'So, you got any idea what the damage is? They've both got their pockets stuffed full of pound coins. Nowt else though.'

The landlord had gone behind the bar and made his way to the far end. 'They've forced the till open, look. That'd be the float money they took.'

'How much of a float are you talking about?' We went across to have a look. The drawer was open. A number of coins were scattered about on the counter and the floor. 'They'd more than a handful of loose change about them, I can tell you. Hundreds at a guess.'

He pursed his lips and shook his head. 'Wouldn't be more than thirty pounds in here, max. Hang on though.' He led us over towards the far side of the room where a fruit machine had been pulled away from the wall a couple of feet. Looking over his shoulder as he peered behind it, I could see the splintered wood where they'd managed to get into the back of it.

'That'll be where they got all the cash,' he said. 'Mind, I had it emptied a few days ago. Maybe a week, let's say. There wouldn't be a huge amount. Like you say, a couple of hundred, perhaps.'

His wife was behind the bar looking up at the shelves. 'There's a couple of bottles of single malt gone,' she said. 'Fifteen-year-old stuff. And some brandy. Oh, and here's one they've dropped on the floor.' She bent to pick it up, then walked across towards the hallway and switched the light on. 'I wonder . . . Ah, thought so.'

I followed her through. There was a cigarette machine there. It had been forced and more or less emptied.

'Yeah but I wonder what they've done with it all,' I said. 'They'd nothing but the cash with them. Unless they've stashed their goodies about the place somewhere.' I looked around. 'How d'you get down to the cellar?'

She led me through a rear door, her husband following us, down a set of stone stairs, and there it was all neatly stacked up at the bottom of the steps next to the metal doors they'd come out of. There were several dozen packets of cigarettes, the malt whisky, a few bags of crisps and nuts – and a crowbar to boot.

'Makes you wonder,' the landlord said as we went back into the bar.

'How's that?'

'Well, risking your liberty for a couple of hundred quid and a few bits and bobs.'

'It does,' I said. 'And to say they've to split it between two of them. But you think about it. Couple of young lads, living at home. It goes a fair way, a bit of cash like that. And they could've got lucky, couldn't they? You could've left the register stuffed full of money; or they could've found the fruit machine loaded.'

I left Ed and Fordy to take the statements from the victims. The dog handler headed over to Malton to cover, just in case anything else should come in while Thommo and I were taking the two prisoners and the property to York, where they would be put in custody overnight and then interviewed by the CID in the morning.

It didn't take us too long. Once we'd booked them, and the property, we were free to return to Malton to write up our reports. We sat together and recorded the details of the incident, the evidence and the arrests. Later we would fax ours and the victims' statements over to York and post the originals in the internal mail. The CID would need their own copies to conduct the interviews later that day.

'Busy start to the week,' I said later as we relaxed over a cup of tea.

Thommo didn't answer at first. Then he fixed me with a hard stare and said, 'See, that's the difference between you heathens and us churchgoers, sarge.'

'Eh? How d'you mean?'

'Well, ye're saying it's the start of a week, and I have to disagree with ye. The Good Book tells us that the Sabbath is the seventh day, ye ken? Not the first.'

What do you say to a fellow like Thommo? The man has an answer for everything. I'd decided some time previously that by and large it's better to say nothing, otherwise he'll blind you with science. 'Aye, have it your own way,' I said.

'That's very gracious of ye,' he said. 'But considering the strength of my case I'd say it's a wise decision. All those Sunday morning scripture classes – I knew they'd come in handy in the fullness of time.' He stirred a spoonful of sugar into his tea and sighed. 'Course, Sunday night has never been my favourite shift. Didn't mind it when I was younger, but at my age? No, I cannae say it fills me with delight and *joie de vivre* to be up all night. Still, that was a heck of a result we had there. Not very often you catch a couple of billy burglars in the act, eh? I dare say that's the excitement over for now. I reckon things'll quieten down for a few nights. Law of averages, wouldn't you say?'

I nearly warned Thommo he was tempting fate. And I reckon I should've done, because it turned out to be an eventful week. Monday night, going into Tuesday, was actually quiet enough until late on, just at the point when I was starting to think of home. That's when I got the call to say that control had had a security officer on the line, in a panic, possibly in shock, after seeing what he described as a big cat, most likely a panther.

Here we go, I thought. Must be Sunday's full moon still messing with people's imagination. The station was empty. I suppose I could've called Fordy or Ed, both of whom were out on patrol – or more likely on their way back to base – but, as I was a wildlife officer, and had a special interest in the case, this was my baby.

The security guy had called from a sort of hostel, out on the edge of town close to the river. It's a place where youngsters, not necessarily offenders as such, more what you'd call wayward and vulnerable youths, are put under supervision while they sort themselves out under the guidance of social workers and the like. But it was well supervised, naturally, and this fellow who'd called in was the night security man. He was a big beefy sort, not at all the kind to be rattled, you would've thought, so I had to take him seriously when he described what he'd seen.

'Oh, it was big,' he said. 'And bold. It was just stood there, looking straight at me. And as it turned its head its eyes were like – like a sort of . . . opalescent green.' Opalescent: I made a mental note to look that up in the dictionary when I got home, then suggested we set off along the riverside, which was where he reckoned he'd last seen the mystery animal, heading downstream towards Kirkham.

Oh no, he wasn't having any of that. For all his shaven head and gold earring and broad shoulders, he wasn't going to risk life and limb in a search for a vicious wild beast. Besides, he couldn't desert his post, could he? Not even to defend his charges against a prowling carnivore.

I'd always been sceptical about this supposed panther, but I have to admit I was a bit jumpy as I made my way down the embankment, flashing my torch into the bushes and across the water-meadows. When a guy that size looks you in the eye and tells you that he's seen a monster, you're inclined to believe him. However, I didn't find much to excite me. Sure, there were some large paw-prints in the mud, but they had the telltale claw-marks that suggested a dog, not a cat. Cats always pad along with their claws retracted.

It was only after I got back to the place and talked with me-laddo again that he told me the best bit. 'I just realised, while you were out there,' he said. 'With a bit of luck it'll all be on t'CCTV, won't it?' And he showed me where they had a camera sited on an external wall, pointed towards the river's edge.

'Well, can you retrieve the film for me?' I asked. 'That'd be a massive help if you've got any decent images.'

This was starting to look very interesting, although in the light of the bet I'd had with Thommo some months earlier it could spell bad news for me. But at least it might shed some light on the mystery.

It didn't take the guard long to get the videotape, and although my shift was almost over by the time I got back to the station I wasted no time in taking it to Jayne, who'd just arrived at work and was standing in for Phil. 'Here you go,' I said. 'Nice little job for you. This innocent-looking cassette could represent history in the making.'

'Less 'ave a look then.' She took it from me and turned it over in her hand. 'Caught 'em red-handed, did you? Bang to rights?'

'Jayne,' I said, 'brace yourself. This isn't some hen party causing mayhem down Castlegate. What you have in your hands could settle once and for all the burning question of the day: have we or we have not got a panther on the loose in Ryedale? I've just been to see a burly, sensible-looking security guard who reckons he came face to face with it this very morning, under the all-seeing eye of his CCTV camera. This could be the first filmed record of the Ryedale panther – and you, Jayne, could be the first person to set eyes on it. Other than him. Think of it. Soon as the story hits the press they'll be after you with microphones and cameras and asking you what you're gonna call your baby.'

'I just hope there's nothing too shocking on it.' She patted her bump. 'If this baby decides to put in an early appearance I'm gonna hold you personally responsible.'

'Jayne, let me put you right on that score. You do not want an early appearance at work – not if my first-aid skills are all you've got to fall back on.'

'Yeah yeah yeah. Go on then, you go and drink your tea and I'll have a butcher's at this. How long d'you think it is?'

'No idea. Six hours, eight, twelve. But with any luck it'll be on a timer. That means you can crank the speed up, can't you?'

'Yeah, course I can. Only thing is, d'you reckon I'll be able to stand the excitement? A film shot at night, and the testimony of a security guard who's just put in an eight-hour shift?' Jayne shook her head. 'I can't see a good outcome.' She sighed and started setting up the machine. 'Oh well, let's see if we can put you out of your misery.'

I left her to it and went to answer the phone, not once but four times. My pal the security man had called *The Press* in York, and Minster FM. Then he'd had a rush of blood to the head and called the *Yorkshire Post*. Which meant that I spent the next fifteen minutes fielding a series of daft questions.

'Is it true there's been a big-cat sighting in Malton?'

'Do you think this is the wildcat we've been hearing about all these years?'

'Is it true that you've got film footage of the Ryedale Panther?

'Do you think there's any danger to the public with this savage killer on the loose?'

'So, Acting Sergeant Pannett, how safe are the public of North Yorkshire with a man-eating lion rampaging around the countryside?'

I played a straight bat. What else can you do? 'Listen,' I told them, one after another, 'we have had a report of a large cat, seen on the outskirts of town, well away from any housing. We're investigating. And as part of our investigations we are looking at footage from a security camera sited in the vicinity of the sight – of the supposed sighting. We are not aware of any danger. Any further developments and I assure you we will let you know.'

'Bloody press,' I said as I went back to see how Jayne was getting on. 'Desperate for anything that'll give them an eye-catching headline.'

Jayne had the cassette in her hand and was shaking her head. 'Well, Mike, if the press get hold of this one you'll be in for some real shockers.'

'Eh? What d'you mean? What you got?'

'Headlines. You know the kind of thing. "Police in Panther Cover-up as Evidence is Destroyed"?'

'Jayne, what are you on about? Talk English, will you? And make it snappy. I'm ready for my bed, mate.'

She wagged the cassette at me – and that's when I noticed the great loops of shiny brown tape dangling from it, strung right across to the machine on which she'd been trying to play it.

'Oh hell.'

'That's what I said – or a rough translation of it. Our machine here has gobbled up the evidence. I was rewinding it and – crunch! I reckon it's chewed up about an hour's worth.'

'Shit. What can we do?'

She reached out and ran her fingers through the tangles, then tugged at a tightly twisted strand that refused to budge. 'Assuming I can persuade it out of the machine we can stuff it an envelope, send it to our central labs, and wait a week, maybe two, maybe a bit longer, until it gets to the top of their pile.'

The question now was, could I communicate this back to our friendly security man without him immediately picking up the phone and talking to the press all over again? The answer was, I couldn't. I knew it, he knew it and Jayne knew it, and by the time I came into work the following night the cat – so to speak – was out of the bag and everyone knew it.

Thommo was waiting to pounce as soon as I walked into the

locker room. 'So, ye going to pay up now, laddie? I mean, hand over the ten pounds and I'll overlook the fact that ye've somehow spirited away the evidence. What d'ye say to that?'

'I say one word, Jock. Patience. I mean, who said anything about evidence? What we got – what that machine chewed up – was *potential* evidence. And as you know, there's a difference. There could've been anything on that film. Or nothing. Trust me, we will get an answer – and one of us will get that tenner – in the fullness of time.'

'All right,' Thommo said, 'so how d'ye feel about voiding the bet?'

'No chance. In fact, I'm willing to up the stakes.'

Thommo wasn't expecting this. I was walking down to the messroom and he was huffing along behind me. 'Up the stakes? Come on, Mr Pannett, what do ye know? What did ye see on that tape before you – before it was conveniently devoured? What did Jayne tell you before she threw the auto-destruct switch, eh?'

'Not at liberty to disclose that, Thommo lad, as you well know. But I've another tenner here in my pocket if you're feeling brave.'

He wasn't, and after a bit of routine banter from the rest of the shift the matter was shelved.

It looked like being a quiet night. That was, until about eleven. I was on top of all my corries, or correspondence, and had gone out on patrol round town. Fordy and Thommo were covering the bottom end of our area, and Ed the top end, when control passed us some information received from an anonymous source. The informant had reported that a young man, known to us, and known by us to have been disqualified after recently being prosecuted for drinking and driving, had been seen in a pub at Terrington. Nothing wrong with that, except that he'd arrived at the wheel of a car, had allegedly consumed several pints of beer, and was giving every indication that he intended to drive off shortly.

You have to be very careful when dealing with anonymous informants. We rely hugely on tip-offs from the public, but we always have to try and establish how reliable is the information on offer and what is the motivation for giving it. Or, to put it more bluntly, are the informants simply fabricating? Are they acting out of malice towards the accused? Might they be trying to divert our attention from something that they themselves are up to, or planning? Having said that, it's quite a common thing for people to ring in and report drink-drive offenders. The days when getting away with that was considered a bit of a lark are long gone. People are fully aware of the seriousness of the offence and the dangers involved, and have absolutely no sympathy with those who try it. They'll inform, but in most cases they prefer to maintain anonymity. Whoever handles a call from an informer will always try their best to get the person's details, especially when they are reporting crimes. But the fact is, people sometimes have good reason not to divulge their identities. And with regard to drink-driving, those accusations are more often than not well founded, and we have to treat them seriously.

As I set off towards Terrington I considered my options. My first priority would be to apprehend the suspect before he could endanger the lives of himself or others on the road. Clearly, if I wanted to secure a prosecution I needed to catch the suspect in his car with the keys on his person. Either that or I could get him opening the car doors – but that would require good timing, or good luck. And I'd need to be positioned so that I could see him but not be seen. The trouble with taking that approach is that you run the risk of the guy getting away from you, which could mean you end up with a chase, and all the dangers that that involves.

Before I put any plan into action, however, I needed an ID on the suspect's car. Right on cue, control came in, just as I was driving along the main village street and approaching the pub. '*Yeah Mike, further info on this suspect at Terrington. Informant says he's about to leave the premises. He's come out of the pub and got into a dark coloured Ford Focus, six years old.*'

'Is that his own vehicle, over?'

'*That looks like a yes. He had a Focus registered to him before the ban. Hang on, Mike, we're just hearing . . . yep, he's driven off in the direction of Bulmer.*'

Even as that piece of news came through I was dazzled by a set of headlights coming towards me. The driver dipped them at the last minute and shot past, heading towards Bulmer village. I braked, stopped the car and watched my rear-view mirror as he sped away. I just had time to see that it was indeed a Ford Focus, and that its registration number matched the one control had given me.

Here we go, I thought. I waited for his rear lights to disappear from view, then turned round and set off after him. You can never be sure that you've been clocked, but I felt there was a pretty good chance he'd spotted me as he came out of the pub car park. Would he know that I was behind him though?

'1015 to control. Just been passed by the vehicle travelling at speed towards Bulmer, over.'

'*That's all received. I'll get you some backup sorted.*'

I needed to play this with great care. According to our information, the guy I was now pursuing had had a bit of a skinful. If he was drunk, he represented a massive danger to any other road users, as well as to himself, so I wasn't going to crowd him. On the other hand, he needed to be caught before he hit the built-up areas, or got out onto a major road – always assuming he didn't come to grief on these narrow country lanes. And God help anybody who happened to be coming towards him. The more I thought about it, the more the possible outcomes filled me with horror. But for the moment all I could do was follow at a safe distance and hope he didn't panic.

The great advantage about giving chase at night, especially out in the country, is that you can see your target vehicle way ahead, far further than you'd hope to in daylight. I was maintaining a good four to five hundred yard margin between myself and my quarry, driving faster than I would've liked to. It had been raining for much of the day, and although the skies were now clearing there was quite a bit of water on the roads. He was really pushing it, and that was worrying me. If he chose to drive like this and ran into a tree or a hedge or a stone wall, that was his choice. Ploughing into somebody's house, or an oncoming car, that was another thing.

We weren't far from the T-junction where you turn right for Bulmer, left for Welburn, when Fordy called me to say he and Thommo were on their way, coming along the A64 and preparing to turn north up towards the latter village, which meant they could well meet the suspect coming towards them.

A moment later control updated me with the news that the night-duty traffic car was dealing with a serious accident over in Scarborough. They had however managed to get hold of a York unit, who were making their way out to the Hopgrove roundabout. This was better news. I sped on between the hedgerows, the way ahead sporadically suffused with a bright red glow as the driver braked, then accelerated away again.

'What the— ?' Suddenly the Focus didn't appear to be moving any more, and its headlights were shining through a thin veil of mist, way up into the sky.

'1015 to control. Looks like he's off the road at . . .'

I rounded a sharp bend and saw an open gate on the left-hand side. I braked hard and skidded briefly as I hit a layer of packed mud that was spread across the road. I could see where the other guy had skidded too – and the car itself, rear wheels on the road, nose in the hedge, the driver's door wide open, the lights illuminating the bare branches of a tall ash tree. But where was me-laddo? That was the question.

I'd just got out of the car and was looking for footprints in the mud when Fordy and Thommo arrived from the opposite direction.

'He's done a bloody runner, lads,' I shouted, and ran across to the gateway. Fordy was already in the field, examining the ploughed-up earth. 'These look fresh,' he called out, shining his Dragon Light on the ground. A few yards further ahead was a set of fresh footprints, and then a trail of them leading up the slight rise towards another hedge over to the left-hand side.

'Right,' I said, 'let's get after the bugger. Thommo, just make sure there are no keys in that car, would you? And disable it. Don't want the bugger doubling back and driving it off. Oh, and stand the York traffic car down, could you? Shan't be needing him now.'

'There he is!' Fordy had shot on ahead, racing over the old furrows like a greyhound, flashing his torch ahead of him. I set off after him, stumbling on the rough ground and cursing the amount of kit I was carrying. It's all necessary, but it doesn't half weigh you down. I heard Fordy shout again, and beyond the hedge, in a grass field, I caught the merest glimpse of a figure racing downhill towards a ragged sort of copse that lined the beck at the bottom.

I stopped for a second or two to get on the radio and see if I could raise control to summon up a dog unit. By the time I set off again Fordy had cleared the sheep-netting and was halfway down the grassy slope, standing still with his hands on his hips. 'Lost him,' he gasped, when I caught up with him. He flashed his torch towards the trees. 'He's – he's somewhere down there. Has to be, but . . .' He tailed off, took a deep breath and clutched his side. 'Got a bloody stitch now.'

'You're sure you saw him go into the trees?'

'No, but that's – that's where he'll be OK. Last I saw he was halfway down, right about where we're standing. So – what's the plan?' he asked, turning towards me.

'Good question.' I was just about to say we'd wait for the dog unit to show when control came on.

'*About the dog unit. Sorry, Mike, but it's still tied up with a search for suspects in Scarborough. Might be free in an hour or so.*'

'Great. Yeah OK, thanks.'

Fordy was looking at me, his face pulled into a sort of questioning grin. 'Helicopter?' he said.

'You know my record with calling for helicopter assistance: no results and two massive bollockings, or "words of advice" as the superintendent would say. No – I tell a lie. There was that time when I got one in to help with the rave in the woods, Sand Hutton. But . . . oh, sod it. This a manhunt, right?' I pulled out my radio, braced myself and asked the question. I was still awaiting a reply when I saw Thommo climbing over the netting and coming towards us, pausing to kick the clods of mud off his shoes. 'I've pulled the leads off the plugs,' he said. 'That car won't be going anywhere in a hurry. So – what's the S.P., as those Cockney cops say on the telly?'

Fordy pointed towards the woods. 'Our man's down there – or was. Mike's trying to get a helicopter in.' He looked at me. 'Any joy?'

'Nah,' I said. 'No good. Humberside's occupied; the Cleveland one's grounded. Mechanical malfunction.' I glanced at Thommo. 'Tell you what,' I added, 'I've got an idea.' I got back to control. 'Yeah, do we have a current address for this lad?'

There was a short silence, then Julie was back to me. '*Got it, Mike.*' She named a village barely three miles from where we were standing. '*It's one of the council cottages, number 6.*'

I knew the place, and so did Thommo. 'OK,' I said, 'why don't you get in your car and head that way – just in case matey decides to slither home across the fields.'

'Will do.' He hesitated. 'What about you two?'

'Yeah,' I said. 'That's a question I was about to ask myself.'

I turned to Fordy. 'Looks as though we're going to have to search as far as we can and keep our fingers crossed.'

Fordy looked down at his mud-covered boots and shrugged. 'I'm lathered in crap as it is,' he said. 'I don't suppose a walk in the woods'll make much difference.'

We gave it forty, maybe forty-five minutes. We beat a path down to the little beck, and worked both sides of it through a tangle of long grass, brambles and fallen trees, covering maybe three or four hundred yards in either direction. But our man had vanished, and was most likely laughing his socks off. We returned to our cars on the roadside wet, muddy and dispirited. It was well gone midnight now. I'd come out without my flask, and neither of us had got any grub. As I rummaged about in the glove compartment and considered what to do next another call came in. Suspected break-in at a newsagent's shop in Pickering.

'Great.' I offered Fordy a Polo mint from a suspect-looking half-packet I'd dug up from between the seats. 'D'you fancy it, or shall I whistle up Thommo?'

Before he could answer I realised that Ed had come back down to cover Malton. He was the handier option; he could be in Pickering in five or ten minutes. I called control and they got on to him. Then I had a think, while Fordy scraped his shoes clean with a stick. 'Y'know,' I said, 'I've got an idea.'

Fordy didn't say anything. He threw the stick away and turned up his coat collar. He wanted to get back to town and dry off. So did I, to tell the truth. My feet were like blocks of ice, my fingers were starting to go numb, and the back of my hand was bleeding where I'd scratched it on a thorn bush. But somehow all that made me more determined to run this man to ground.

'Come on,' I said, 'get back in the car.' He plonked himself down beside me and shut the door. 'Y'know what I reckon?' I said. 'I reckon he's probably not too far away.'

'What? After all this time?' Fordy sounded almost

exasperated. 'He could be miles away.' He looked at his watch. 'Well, a couple at least.'

'Yeah, he could be. On the other hand . . .' I tapped my forehead. 'If he's using his old noggin he'll have figured that we won't search for ever. So maybe, just maybe, he's found a nice little hidey-hole up the beck somewhere and he'll come out when he thinks the coast is clear. All we have to do . . .'

'Right. Is sit here and freeze our nuts off.'

'How did you guess?' I looked out through the windscreen. The sky seemed to be clearing and the moon, although it was on the wane, was giving out plenty of light. 'You wait here, and keep obs on the suspect vehicle. He might think we've cleared off anyway when Thommo drove away. I'm going to find myself a little patch of high ground and keep an eye on this field. I got lucky this way once before. Sat in a graveyard and nabbed my friend Ronnie Leach. Or was that before your time? Anyway, I've a gut feeling he'll show before too long.' I pulled out my woolly hat, tugged it down tight over my head and stepped outside.

'Don't forget your hip-flask,' Fordy said.

'Yeah, that would be nice, wouldn't it? Tell you what, though. Pass me that rainproof coat off the back seat, will you? Might as well stay dry.'

I went back into the field, turned right and climbed the hill towards the top corner, keeping tight to the hedge line. There was a broad grassy headland there. I spread my waterproof out, sat down on it and waited. After a while I got up, went over to the hedge and lit a cigarette. It was a still night and, as much as I could overlook the cold, a beautiful one. As the temperature dropped further my breath started to come in clouds. Across the hedge in the next field the long grass reflected the moonlight. I wondered whether a frost was forming, and then cheered myself with the thought that if I was cold so was our friend.

I must have sat there for forty-five minutes, maybe an hour. Twice I got up and did a few knee-bends, whirled my arms around like windmills, trying to warm up. Twice I radioed Fordy to pass the time. On the second occasion I suspected I'd woken him up. No danger of my falling asleep, the way I was shivering. I called Thommo, over at the suspect's home address, but he had nothing to report, so I sat and watched some more, marvelling at how much you can see once your eyes are really accustomed to the dark. I remembered reading somewhere that they take twenty minutes to adjust fully.

It had just turned one o'clock. A pair of roe deer had come out of the copse and started grazing in the long grass at the edge of the pasture. I watched them for five or ten minutes before something startled them and they slipped quietly back to where they'd come from. I felt myself tense up, wondering, hoping – and suddenly there he was, our man, stumbling out from among the trees, just to the right of where we'd stopped searching, and making his way slowly up the rise towards me.

I got on the radio and whispered to Fordy. 'Stand by, stand by, contact contact. He's on his way towards you.'

By ducking down I was able to keep out of sight and scamper along the edge of the field, back to the gateway where Fordy was waiting for me.

We could hear the suspect well before he appeared. He was actually singing to himself – quietly, and tunelessly. I think he was trying to keep warm, because a breeze had got up now and it really was bitter.

Fordy grabbed him as he arrived at the gate. It was the last thing the guy was expecting. He gave a startled yelp, then shook his head and held his hands out. Covered in mud, half frozen, with his trousers torn, he looked a sorry sight. Gary formally arrested him for driving whilst disqualified and put him in handcuffs. There was no way he was getting away a second time.

The night duty inspector over in the force control room at Northallerton had been listening in to our job and was delighted. He let us know that he'd organised for the vehicle to be recovered and kept secure for the SOCO to gather evidence from it in the morning, just in case our man decided to deny that he'd driven it. We took the prisoner to York custody where he blew nearly three times the legal limit on the CAMIC machine. We left him to be interviewed by the early turn there, after he had fully sobered up. When we got back to Malton it wasn't far off home time.

It wasn't until the next night, then, that we heard that the suspect had confessed to driving the car. As I remarked to Fordy when he came on duty, it was the sensible decision. The guy knew he was in trouble, and he knew that it would go easier for him if he admitted the offences.

Throughout the rest of that week I had a lingering good feeling about this case. To me it was an object lesson in the need for perseverance. OK, you could say that we were lucky in that we didn't get called off on another job, but I would counter that it would've been so easy to have walked away from that field, cold as we were. Sure, we could've caught up with the guy later at his home address, but by then he would've been clean of any alcohol and would've denied any knowledge of the car – and we wouldn't have been able to prove a thing. So, a tidy end – except that we never found out who our informant was. That remained a mystery.

Chapter 11

The Rescuer Rescued

There was no question about it. Winter had arrived. The trees
lining the track that led down to Keeper's Cottage were coated
with a thick rime of frost, the puddles were covered in ice, and
when I took Henry out for his walk I had to be careful not to
stumble on the hardened ruts in the gateways that led from field
to field. Not that I was complaining. I like winter. I mean proper,
old-fashioned winter: a good hard freeze to kill the germs off,
ice on the puddles, and a bright sunny morning like this to send
you out of the house with a spring in your step. After two
months of sploshing about in the wet it was a real pleasure to
be striding across the countryside and know you'd be coming
home with your boots still nice and clean.

I had the day off, and decided to enjoy a decent leg-stretch.
It was just me and the dog; Ann was snuggled up in bed, part
way through a week of nights. Henry and I walked halfway up
the hill towards the metal gate where the path angles across
towards Burythorpe, past the church where Soapy got married,
and then took a bit of a yomp over the fields to complete the
circuit, coming in at the west end of the village. After calling
in at the shop for a few essentials, we hurried home. When I've
had a walk like that I only have one thing on my mind. Food.
Real food. A good old-fashioned fry-up. I'd just put three or

four slices of bacon and a couple of sausages in the pan when the phone rang.

'Now then, lad.' There was no mistaking Walter's voice, only he sounded a lot quieter than usual – sort of hushed, as if he didn't wish to be overheard.

'What can I do for you, mate? Only I'll have to hurry. I've got me breakfast sizzling away—'

''Ow much room d'you have in that freezer of yours?'

'Me freezer?' I was still by the stove, cutting mushrooms one-handed as the bacon started to curl up. 'It's about half full, I'd say. Why, what's on your mind?'

'There's been an accident, d'you see? And I need somewhere – somewhere to stow t'body.'

'Body?' I paused, halfway through cutting a tomato. 'What in God's name are you on about?'

He lowered his voice, almost to a murmur. 'Eh lad, between you and me there could be a few bob in this if we play our cards right.'

'No no no – tell me about the body first, and never mind the commercial potential. Number one: who's dead?'

There was a moment's silence. Then, in a hushed, conspiratorial tone, he said, 'It's not a who, lad; it's a what.'

'A what?'

'Aye, like I said. A what, not a who.'

'Walter, me old mucker, I'm afraid you're going to have to gimme another clue.'

'It's an animal. A bod.'

'Nah, you're going to have to explain yourself. Listen, why don't you slip your clogs on and get yourself down here. I'm having a serious fry-up, and because the sun's shining and I'm in such a good mood I'm inviting you to join me, OK? Hey, and maybe bring some of your sister's home-made marmalade.'

He didn't answer, just rang off. I grabbed another handful

of pork products, bunged them in the pan and put the kettle on.

He arrived just as I was frying the eggs and scraping the burnt bits off the edges of the toast. 'Right,' I said, 'the order of the day is, keep the volume down, OK?' I pointed to the ceiling. 'Ann's asleep. Now, grab them plates I'm warming, and start dishing up. Hey, and don't forget: you load, I choose.'

I waited till I'd taken the edge off my appetite and got my first cup of coffee down before I asked him to explain himself. 'Come on, then. Tell us the tale. Where's this body? And what exactly is it?'

'Just hold your hosses, lad.' He shoved another half sausage in his mouth and winked at me. 'It's outside. You'll see soon enough.'

I didn't have long to wait. When I get stuck into a plate of fried stuff I don't hang about – and neither does Walt. After he'd wiped the grease and tomato pips off his plate with his middle finger and licked it clean, he stood up and loosened his belt a notch. 'By, that was a bit of all right, lad. What's for afters?'

I was already opening the back door. 'Never mind afters,' I said. 'You get yourself out here and show me what you've got.'

There was an old hessian sack crumpled up against the water-butt. He walked across to it, bent down and undid the string that was tied around its neck. I was peering over his shoulder, wondering what the hell he'd got in there.

'An owl? Walt, what the hell you doing with that?'

'Like I said, lad. There was an accident. Right outside me house. I heard this car racing down the hill, and then he slammed the anchors on, so I went out to investigate. But he'd gone. Just left this on t'side of the road. He must've just clipped it with his front end, I reckon. Cos it's not damaged, is it?'

'No,' I said. 'It isn't. Apart from the fact it's dead as a door-nail.' I stood there looking at it. It was the first time I'd ever been that close to a barn owl. I'd seen plenty of them in flight, of course. There was one that lived in a hollow tree not four hundred yards from home, and I'd seen that many a night, flitting silently across the sky. Watching a barn owl as it scours the fields and hedges looking for its supper is a wonderful sight. Breathtaking. But here was one laid out on the frosted grass: pale, exquisite, but utterly lifeless. I reached out and ran my finger over the downy white feathers around its face. 'But why d'you want to put it in my freezer?' I said. 'You're surely not – not thinking of eating it, are you?'

'Hey, gerroff you little bugger!' Henry was sniffing around, and Walt was fending him off with his outstretched foot.

'So what are your plans?' I said, grabbing the dog's collar and locking him in his run.

'Aye well, this is where the money comes in, d'you see?'

'I don't, but I think another cup of coffee would help me follow your line of argument.'

Back inside the house he told me his plan. 'I've a friend over at Westow, see. Except he's in Australia just now. One of them taxi-whatsits. I'm going to get him to stuff it, then we'll tek her over to this cabinetmaker I know and put it in a glass . . . you know.' He seemed to be struggling for words, and tried to describe what he meant with his hands.

'Ah – you mean like a display cabinet?'

'Aye, same as that pheasant I have up at the house.'

'That's as old as the hills, that thing. And all covered in dust. Dare say it's got moths too, hasn't it?'

'Aye, that's me point. It's been around a good while. And folks – city folks – they'll pay owt for antiques, y'know.'

'They will, Walt. But there's a problem, isn't there?'

'What's that?'

'Well, antiques – don't they have to be old?'

Walt chuckled. 'Course they do – and don't you worry. This bugger'll be old as the hills by the time I'm done. First off we'll fix her up in a nice cabinet' – he paused and gave a little laugh – 'made out of antique wood, lad. Aye, I've all sorts of furniture in me shed. There's a wardrobe or two, couple of sideboards and one of them commode jobs. Came out of me auntie's place when she died, and she got it off her gran, so it goes back a bit. She lived to ninety-seven, did t'owd lass. And me-laddo over at Thixendale, the cabinetmaker, he'll break everything up and make us some brand-new antiques. D'you see?'

'I do. Just so long as you don't go making fraudulent claims, my friend, that's all I can say. Cos if you do, I know nowt. Remember that. And by the way, your pal in Australia? Hasn't been shipped out for nefarious activities, has he?'

'Nefar . . .? Nefar . . . What's that mean?'

'Bad stuff, Walt. What they used to transport convicts for.'

Walt polished off the rest of the coffee, helped himself to some more toast and made a sizeable dent in the jar of marmalade he'd brought down. Then we put the owl in our freezer and he took himself off home, with the sack draped across his shoulders. It was only after he'd gone that I remembered Ann had told me to ask him how he was getting on with the mobile phone. But I was pretty sure I knew the answer to that one.

The frosty weather held for the next few days, and things went very quiet on the streets. Not that it surprised any of us. It seems to go that way every year, and as usual we were speculating about the villains: were they waiting for the season of goodwill, when houses would be loaded with tempting goodies? Or were they just staying home in the warm? Either way, we were feeling restless and fidgety.

Still, as I pointed out one particularly quiet two-to-ten shift, a slack period is an ideal opportunity to catch up on all those annoying little tasks we keep putting off. Keeping on top of paperwork, for example, or clearing out our trays. Or, if you were on top of that, taking the hand-held speed gun out to the villages where we'd had complaints about speeding. As for me, I had an absolute killer of a job waiting. The lab had sent back the CCTV film we'd managed to tangle up a few weeks previously – the one from the juvenile unit where the nightwatchman reckoned he'd spotted the Ryedale Panther. Thommo would love this, of course. And true to form, as soon as he got wind that the film had arrived back he was at me.

'Looks as though you didn't do such a thorough job after all,' he said.

'What's that supposed to mean?'

'I mean destroying the evidence. It looks as though our friendly tech-heads have salvaged the vital footage, enabling us to unravel the mystery, so to speak. I just hope you've authorised Ed to hand over the tenner to me. Aye, it'd be an awful shame not to be making interest on our bet, ye ken what I mean?'

'Tragic, Thommo. but you should be more worried about Ed, mate. He was holding the cash, remember? And he might have spent it on stocking-fillers for his kids by now.'

Thommo ignored the remark, 'So . . .' he said, 'd'ye want me to sit in, just to ensure there's no foul play? No mysterious wiping of crucial evidence? Not that I'm suggesting it could happen twice, y'understand.'

'Thommo, mate, you know as well as I do that those images, coming as they do from a home for juveniles in care, may contain confidential or sensitive material and must be viewed in private by the officer concerned with the investigation – namely, *moi*. And you'll have to rely on *moi* to abide by my usual standards of fair play and honour. You get yourself out on patrol and I'll keep you posted, matey.'

Before I started the tedious business that lay ahead, I checked on Ed and Fordy to see what they were doing. Ed wanted some time to get on top of his corries and Gary was busy with a bit of Country Watch business. He was showing a real interest in rural policing, and I'd been looking for a chance to get him more involved, so when I realised that we needed an updated newsletter I briefed him as to content and put him on the case. While he got on with that I took the repaired cassette into the CCTV room with a mug of tea and a packet of biscuits. If I was destined to sit through 'Twelve Hours in the Life of a Row of Waste Bins', featuring an in-depth study of a board fence topped with barbed wire, I might as well be comfortable – even allowing for the fact that I was constantly winding it on. In the first hour I was roused to a fever pitch of excitement and had to replay a whole sequence when a lass in a white coat emerged from a side door and dumped a bag of kitchen waste in the bins. Some time later I could've sworn I saw a rat stick its nose out from behind a drainpipe. Could I stand the pace? Evidently not, I realised as my own snoring woke me up. I'd slept through a full ten minutes of action-packed footage and would have to rewind. So when Julie from control broke the spell I was out of my seat and ready for action like a greyhound coming out of the trap.

'*Units to deal. Reports from the fire service of a house fire in Malton, just off Showfield Lane. Possible person still in the premises.*'

Even as she gave me the address the three of us were making for the door. Without thinking I said, 'Hey Fordy! Grab a fire extinguisher, will you?' We have a number of different types of extinguisher dotted around the building – water, carbon dioxide and so on – and I'd just reacted instinctively. If we got there before the fire brigade at least we'd have something to fight the blaze with. Fordy took me at my word, grabbed a large extinguisher – the water-filled type – and yanked it, pulling its mountings clean out of the wall. He looked at the shower of plaster that fell onto the floor, then hurried after me, through the door and out to the car.

It barely took us a couple of minutes to get down to the mini roundabout, back along Highfield Lane and on towards the estate. It was just starting to get dark now, and was bitterly cold. A breeze had got up and the sky had clouded over. There were even one or two snowflakes flying in the wind. When we turned into the cul de sac we could see the house immediately. Smoke was coming out from under the eaves and rolling away towards the orange street lights. We could see that the downstairs was ablaze, and the curtains on fire.

'1015 to control. We're just arriving at the scene, Julie. Any news on the fire tender? The fire's got a serious grip, over.'

'Should be with you shortly, Mike. We've just had a further report of a female trapped in the house, upper floor; at the back, apparently.'

'Received. Confirm ambulance has been called?'

'That's a yes, Mike.'

Outside the front of the house a cluster of neighbours was standing at the gate, facing us. As we approached one of them ran towards us. 'She's round t'back!' she shouted.

I dashed out of the car. Fordy and Ed were right behind me. We ran to the side gate, shoved it open and went through into the little enclosure at the back.

'Oh shit!'

Some twenty feet from the ground a young woman had climbed out of the bathroom window. Her arms were stretched out above her head and she was clinging to the top of the frame with her fingernails. Her toes were on the narrow plastic sill below. Smoke was seeping out from the partly open window and she was pressing herself against the glass. To say it was a precarious position would be to understate it massively – and she hadn't a stitch of clothing on her. Even from several yards away I could hear her sort of whimpering. 'Oh hell!' I said. Then I heard myself say, 'Hold on tight, love.' I turned to one of the neighbours who'd followed us through the side gate. 'Have any of you got a ladder handy?'

'Not sure. I can go and check me garage if you like.'

'OK – as quick as you can, and can you fetch me any duvets or cushions? As many as you can grab hold of.' I turned to Fordy who was standing beside me. 'Go with her, mate, and see what she's got. Anything we can pile up, OK? Give her a soft landing if she . . .' The patio we were standing on, right below her, was paved with stone slabs. If she did fall it could be fatal.

'I'll go and see.' The woman ran next door, and Fordy followed. I could hear Ed out the front keeping the bystanders from pressing into the garden and asking around for big ladders. I glanced up at the girl. She was still clinging on. 'Try to keep hold,' I said. 'Won't be long now. We'll soon get you down from there.' As busy as I was reassuring her, I actually felt helpless. I thought for a minute about running into the house to save her, but the fire had taken hold and my fear was that the minute I opened the door the inrush of air would fan the flames right through the place.

'*Control to 1015. Fire tender about two minutes, max.*'

'That's received. Can hear them in the distance, over.'

The sirens weren't far away. As well as alerting road users to give way, they serve to let people in trouble know that help is on its way. It's often that realisation that gives someone who's in trouble the extra bit of strength that enables them to cling on. It can be the difference between life and death.

But even with help about to arrive, I didn't like the look of this one little bit. I carried on trying to reassure the young woman. 'Any minute now and they'll be here,' I was saying. What I was thinking was, 'Don't fall, love; please don't fall.' I knew she must be in considerable pain, and freezing cold too. I could see where her skin was burnt, on her back and her bottom; she must have been in a great deal of pain. Never mind her embarrassment. Through the downstairs windows I could see the flames rising ever higher, while right beside her smoke was starting to pour out through the open window. I looked around the patio. Where the hell were the ladders and duvets?

Why hadn't I asked for a mattress? I glanced at a set of steps that led up from the lawn with a low brick wall to either side. I grabbed hold of a concrete planter and hauled it out of the way. Didn't want her landing on that. 'How are you doing up there?' I'd not heard a word from her yet. I was worried that she might have gone into shock and might slacken her grip at any moment. 'You gonna be OK?' No answer. 'Listen, it shouldn't be more than another minute now. We'll soon get you down. You're gonna be fine. Just – hold on.'

When she finally spoke it was a thin, quavery voice. 'I don't think – don't think I can hold it much longer.' Then the smoke wafted over her head and she coughed. I really thought this was it, that she was going to lose her grip.

'Listen, love – just hold on. What's your name?'

'Diane.'

'OK, Diane. Listen to me. You're doing brilliantly. You've done fantastic to hold on so far. Don't let go now.'

I could see her grabbing at one of the hinges on the window with her left hand. She got a couple of fingers to it, then let go. I held my breath. For an awful moment she was holding all her weight with her right hand. Well, I was thinking, at least she's only slim. If she does fall, or lets go, there's not a lot of her. I tried to position myself so that I could break her fall the best I could, but I knew that if she landed on me we'd both be in trouble. This was getting desperate. She was trying to grab that hinge again, but kept withdrawing her hand. 'It's hot. I can't . . .'

'OK, don't worry. Just . . . as you are.'

She'd grabbed the plastic lip at the top of the window-frame once more, and seemed to be holding on with grim determination.

'Here they come, Mike.' As Fordy spoke I realised the fire tender was in the cul de sac, sirens screaming, engine thrumming. Come on . . . come on . . .

'Hey, grab these will you?'

The voice startled me. Ed was there with several of the neighbours. They'd brought out a stack of bedding, handfuls of cushions and a slim mattress like you get on a bunk bed. We stacked them up carefully on the ground, arranging them directly under the poor lass. Then I heard some shouting from behind me, turned and saw the fire crew bursting into the yard.

'Here you go, Diane.' I stepped aside. There was a loud clattering as they opened up the extending ladder, quick as a flash, then lined up the top level with the girl's head and set its feet firmly on the icy slabs.

'OK, love.' It was a young fireman who spoke. 'I've got a ladder right beside you – to your right, OK? Just hold on, and I'll soon have hold of you.' Even as he spoke he seemed to be gliding up the ladder as if on a set of runners.

'Oh, thanks.' The women from next door had handed me a large, dark blue blanket. I watched as the fireman reached out to put an arm round the girl's waist and scoop her in towards his body, holding her tightly as he brought her down almost as smoothly as he'd climbed up thirty seconds earlier. As they reached the bottom step I put the blanket over her. She stepped away from her rescuer and wrapped it quickly around herself. Only then did she start sobbing, her head bowed and her shoulders trembling.

That's when one of her neighbours came up to her. 'Come on, Diane,' she said, and bent down to put a pair of blue fluffy slippers on her feet. Then she ushered her out through the gate and away to the house next door, just as the ambulance arrived and the two paramedics followed them inside.

By this time the fire crew had got hoses into the house, front and back, and were busy trying to douse the fire. With them now taking control, and nobody in danger, it would be up to the brigade to ascertain the cause of the fire. They would conduct the investigation. We would only get involved if it turned out that any offences had been committed.

I could now take stock of the situation. Ed had already been called away to a shoplifting case in town, and Fordy was getting a few witness details. I was all set to go back to the station, but first I wanted to see how Diane was doing.

She was clearly in shock, and was shivering violently, despite being smothered in blankets and hunched over an electric space heater. She told me she'd come home off an early turn at the hospital, lit a candle in the living room, then decided to take a shower. 'Must've caught the curtain or something,' she said. 'Can't believe I was so daft.'

'Listen,' I told her. 'These things happen. Let's just be glad you've come out in one piece. It could've been an awful lot worse, couldn't it?' Before I left I had a word with the paramedics. According to them, her burns were only superficial, but they would be taking her to York District Hospital to get them treated.

I left the house and stepped out into a proper wintry scene. The wind had really got up now, and the snow was starting to fall in earnest, piling up in shallow drifts along the kerbs. I drove back to the station along deserted roads. Thommo was just getting out of his car as I pulled into the yard. 'What's the forecast, Thommo? Do you know?' I asked him.

'Aye, I heard it. If ye can call it a forecast. By the time I'd unravelled all the tosh and the hype, I got the impression they're expecting the world to come to an end.' He slammed his door shut. 'Some time in the early hours, they reckon. Earlier if you live in Scotland. Three inches of snow and it's panic stations. Ye wonder what they'd do if we had a proper snowstorm. Like when I was a bairn in Lanarkshire.' We made our way across the car park to the rear door. 'Anyway,' he said stamping the snow off his boots, 'never mind the apocalypse. What's the news on that panther? Has he emerged from his lair yet? Or is he camera-shy?'

'Thommo, mate, when I've reviewed the evidence, you will be the first to know. That I can promise you.'

The rest of the shift was quiet, thank goodness. We both kept an eye on the weather, and it didn't look as though it would get any better; in fact it was now a full scale snowstorm. As it got towards eight o'clock I checked the duty shift roster, to see who was working nights and where they were travelling from. If they were coming from far it might mean one or more of us having to stay on just in case they had trouble getting in. By nine thirty, however, the night crew had all made it in with various tales to tell about their journeys, although they reported that the gritters and ploughs were out in force and the roads around town were passable at least. The last thing I had to do before handing over was to pass on the orders of the night duty inspector, that we were to 'fire brigade' it until conditions improved – that is, only leave the station when or if we were called to an incident. There was no point at all in patrolling empty, snow-bound roads and putting staff at risk unnecessarily. But the good news was that if we did have to go out we had two 4x4 vehicles available, one at Malton and another at Pickering. All of us off the late turn were now preparing to brave the elements and head for home.

As Ed got his coat on and turned the key in his locker he said, 'What about you, Mike? Gonna be wild out in your neck of the woods. Y'know you can stay at ours if you want.'

'Yeah, cheers Ed but . . .' I glanced through the window at the snow, horizontal now and sticking to the trunks of the big trees out front. 'I should be okay. Front-wheel drive . . .'

'Up to you, mate. You know you'll get a decent breakfast.'

'You're tempting me, but nah, I'll be fine. Take my radio with me just in case.'

'Your decision, bud.'

The fact is, I cannot resist an adventure; and I love snow. Always have done, right since childhood. The idea of ploughing a lone furrow up Welham Road and onto the wolds – well, it got my pulse racing. I had a shovel in the back of the car, and an old sleeping-bag – although the last one to use that had been Henry. If I refilled my Thermos before I left the station, I'd be right as ninepence. Man against the elements. My kind of fun. To be honest, I was more concerned about Ann, trying to get in to work. I was hoping she wouldn't try, but before I left I called home. No answer, so I rang her on the mobile and discovered that she was already in York. She'd seen the snow coming down, set off early, and had just missed the worst of it. So that was one less thing to worry about. She told me to take care, and suggested that if I had any sense I'd stay over at Ed's. Yes, I said, that's not a bad idea. And got into the car.

By this time it was gone ten thirty, and outside was just a sea of white. Somebody had preceded me along the road out of town. As my windscreen wipers struggled to keep ahead of the fast-falling snow, I could just make out a single set of ruts in front of me. They were barely visible, they appeared to keep veering to left and right, and where the snow was pouring onto the road through gaps in the hedge bottom they were totally obliterated. I pressed on, ignoring the occasional swerve, maintaining a steady fifteen to twenty in third gear. It's best to keep going in these conditions. Stop, and there's a fair chance you'll be stuck.

It wasn't long before I thought I could see the flickering lights of Leavening in the distance, but my speed was dropping all the time. The tracks I'd been following were no longer there, and the snow seemed a lot deeper than it had been. It was already scraping against the underside of the car. The wipers were barely doing their job and despite me having the heater on full blast the windscreen kept steaming up. I lowered my window a few inches, and the snow that had built up smacked against the side of my face, penetrating my right ear.

I'd now reached the point where the road turned off towards

Burythorpe. There at the junction I saw the outline of a car, rear lights glowing dimly through the swirls of snow, a few puffs of exhaust being whipped away by the wind. The last thing I wanted to do was lose valuable momentum, but I couldn't just drive by. These people could be in trouble. I stopped short, so that I was still on a downhill stretch, got out and plodded through the snow towards the stationary vehicle.

'Now then, you stranded?'

They were a middle-aged couple, they lived in Burythorpe, and, yes, they were stuck.

'So how long you been here in this lot?' I shouted, hunching my shoulders against the wind.

'Only about twenty minutes. We thought about walking to the village if it eases up, but . . .' He tailed off.

'No, you don't want to be walking in this,' I said. 'Anyway, you've fallen lucky. I'm a police officer, just come off shift. I'm going to call my colleagues, get them to come out to you. They've a four-wheel drive. Should get through here, no problem, and see you safely home – OK? So long as you're prepared to wait.'

I got back in the car, pulled out my radio and spoke directly to the night duty sergeant.

'Mike?' he said. 'That you? Thought you'd gone home.'

'Yeah, just on my way now but I've got my radio with me – and a good job I have. I've got a couple of motorists in a spot of trouble.' I passed him the exact location. He told me that one of the four-wheel drives was out on the A64, at the bottom of Whitwell Hill, dealing with several vehicles that hadn't made it up the incline. As soon as the gritters had gone through they would head over and deal with the stranded couple, maybe in thirty minutes or so. I trudged back through the snow and tapped on the car window.

'They'll be with you within the hour. So my advice is, wait here for them. What d'you reckon?'

They didn't need any persuading. They would stay where they were, warm and safe. They had a phone with them, and plenty of fuel. 'OK,' I said, 'and listen – pop out every now and then to make sure your exhaust doesn't get covered up.' They told me they'd already done it once. They seemed sensible enough, and I needed to get home before the snow piled up any higher. I went back to my car, slipped it into second and heaved a sigh of relief as it edged forward and on up the hill towards Leavening. I managed to get a bit of speed up and slipped it into third, but by now I was ploughing my way forward, and it was only a matter of time before I came to a complete standstill. I'd probably travelled four or five hundred yards. Once, twice, three times I got out, shovelled the road clear in front of me, then backed up and took a run at it, but the snow was now too deep. I knew I was fighting a losing battle. I put in reverse one final time – and spun round ninety degrees. That was it. Time to give it up as a bad job. I managed to get the car off the road by backing into a gate-hole, then set off on foot. I thought about radioing in for help, but as daft as it seemed I didn't want to admit defeat. What Ann would call stupid male pride. But then she didn't have to worry about Ed. If I sent for help he'd be badgering me about it for the rest of my career.

Anyway, there was only a couple of miles to go, if that. Surely no more than an hour if I cracked on. The trouble was, this was not walking weather. I was wading through a foot of snow. In places it was two feet deep; and the wind was shoving me across the road, threatening to knock me off balance. At least I had the roadside hedges to guide me. Under a sprawling elder tree I leaned against the embankment and took out my phone. Yes, a signal. I peeled off my glove and punched in Walt's home number. Above the sound of the wind whistling through the bare branches I could hear it ring, and ring, and ring. No answer. Where the hell could he be on a night like this? Out at Muriel's? Surely not. He has a keen weather eye; he'd have seen this lot coming. No, he was probably in bed and fast asleep, saving electricity and coal. As a last resort I tried his mobile number, but that really was a shot in the dark. The chances of him having that switched on were about as good as my chances of meeting a string of camels around the next bend.

I put the phone away and staggered on, occasionally making a few yards of rapid progress, but always stumbling into a drift, or another blast of Arctic air. But, as I said before, I do like a challenge. I knew I had to keep moving and stay warm. I'd taken my police reflective jacket and my high-visibility woolly hat from the station, so, as cold as it was, I soon began to sweat. Despite it all, I couldn't help laughing out loud when I wondered what sort of reaction I'd get if some stray motorist came by and saw a police officer in full uniform leaping through the snow in the middle of the road.

It must have taken me the best part of half an hour, perhaps more, to make it as far as the edge of the village. Once I got there, I felt a surge of energy. Now I knew I'd make it. It was gone midnight but there was still a light on in the Jolly Farmers. At the entrance to the car park I hesitated. Surely if I tapped on the door they'd let me in. But would they? Would I be disturbing a lock-in? No, it'd most likely give the landlord a heart attack if he saw me knocking on the door at this time of night. All I had to do was get up that hill, and down the lane, sheltered by the woods. With a bit of luck I could be home in twenty minutes.

Reluctantly, I walked along the side of the pub and its welcoming yellow light. But I couldn't resist the temptation to stoop down and peer through the window. There indeed were a couple of figures seated at the bar with pints in their hands, their faces lit up by the cheery glow of the fairy lights.

Sod it, I thought, retracing my steps. Embarrassment or not, this was an emergency. A nice pint and a sit-down by that fire would be just the job. I actually had my fist poised to rap on the door when I heard an approaching motor.

Stepping out towards the road I caught sight of a dim pair of lights approaching me from up the hill towards home. Was this the four-wheel drive coming to the rescue? No, they wouldn't be coming from that way. Surely not. Or had that couple in the stranded car tipped them the wink and sent them off in search of me?

No, it wasn't Ryedale police riding to the rescue. As the vehicle came closer I was just about able to make out the familiar front number plate. BAG 67.

'Walter, you daft old bugger! What you doing out in this lot?'

He wound down his side window, screwed up his eyes against the wind and snow. 'Why, what sort of greeting's that after I've risked life and limb to rescue you?'

'Well, how did you know I was stranded?' I was round the other side of his Land Rover and in through the door, holding out my frozen hands to the heater vent.

Walt eased the vehicle forward and started to turn it around in the pub car park. 'Why,' he said, 'I called t'station and they told me you'd set off. Doesn't tek much working out to realise you'd likely get stuck, does it now?'

As he spoke he was fishing in his coat pocket. 'Aye, but I'll tell you sommat else, lad. This here mobular phone or whatever you call it, why, come an emergency like this it's neither use nor ornament.'

'What, you tried to use it?'

'Course I blooming well did. That's what she's for, isn't it? Didn't you give it me in case of emergency?'

'Well, yeah. That was the point. So you remembered my number, did you?' I wasn't going to tell him, but I was mightily impressed.

'Aye, I have it chalked up on t'kitchen wall. Only took me a week or two to learn it off, like. But this daft piece of . . .'

Walt had it in his hand now. As we drove slowly out onto the road again he held it up for me to see. 'I lost count of the times I put your number in, but would it have it? Would it heck. Here, you may as well take her back now, lad, before I'm driven to distraction. Bloody modern technology. You're as well off wi' a carrier-pigeon.'

And with that he thrust into my hand . . . his television remote.

Sometimes I have more self-control than I ever give myself credit for. I took it from him without uttering a word. But a moment later I couldn't help myself. I started laughing.

'Why, what's so funny?'

'No – nothing, Walt. Must be the relief of seeing you show up.' And just you wait, I was thinking. I'm going to keep my powder dry. Then next time you get up on your high horse, down the pub, this is a story that will have to be told. And I chuckled again. It's always nice to have a bit of spare ammunition in your locker.

Walt dropped me off at Keeper's Cottage and made his way home. Before I went to bed I rang Ann in York to tell her that the road was impassable and she should wait until the snowploughs had made it to the back roads. I said I'd set the alarm and go out to have a look before she set off. That meant getting up early, but I needed to do that anyhow, to go and rescue my car.

I was surprised, when I set off next morning just as it was getting light, to find that the road down to the village had already been ploughed and gritted. The council had done a brilliant job overnight – and one or two intrepid locals were already out and about. One of them just had to be Algy, of course, pulling up beside me in his huge four-by-four.

'Michael, my dear fellow! You seem to be afoot.'

'Full marks for observation, Algy. Now, are you going to sit there and assess the likelihood of me getting frostbitten, or are you going to offer me a ride?'

'Of course, of course. Do step inside.' He leaned across and opened the passenger side door. 'Where to?' he asked, as I made myself comfortable.

I showed him where I'd left the car, and to be fair to him he pulled a shovel out and helped me clear away the mound of snow and slush that the ploughs had dumped in front of it. The sun had come out, the wind had dropped, and we soon warmed up.

'Which way are you heading?' Algy asked as I scraped the windscreen clean.

'Just need to take this back home – or at least to the end of the lane. Don't have to be at work till this afternoon. But I need to give Ann a quick ring to let her know what's what.'

'Righty-ho. I'll follow you down there, just in case, shall I?'

'I'd be much obliged. Thank you.'

Back at the house I waited for Ann to make it home safely, and had a coffee ready for her when she landed. She had got lucky: managed to follow the second snowplough heading into the village. I took it easy the rest of the morning, and set off for work not long after midday. It's nice to get in early, let the first shift get away in good time. Of course, I knew what I was in for, but there's only one option in a case like this: take it on the chin and keep smiling.

From the moment I set foot inside the station I got it from all sides.

'The lengths some blokes'll go to to get their hands on a naked female! Hey, if I'd known you were that desperate, Pannett . . .'

'Desperate? They told me he threw that fireman off the ladder so's he could be first in line. Sommat about rescuing a damsel in distress.'

'Very funny,' I said. I'm not usually lost for words, as anyone'll tell you. There were a few remarks I might've made, not many of them printable. I could've pointed out, for example, that it was the firemen who'd had the privilege of bringing the poor lass out; but maybe this was about reputation – my reputation for being in the right place at the right time. I let them have their bit of fun and when they'd run out of steam, I said, 'You know, I'd really like to share the secret with you – seeing as we're all comrades, like – but I've come to the conclusion it's a gift. You've either got it or you haven't.'

'Got what?'

'Charisma, mate. Big word, and I can only explain it by saying that when you have as much personal magnetism as I have – I dunno, good things just . . . they just drop into your open arms.'

I would've got a nice lot of abuse for that, but Birdie came to the rescue. 'Ah, Mike,' he said, coming into the parade room for briefing, 'Good to see Ryedale police in the news again – in a positive light. Well done.'

That put an end to it for the moment. I knew it'd rear its head again in time; but for now I had other things on my mind. With luck, and a following wind, I would surely get through the rest of that CCTV tape – and who knows, I was thinking, maybe at last I'd make history and win some money off Thommo.

We were barely two hours into the shift when I found what I wanted. And as luck would have it, my man was skulking around the station. I found him in the parade room, dunking Hobnobs in a mug of tea and dabbing his nose with a tissue. 'How do you get away with it?' I asked.

'What d'ye mean, laddie?'

'Oh, just that most people, when they're having a crafty skive, they scatter a few forms around and grab hold of a pen or a clipboard. Try to look busy, at least.'

'I am busy. Busy thinking.'

'Oh. About what, exactly?'

'About the course I've just been on. I've been pondering. I mean, how they can pump all that money into gathering together a bunch of experts who spend three whole days telling us what we knew before we walked in the door?'

'Ah. Yes. Not 'maintaining professional standards', was it?'

'The very same. A complete waste of time and resources – although, mind you, the catering was first-class.'

'So what you complaining about? You had three days away in a nice warm classroom, free tea and biscuits, a new audience to bore witless with your memories of Glasgow in the 1970s . . .'

'Aye, trouble is there was a fresh bunch of germs to negotiate. Southern germs. Wouldnae surprise me if I came down with a stinker any day now. Knowing my luck it'll turn to flu.'

'Well, Thommo, that's the risk you run when you volunteer for these courses. However, before you go sick on us, I've got something here that'll cheer you up. Just step into the CCTV room, will you?'

'You're no saying . . .?'

Thommo was out of his chair in a flash, brushing past me and heading for the door like a man half his age.

'Now,' I said, resuming my seat and winding the tape slowly back to where the good stuff started – and then a bit more. 'Sit tight and watch carefully, because I can promise you, this cat doesn't hang about. Blink and you'll miss it.'

I pressed PLAY, and leaned back in my chair. There was a good bit of not-very-much to sit through – but I sat there with my hands behind my head. I was loving this. I'd had my fill of watching these waste bins and drain-covers over the past night or so. A couple of minutes wouldn't do Thommo any harm. He, on the other hand, was getting edgy. 'Well, where is it, mon? Where's this panther?'

'Patience, my friend. And vigilance.' I had my eye on the timer and was braced for the good stuff. 'Now,' I said, leaning forward toward the screen, 'watch out for a sleek, slender, black thing moving like – like a will o' the wisp.' I reached out and put it on slow play. 'Here,' I said, 'here's where it is. Any moment now. Frame by frame. The crucial evidence.'

He sweated through another minute or so, shifting in his seat and tutting impatiently. The only action was the occasional puff of steam emerging in slow motion from a flue. And then the moment I'd been waiting for. I could hear Thommo catch his breath as a dark form emerged from behind one of the bins and leapt to the top where it dived into the bin under a half-open lid.

'But that – that's no more than wee domestic moggy!' he spluttered.

'Not so wee,' I said. 'In fact, I'd say it was quite a clonker really. Had to be to rattle a sturdy lad like our security man – and well worth waiting for, wouldn't you say? Aye, a clonker, but not exactly a panther.'

It was perfect timing. Ed had just landed for his break and a warm-up after taking a walk around the cattle market.

'Ah, Ed. Could you do the honours, mate, and hand over that money you've been holding for us?'

'What, have we got a result?' he said.

I didn't answer, just wound back the tape and replayed the crucial bit. Thommo scraped his chair back and stormed out of the room. 'Oh, while you've nowt else on,' I called after him, 'd'you want to give our security guard a bell, tell him he can rest easy? Then maybe give an update to the press?'

But he'd found other things to occupy him – somewhere he said, that was well away from big-cat country.

Chapter 12

Children In Need

Christmas came and Christmas went – and this time it left us with very few memories. That's the way it is some years, when you find that your shifts are at odds with your partner's. Ann and I had been lucky so far; since we'd been together we'd always managed to get one or two days off at the same time over the holiday period. I think we'd got used to it, and started to take it for granted that the rosters would just fall right every year. But this time our luck ran out. Not a single one of my days off coincided with hers. The truth is we'd both been a bit slow putting in our requests for leave, and been beaten to it by the officers with kids – who are notoriously quick out of the blocks when it comes to booking time off at Christmas. But who can blame them? It's a family time of year, so good luck to them.

What all this meant was that we'd both ended up working all over the holiday period. We did eventually manage a weekend off, but it wasn't until a couple of weeks into January. However, as so often when you draw the short straw, there were compensations, in our case a bargain low-season holiday cottage just outside Whitby that Ann found on one of those late-booking sites on the internet. We drove across the moors on the Friday evening and next day, after catching up with our beauty sleep, took the bus down to Scarborough. On a beautifully clear, frosty day, we hiked back along the coast. Along the way we found ourselves a sunny spot and picnicked. We even managed to light a fire on the rocks down at Hayburn Wyke, near Staintondale, a reminder of the sort of days out I enjoyed as a boy when I used to holiday with my relatives there. We enjoyed ourselves so much along that stretch that in the end we had to hurry to get back to Whitby before dark – just in time to enjoy one of those monster seafood dinners for which the little fishing port is famous.

Neither of us was due to return to work until late on the Monday, so we indulged ourselves with a long lazy Sunday, doing just as we pleased. For Ann that meant only one thing. Give her a bit of spare time and she'll settle down to read. Always has her nose in a book when we're on holiday. I'm more the restless type. Can't sit still for long and always want to know what's happening next. But I do have my reflective moments. When a new year dawns I generally find myself thinking back over the previous twelve months, remembering the cases I've had to deal with. Sometimes – and you'll have to forgive a very bad pun here – a copper's life is a bit of a plod. Or 'same old, same old' as they like to say these days. Ann laughed at me, but when she pulled out one of her 600-pagers – it was American, all about the Hells Angels – I decided to just sit and ponder recent events. 'Hey, never mind the superior look,' I said. 'Each to his own and all that.' At which she gave me what I call her 'Yes, dear' smile.

It's a useful exercise, glancing back over the previous twelve months' work. It reminds you of the sheer variety of cases you've handled, and the fact that every year throws up new aspects of policing. After ten, fifteen years in the job it's often tempting to think you've seen it all. You hear a lot of old hands saying the same thing, that there's nothing new under the sun. Not me though. I reckon you really do 'live and learn' on this job, day by day, year by year.

As well as reminding myself what sort of year I've had I find myself trying to assess it, reflecting on the cases that went well, as against the ones that didn't. How successful had I been? Had I improved as a copper? I can usually find a few standout successes, like the time we caught that gang of break-in merchants who were burgling shops all over Ryedale, or the time Ed and I stumbled upon the cannabis plantation out in the country. That was a good bit of old-fashioned police work – with a very satisfactory outcome. And then there were the trailer thieves I collared while off duty one night.

Arrests like those give you a huge buzz at the time – and a deeper satisfaction when you look back on them. At the same time, of course you're always aware of the crimes that haven't resulted in a conviction, of the wrongdoers who are still on the loose, probably laughing their socks off at our failures or preening themselves over their own cleverness as they plan the next hit. But I always cheer myself up by recalling a thing my old primary-school teacher said one time. He was a lay preacher, and he loved to quote from the Bible, particularly the Book of Proverbs. He knew it back to front and seemed to have one for every occasion. And he had a knack of making it relevant to the individual he was targeting – in this case me.

'Pride goeth before a fall,' he intoned one morning as we sat down at our desks and prepared for our first lesson – and by heck, it made me sit up and take notice. I always remember that. He was looking right at me as he said it, and he immediately had me sweating. Oh dear, what had I done this time? I remember I'd been a bit full of myself that week, having got top marks in the mental arithmetic test, so maybe he was trying to deflate me. I could think of plenty of mischief I'd been up to, naturally enough, but what exactly was he referring to? Chalking my name on the wall of the girls' outdoor toilet? No, that was ages ago, and the rain had washed it off by now. Sticking my chewing gum on his seat for a bet? No, that was the week he went sick. It was his stand-in who copped it – and I copped six of the best. So was it scrumping apples? Oh yes, that would be it. It was only a few days previously, and the owner of the orchard had chased us through the village waving his Dutch hoe at us. But how did old Mr Jennings know about it? Had someone snitched on us? Had he got the second sight? And what did it mean, anyway, this business of 'pride' and 'a fall'?

As soon as I got home that afternoon I took out the family Bible that lived on the sideboard next to the chiming clock, and turned to the Old Testament. It took me long enough, but I eventually found the relevant passage. Next day I couldn't wait to tell the man himself – in front of the whole class – that he was wrong. Straight after morning assembly, when we were all settled in our seats, up went my hand. 'Sir, sir, I looked it up, sir, that proverb sir, and it's "Pride goes before destruction, and a haughty spirit before a fall", not what you said, sir.' Fair play to him: he acknowledged the error, but of course he had to have the last word. Teachers always did in those days. He told me I was a cheeky young beggar and just to make sure he never got it wrong again, would I mind writing it out in full. Fifty times. No good protesting with Mr Jennings; he always had the same answer: 'Think of all the things you've done over the year, Pannett, and not got caught.' I had no answer to that. It was, you might say, a fair cop.

Well, I'm straying from the point, which is that if one thing leapt out at me from last year's incidents it was that two particular teams were still getting away with it on a regular basis. We had signally failed to rein in whoever was responsible for the country house break-ins – which our CID man was still working on, full time near enough, with the crime analyst. And I particularly felt for my friends out on the farm, Helen and Jim, whose home had been violated on two occasions and who were still nervy about their security every time they left the house unoccupied, even for a trip to the shops. But I'd always maintained, to anybody who'd listen, that I felt this was a different team from the country house lot, and that they would be caught in the end; either through their own carelessness, or perhaps after a display of that 'haughty spirit' that the Good Book tells us about; or, failing that, our twenty-first-century century friend, forensics.

It was early in February when it happened, and it really was down to sheer good fortune. When I heard the news my first impulse was to pick up the phone and call Helen and Jim, but I always prefer to deliver good news in person – especially when, as in this case, the news carried a bit of a sting in the tail. And of course, being as cunning as a fox, as someone once said of me, I managed to pull into their yard just as Jim was stepping off his tractor and making for the kitchen door.

'Always time it right, don't you?' he said. 'I suppose this is going to cost me half my breakfast, is it?' He ushered me through the door and into the kitchen. 'You see who's turned up?' he called out. Helen was just opening the stove door and pulling out a tray of bacon and sausages.

'Don't fret. There's plenty for everyone.' She put a hot china plate in front of me and scooped a couple of fried eggs out of her pan. 'It'll do you good to cut down, Jim.'

'So what's this in honour of?' Jim seemed to have satisfied himself that we all had fair shares and was starting to dig in. 'Hey, don't get me wrong, Mike: it's good to see you. Been quite a while, hasn't it?'

'That's cos I'm on a diet, mate. No – only joking. And anyway, I hear you have a newfound friend in PC Ford, ever since I told him to keep his eyes peeled around this area. Tells me he calls by every week and you're treating him as one of the family.'

Jim glanced at his wife. 'Oh she does, Mike. Wouldn't be surprised if she puts in to adopt him. And I tell you what, he can't half put it away.'

Helen raised her eyebrows. 'Don't listen to him, Mike, the young lad's too shy to stop long.'

'Aye, all right, so I was exaggerating,' Jim said. 'He does drop in for the odd cuppa now and then. Never stays for more than a few minutes though.'

'That lad worries me sometimes,' I said. 'He's showing all the signs of shaping up to be a good rural copper. Has the nose for it, I'm telling you – can sniff out a chance of free hospitality like a veteran. He'll be after my job soon, you wait and see. Anyway,' I said, 'getting down to business. I've two bits of news. Number one, the results from your stolen guns.' Jim raised an enquiring eyebrow. 'Threw up the evidence I hoped they would.'

'Oh, that's good,' Helen said.

'Yes, they found some DNA that matches the samples our SOCO found when he examined your place after the second burglary – remember?'

'I do,' Jim said. 'Big lad. Sweated a lot.'

'That's our Stuart, aye. It's taken a bit of time to find the match, but it's resulted in us arresting the guy, and I reckon we've got a solid case against him.'

'Well, that's good news,' Helen said.

'Ah, but there's more. A bonus.'

'We're all ears, Mike.'

'Well, when Humberside made the arrest, his girlfriend was in the house. Then when our CID picked up the case it turned out that she matches the description of the girl you saw, Helen – in the car.'

'Oh, that's brilliant, Mike.'

'Well yes, it is. But. There's always a but, isn't there? When she was interviewed she denied any involvement. And that's another reason I'm here. I was wondering how you felt about trying to pick her out on an identity parade.'

'Oh dear.' Initially, Helen was very concerned about the idea of coming face to face with someone who might have been responsible for causing her family so much hurt and anxiety. And who could blame her? However, we really needed her to help us, so I went through exactly what would happen and how it would work.

'Rest assured,' I said, 'you will not – cannot – be seen by the suspect. You'll be a hundred per cent screened off, so you won't come into direct contact with the woman.'

Helen was silent for a few moments. Then she said, 'You know, I'll never forget that woman's face when she passed me. I can still see it sometimes when I think back. Nasty looking sort.' She thought for a moment, then said, 'All right, Mike, if it'll help you to get a conviction, I'll do what has to be done.'

'That's brilliant, Helen. I just need to report that back, get a date for the parade and it'll happen. Tell you what, I'll get our CID to give you a ring and organise it with you. How's that?'

I finished my breakfast, left them to ponder their changing fortunes, and hit the road. It's always a pleasure to bring good news to people, and I could see the relief and gratitude on Helen and Jim's faces. It's times like those that really make a policeman's job worthwhile. That's when you know you're doing a real service to the community.

The warm glow, however, didn't last long. A few days later I was faced with one of those situations that test your abilities as a police officer and demand that you make good judgements in the most trying of circumstances. I'd arrived at work for a Sunday night shift and was going through the usual handover with the outgoing late-turn shift sergeant. He particularly wanted to flag up for me a job they'd dealt with earlier. One of his officers had been called out to an address over Kirkbymoorside way, just after eight o'clock in the evening. It was one of those tiny villages that sit between the river Rye and the Severn. No shop, no pub, just a cluster of houses and a church. The family were marked up on our intelligence system as on the 'at risk' register, and Social Services had taken up their case. It seemed there had been some sort of mental abuse – not physical abuse, the sergeant stressed – due to the mother's behaviour towards her kids. A call had come in from one of them, stating that her mother was threatening to take an over-dose. On arrival the officer had spoken to the girl, the eldest of three sisters. She'd been really worried, but her mother denied the accusation and claimed that she had no intention of doing any such thing. She said she'd been upset. She'd had a phone call from her estranged husband who had told her that Social Services could take the children away. This, she said, and the fact she was short of money, had upset her and things had got a bit heated. The officer felt that his arrival had calmed things down, and that no further action was required that evening. However, on his return to the station he'd filled out the relevant paperwork to alert the FPU, or family protection unit on Monday morning, and they would liaise with Social Services. 'Not ideal,' the sergeant said, 'so this is just to forewarn you, if you get another call out there. But from what my officer said it should be all right.'

'Famous last words,' I said to him as he completed the hand-over and got ready to go home.

Situations like that are difficult and delicate. The last thing you want is for everything to kick off on a Sunday evening, when it's notoriously hard to get hold of the right support teams. I read through the officer's report and noted that when he'd left the house the mother was more settled and the kids were in bed. To be fair to him – and he was one of our senior officers – he'd spent a long time at the house and tried to ensure that the kids were safe. So, perhaps it would be all right after all.

By the time I walked into the parade room Jayne had made everyone a brew and was enjoying some banter with the rest of the crew. I had a quick catch-up with her before she headed off home. It seemed she was missing us as much as we were all missing her, but things were going well with the pregnancy, and her partner was settling into his new life in North Yorkshire.

Once I'd given the briefing and updated my team on the day's events I gave out the postings. Thommo was back from a few days off with flu so I was going to pair up with him for the evening, covering the top end over at Pickering. Fordy and Ed would cover the bottom end and Malton. Before we'd even set out on patrol, however, we got a call from Julie in the control room.

'*Mike, we've had another call from the address attended earlier. The woman who was threatening to take an overdose?*'

'Go on, I said.'

'*We've had her daughter back on, distraught. Can you attend, over?*'

'On our way, Julie, me and Thommo.'

'This is not going to be easy,' Thommo said, as we got into the car. 'Trust me, I know these people.'

'You had dealings, have you?'

'I have indeed. I was called out when she and her husband were splitting up. They were having a set-to – I mean a really vicious row. In front of the bairns too. He was wanting custody and she wasnae having it, so you can imagine what it was like.'

'Oh dear. It doesn't sound good, mate.'

'No, she's – let's say she's a difficult customer.'

Thommo wasn't exaggerating. As soon as the woman answered the front door she greeted me with, 'You can f*** off for a start. I s'pose that stupid daughter of mine called you out again, did she?'

She'd clearly been drinking. I could smell the alcohol on her breath, which was coming in clouds in the cold night air. She actually looked unsteady on her feet. I explained very calmly that I was concerned for her and her kids' welfare, and wanted to come into the house to see that everything was all right. It didn't do a scrap of good. 'Listen, I've got enough trouble on me plate with that twat of a husband on my case. I don't need you bastards sticking your f***ing noses in. Go on – piss off, the pair of you!' She had hold of the door handle and was trying to shut me out. I stepped deliberately forward and put my foot inside, pushing my forearm against the door to prevent her from closing it.

The shoving match lasted a few seconds before she turned and stumbled away, across the hallway and into the living room. I followed her in, with Thommo closing the door behind me. I wasn't going to let her out of my sight if I could help it. People can be very unpredictable when they've been drinking, especially when there are emotive issues to be discussed, and I wanted to make sure she wasn't going to do something stupid like grabbing a knife and turning on us. Believe me, it happens. In this instance, though, the woman was more intent on grabbing the glass she'd been drinking from, and a packet of cigarettes.

As she fumbled with her lighter I looked around the room. Clothes – some clean, some dirty – were draped across the backs of chairs or piled up on the floor. On a table under the window was a collection of dirty mugs, a saucepan encrusted with dried-up spaghetti hoops, and three or four plates, one of them containing a half-eaten steak pie. There were crumbs everywhere and a couple of yoghurt pots with spoons in. On a coffee table beside the telly I spotted a packet of paracetamol tablets. I went across and picked it up. Empty. 'Have you taken any of those?' I asked. She just leaned forward and flicked the ash off her cigarette onto one of the dirty plates. 'What the f***'s it got to do with you?' she said. 'Is it a crime to have a headache?' Then she looked up and saw Thommo entering the room. 'And as for him – he can f*** off too. Had him in here before and I don't want him again – you got that?'

While she was carrying on a young girl had half entered the

room from the kitchen. She looked about fourteen. She was standing at the doorway, obviously not sure whether to come in or not. She was wearing a thin dressing gown and was shivering.

'Now then,' I said. 'I'm Sergeant Mike Pannett from the police station. We've just come to make sure everything is OK. Are you OK?'

She didn't answer; just looked at her mother, who spat out, 'Didn't I bloody well tell you to keep your nose out of it? Didn't I?' No answer. 'Well, you gonna answer or what?' The louder the mother shouted, the more the girl flinched. Finally she backed away and slipped into the kitchen.

'Hang on,' I said. 'She was probably frightened.'

'What's she got to be frightened of? She ain't bloody frightened of me. Does as she pleases. Don't let the innocent face fool you.'

'No, not frightened *of* you,' I said. 'Frightened *for* you. I think she's worried about you.' I walked across to the door and went into the kitchen, leaving Thommo with the mother.

The girl seemed weary, and was clearly traumatised by everything that was going on. She began to cry, then handed me a bottle of tablets she had in the pocket of her dressing gown. 'I took these from me mum's bag,' she said. 'I didn't want her hurting herself.'

'No,' I said, 'of course not.' I looked at the bottle. More paracetamol. 'And what's your name?'

'Kylie,' she said. 'What's going to happen to her?' she asked. 'What you going to do?'

'Don't worry, Kylie,' I said. 'We're here to make sure that everyone's looked after – including you.' I asked her if her mother had taken any of the tablets from the bottle. It was half empty. She didn't know. The trouble with paracetamol is that they take a while to have an effect; you can overdose on them and show no symptoms for some time. When the effects do kick in, they can be severe. If a person doesn't get to hospital within twenty-four hours their liver can start packing up.

The girl was crying now. I tore off a piece of kitchen roll and handed it to her. 'Look,' I said, 'don't worry. I'll sort things out. Now, what about your sisters? You've two, I believe.' She nodded. 'Where are they?'

She wiped her eyes. 'They're upstairs, hiding. They always hide when she starts shouting. They hate it.'

I asked her if she had any relatives living nearby, somebody I could call on to come round. No, she said, they all lived in Middlesbrough. This was starting to worry me. I wasn't sure what was best to do. Of course you'd always prefer the kids to remain in their home, but right now I couldn't see that their mother was in a fit state to look after them.

'Why don't we go and check on your sisters,' I said. 'See if they're all right, eh?' She didn't need any more encouragement, and was off upstairs before the words were fully out of my mouth. Her mother, on the other hand, was on her feet, shouting and swearing at Thommo. 'Just get out, get out of my f***ing house!' Thommo was doing his best to calm her down, but every time he opened his mouth she got more riled up. I could see her becoming violent if this went on much longer. So could Thommo, who was backing away from her as she came towards him, her half empty glass in one hand, wagging her finger at him and maintaining a torrent of abuse.

'Hey, listen,' I said, 'why don't you sit down and calm down. All this shouting isn't getting us anywhere.'

But she wasn't having any of it. She turned on me now. 'And you – you can leave my kids alone. They ain't going nowhere. I'm telling you that right now, got it?' Thommo tried to hold her back from launching herself at me, and that was when she simply blew. 'That's it, that's f***ing it!' she screamed, throwing her glass to the floor, and lunging at me with her outstretched hands. As I backed towards the door Thommo snatched hold of her arms from behind and held her tight. It's never good to get into that situation where you're physically restraining a mother with the children in the house but there simply was no alternative. I got the handcuffs on her and between us we managed to sit her down on the sofa. For a moment she was quiet. I was wondering what to do next. Should I arrest her for a breach of the peace or what? There's actually not a great deal you can do within someone's own home. Your options are limited. I couldn't arrest her for being drunk, for example, nor under the Public Order Act, nor even the Mental Health Act. All of those laws allow you to arrest a person in a public place, but there is actually no law against being drunk in your own house.

I told her that she was under arrest for a breach of the peace, then went outside. I radioed for control to call an ambulance, and to get hold of Ed and Fordy to bring the van and a spare car over – not to transport the mother, but to remove the kids from the house. There was no doubt in my mind that they needed to be taken somewhere safe.

Given the ongoing problems with this family – which I had now witnessed at first hand – my mind was made up: there was no way the kids were staying. When I weighed up the facts – that the mother had threatened to take an overdose, that she'd been drinking, that it was impossible to have a conversation with her without her screaming and shouting – I felt I had sufficient fears for the wellbeing of her and her children to consider using a PPO or police protection order. It's not something I'd used very often in my career. In fact, I'd probably resorted to it twice, and that was a long time ago, when I was in London.

I left Thommo with the mother while I went upstairs to speak to the daughter. The upstairs was as big a mess as the living room and kitchen. There were more clothes, shoes and toys lying around, and one of the beds was lying at a crooked angle, with a leg missing. But where were the children? There was a loft access in one of the bedrooms, and the ladder had been pulled down. I climbed up and found the attic in total darkness, with no light switch anywhere that I could see. I called out, 'Kylie! Are you up there?' There was no answer. Great, I thought, as if things weren't bad enough without me having to crawl around the attic searching for them.

Just then control came on to say the ambulance was only a couple of minutes away, likewise Ed and Fordy. I went down and waited by the front door, which was at the bottom of the stairs. If the kids did decide to come out and make a run for it I should be able to catch them. It's hard to predict how a child will react in a situation like this. They might do anything on impulse. Maybe they were planning to run to a friend's house.

My lads and the ambulance both turned up within a minute of each other. I explained to the paramedics what had happened, and left them and Thommo to deal with the mother. Then I briefed Ed and Fordy on what was happening, and explained that we needed to get the kids out of the house. I told Fordy to grab his Dragon Light while I got back to control. I wanted to speak with the emergency night-duty social worker, and work out where I was going to take the children. Getting them out of the house was one thing, but what was the best place for them to go? I didn't want to be taking them to the police station, but as things stood it looked like the only option. Control told me where the father lived, but I wasn't going to drop them in on him without first making contact.

'Right,' I said to Fordy, 'let's go and find these kids, shall we?' I followed him back into the house, where the paramedics were struggling to get the mother to cooperate. They were getting the same abuse she'd dished out to me and Thommo. She hadn't taking any effing tablets, and there was no way she was going to no effing hospital.

I left them to it. There were three of them standing over her and they ought to be able to manage. Upstairs, Ed and Fordy and I searched all the bedrooms. 'Well,' Ed said, after we'd checked them all, 'where d'you reckon they've got to? Not slipped out the windows, surely?'

'I don't think so,' I said and pointed to the loft. 'Pass us the light. They've got to be up there.' I climbed up the aluminium ladder again, poked my head through the hatch and shone the lamp around. Way over in the far corner there was a crumpled grey duvet, and as I played the light on it it moved to reveal three tousled heads.

'So that's where you've been hiding,' I said. 'Very good. But by heck it's cold up here, don't you think? You'll freeze to death.' The oldest girl, Kylie, had sat up. Her two sisters were on either side. Now that I could see their faces I reckoned they were no more than eight or nine years old. They were shielding their eyes from the light of my torch, even though I was actually shining it at the ceiling so as not to dazzle them. The last thing I wanted was to frighten them unnecessarily.

'Come on, girls,' I said. 'Let's have you downstairs where it's warm at least.'

'No, why should we?' It was the oldest one who spoke. 'You'll only take us away to some stinking home. We aren't coming.'

'Look,' I said, 'you have to understand – I can't let you stay here all night with nobody to look after you. Can I now?'

'Why, what's happening to our mum? Where you taking her? Where is she?' As she spoke one of the little ones started crying.

'Look, your mum isn't well. And she isn't going to get better till she can get to see a doctor. She won't want to be fretting about you, will she? She wouldn't want to leave you all alone. Now, come on, before you catch cold and give her something else to worry about. If you let me take you to the police station we can get you warmed up – get you a drink of something.'

The thing with kids is, as any social worker will tell you,

that no matter what's going on at home that's where they want to be, with their parents. It's what they know. Everything else, every other alternative, is unknown, and therefore frightening. These three knew that something serious was happening, and were digging their heels in. And I was afraid that they weren't going to come down without a deal of coaxing on my part.

To my surprise, however, I managed to persuade them to come out fairly quickly. Maybe when they saw Fordy they felt a little easier. He was young enough to be their big brother and you could see them responding to him. Between us we saw them safely down the ladder and Fordy led them downstairs one by one. It was when he got them to put their coats on that things kicked off.

Their mother was lashing out furiously with her feet and screaming at the medics, who'd backed off. Thommo had jumped in and was holding her in the chair – just. 'You've taken my kids! You've taken my kids, you bastards!' she shouted. 'Where you going with them?'

'All these people are trying to do is to get you to hospital so that you can be looked after properly,' Thommo was saying, but she wasn't having any of it.

'You won't get me in no f***ing hospital, you bastards!' she screamed. 'I know what you're up to, putting a wedge between me and my kids. If that husband of mine put you up to this I'll kill him.'

'Now, listen to me,' I said. 'The fact that you're behaving like this leaves me with no choice but to remove them. You're just not in a fit state to take care of them at the moment. I'm not happy leaving them here tonight – or you, either. What you need to do is calm down and think what you're doing. For their sake. Now, are you going to get in that ambulance?'

'Just f*** off and leave me alone, will you.'

I went outside where Fordy was getting the girls into the big van. He'd put them in the seated area just behind the driver and had the engine on, the heater going full blast.

'Gary, you take them back to the station and I'll follow you down, mate. I'll get Ed and Thommo to take the mother to York. OK?'

'Will do, Mike.'

I watched him ride off and went back inside where Thommo was still having to restrain the woman. It was clear to me now that the ambulance crew weren't able to handle her. The fact is, you can't force people to accept medical assistance. On the other hand, leaving her alone in this state was not an option, especially where there was the possibility of her harming herself. Between us, Thommo and I got her to the spare car they'd brought down. Thommo sat with her in the back and Ed drove them to the station. There she would be booked in and supervised before the custody sergeant called out the doctor to examine her. By then, with a bit of luck, she might have sobered up, and would be thinking more clearly.

I drove back over to Malton and reflected on what was a dreadful situation. Seeing those girls cowering in the loft was a sight I would never forget. And their mother's shrieks when we took them out of the house – well, it's not a sound you like to hear. Part of you sympathises with a mother in distress, while another part knows that you have a job to do. Because nobody's going to do it for you. A case like this is really, really distressing, and you always ask yourself whether you could've handled it better. Should I have left the girls in the house? It was their home, after all. But it all came down to their welfare and safety. That's always the first consideration. And the fact is that for the moment at least we knew they were safe. What we had to think about now was what lay ahead. Would they be able to go to school the next day? Where were they going to stay tonight?

Back at the station Fordy had made a drink of orange for the girls and raided the team's biscuit supplies. He'd even gone into the community support officers' place and found a couple of videos suitable for them to watch. When I looked in on them they were all huddled together watching the TV. They looked very small and very young. Thank goodness they had each other, I thought.

My next job was to get hold of the night-duty social worker, who had bad news for me. They had nowhere at all to house the three of them at this time of night. But she would review the children's case file and ring me back. As I remarked to Ed, it was about par for the course for a Sunday night.

I didn't have long to wait before the social worker called again. She hadn't found a place in any of their care facilities, but she had got hold of the girls' father – and he was happy to have them. Having read over the file, she was satisfied that they would be safe with him. If everyone was agreeable, the social worker would liaise with our FPU and hold an emergency meeting in the morning to work out the best course of action. Meanwhile, I delegated Fordy to tell the kids the news and drop them off at their father's place in Pickering.

We were into the early hours of the morning when Ed and Thommo returned to report that after two or three strong cups of coffee the mother had finally calmed down. That's when the full impact of all that had happened hit her. She had been seen by a doctor, who assured us that she was not likely to harm herself; neither did he think it necessary to conduct any further assessment of her state of mental health. She was sober, rational and feeling pretty regretful about everything. She'd already been released from custody, and Ed and Thommo had dropped her off at home. Thommo made a brew and sat down at the parade-room table to write up his notes. 'Ye know,' he said, 'that woman was amazing.'

'How d'you mean?' I said.

'Well, the way one minute she was trying to take me off at the knees, threatening me with destruction, and then on the way home she was gentle as a wee lamb. Even apologised to us, didn't she Ed?'

Ed shrugged. 'I reckon she realised how close she'd come to losing her kids. That's what sobered her up, if you're asking me.'

Miraculously, I got away on time at the end of the shift. All the way home on roads slicked here and there with ice, I could feel sleep beckoning. But when I got into bed I struggled to get to sleep. I kept thinking of all the ways that scenario might have unfolded, and thanking my lucky stars that it came out as it did. It could have been so much worse.

Chapter 13

Into the Future

It had been a good week at work, a calm week. No real drama, no destruction, and no deaths. In fact, we'd had cause to celebrate, having got closure on the break-in at Jim and Helen's place. Helen had made a positive identification of the woman on the ID parade, and a match had been made between her boyfriend's trainers and the print so carefully lifted by Stuart off the front door where he'd kicked it open.

And as if this wasn't enough there was more good news. Jayne had safely delivered a baby boy weighing in at a healthy eight pounds three ounces. As we all pointed out to her, he would be able to play cricket for Yorkshire under the old rules of qualification – despite being half Cockney. We had the traditional whip-round at the station, and got a rare sighting of Thommo coming over all touchy-feely and pulling out his wallet – cobwebs and all – to contribute towards a huge bunch of flowers and some Mothercare vouchers.

On the work front we finally got a result on the series of country house burglaries that had been plaguing us for much of the previous year. I'd called in on Des to see whether there was any progress, just on the off-chance, not really expecting anything.

'Ah,' he said, 'nice timing, Mike. Amanda and I have just got a lead on that hire van.'

'You mean the one my Country Watch guy spotted?'

'The very same. Remember we had two suspects, and a girlfriend?'

'Yeah.'

'Well, it turns out she was the one who hired it. And a number of others across the county. All from different firms.'

'Clever move,' I said.

'Yes, but.'

'I was hoping for a "but".'

'Right, well, she made one big mistake: using her real name and driving licence on each occasion. Amanda and I have spent months piecing all this together – and we've also come up with a lock-up that we'll be searching. Pretty sure that's where they're stashing the stolen goods.'

'Well, that's brilliant,' I said. 'Funny though, we've just had a result on the shotgun burglary and the 'two-in-one job.'

'Oh yes?'

'Yes, a girlfriend was heavily involved in that as well. Funny how times have changed.'

'They have indeed. Anyway, I haven't finished yet. There's more. We've managed to link each hire with the date and location of a specific burglary, and we've connected two other suspects with the vans. One is the lass's boyfriend, the other is her brother.'

'Fantastic. So what's your next move?'

Des leaned back in his seat and put his hands behind his head. 'I think an early morning wake-up call, after which they'll all three be arrested for conspiracy to burgle.'

I was chuffed to bits over this – apart from anything because of the role my Country Watch colleagues had played. I'm sure they sometimes feel that they're being asked to deliver us meaningless snippets of information that get swallowed up in the blizzard of paperwork we have to deal with. But here was the living proof that it all counts, that the smallest trifle can yield a result. Just spotting that hire van was what had triggered off this whole line of enquiry.

So, with the Easter weekend looming all was well with life – apart from a couple of things that were gnawing away at me. One was the part two exam for promotion to sergeant. It was a couple of months since Jayne and I had taken that, and neither of us was as confident as we'd been with the part one. What we'd sat was OSPREY, another recent innovation. It stands for Object-Specific Performance Related Examination part 2. It was based on a series of role-play situations where you were marked by an assessor who judged you not just on your knowledge but on your acting ability as well. My mother sometimes used to say I should have gone to RADA – but, like a lot of hopeful performers, I went to Bradford. Not the Alhambra, where all those music-hall stars strutted their stuff, but to a drab hotel on the outskirts of the city. The examiners had taken over a number of rooms, in each of which were a different set of assessors and various actors whose job it was to play members of the public, suspects or police officers, as required by the situation.

Before you entered each room you were given a few minutes to digest a short outline of the situation you would be dealing with. There was precious little thinking time. The whole business operated like a sort of carousel – or, as Jayne remarked, like *Whose Line Is It Anyway?* – with only one candidate in a room at a time. Once your five minutes was up a buzzer would sound and you had to stop, walk out and go to the next room, finished or not. It could've been an absolute nightmare, but Jayne and I had come up with a strategy – that if we could squeeze in as many of the current management buzzwords as possible we'd surely score enough points to pass. I was sure that that was what the examiners would be looking for.

To be honest, the whole thing was a bit of a blur, although I do remember one particular scenario. I was face to face with an actor playing the part of a senior PC who was suppose to be nearing retirement. My brief was that he was being disruptive on shift, was totally unmotivated, constantly going sick and refusing to complete his PDR. He reminded me of Thommo on a bad day – although on that last point, the PDRs, I had every sympathy. For the first two or three minutes all I got in reply to my questions was a nod of the head from the actor and even less from the two assessors, who sat chewing their pencils. I suppose I could've panicked. Instead I got angry. Right, I thought, you want me to play the game; I'll bloody play it. I started on about 'action plans' and 'smart objectives', 'catching the train that was about to leave the station', 'the policing family', 'transparency' – all that baloney we moaned about in the messroom every time we got a new directive from above. Suddenly we were up and running, with the stooge throwing answers at me and the assessors' pencils scratching away on their pads.

By the time I came out I was full of myself. Unlike Jayne, who was convinced she'd blown it. 'Listen,' I said, 'you threw in plenty of jargon, didn't you? And we had all that practice. What's there to worry about?'

We soon found out. It was the waiting. To be fair, after you come out of that exam room they do warn you that it'll be some time before the results come through. Some time? Two months had gone by, and still no news. I was starting to wonder whether they'd forgotten all about us. My confidence was being eroded as the weeks went by. I started reliving every question, every situation we'd gone through, and the more I thought about it the more convinced I was that I'd simply ballsed it up. Ann tried to bolster my confidence, reminding me how upbeat I'd been when I came home that afternoon, and for a while I started to believe in myself again, but as the weeks went by the doubts started to creep in once more. I even went so far as to call Human Remains – or rather Human Resources – but was told it could be several weeks yet. It was a Friday and I'd been on an early shift. I'd gone home and was slumped on the settee feeling sorry for myself when the phone rang. I cast around for the handset. Where the hell had it got to? Ann, coming in from the kitchen, raised her eyebrow as she retrieved it from under the recliner.

'If you'd ever put it back where it belonged,' she muttered as I put it to my ear.

'Michael, m'boy!'

'Oh God, Algy. Not so loud, please. I was half asleep there. What can I do for you, mate?'

'Ah, well . . . bit of a ticklish one, I'm afraid. The fact is, I'm under the threat of prosecution.'

I sat back down on the settee. 'Let's have it. What have you done this time?'

'Nothing, that's the point. It's those snooping, conniving, worthless chaps at the planning department.'

'What? Algy, what you talking about?'

'Remember that business when they came after me for exercising my rights as a Yorkshireman?'

'You mean when you flew the flag with the white rose on it?'

'Exactly. They've been looking for any excuse to come down on me ever since. And now they've found one – or so they say.'

Before I could answer, Ann started signalling to me. She was off to town to get some groceries or something.

'Look, Algy,' I said, 'I'm on my own for an hour or so. Get that kettle on and I'll come over.'

Algy was a lot calmer when I got to his place, and ready to explain what had happened. It seemed that the Ministry of Farming, Fisheries and Food, as he still insisted on calling them, had been checking the satellite images they took as part of their crop regulation and allocation scheme. They'd discovered a large, newly built property next to Algy's orchard. They'd passed the information on to the planning authority, who had written to Algy to ask why he'd erected it without permission.

'Look here,' Algy said, getting up a fresh head of steam as he waved a portfolio of documents in my face. 'See – they even mention a large wooden door. I mean, they can see everything now you know. Big Brother has arrived – and for all I know he has photographs of Algernon in his bathtub.'

'Hang about,' I said. 'What building are they on about?'

'See for yourself, Michael. Take a good look at Exhibit A.' He produced a large black-and-white aerial photograph.

'There's nowt there,' I said. 'Just your house, your outbuildings and your orchard.'

'Aha! Now turn your attention to Exhibit B, taken a few weeks later.'

'Strewth. What's that?' Next to the orchard was a huge rectangular building with what looked like a white roof.

'Don't you see? The damned fools have flown over in their stealth bomber or whatever they use – on Soapy's wedding day.'

'Fantastic. You couldn't make it up, could you? I presume you've told 'em?'

'No. I'm still digesting the contents of Exhibit C.' He produced a third document for me to read.

'What! You've to demolish it within ninety days? Bloody idiots. I mean, there's nowt to demolish.'

'Precisely, old boy. But I shall dangle them on a rope for a while before I flourish the evidence of their incompetence in their smug faces. Mark my words, I'll have them squirming.'

I shook my head. 'Algy,' I said, 'I think it's right what Ann says. You really have got too much time on your hands.'

Algy laughed. 'Maybe so – and how is the delightful Ann?'

'Ah. I'm glad you asked me. Because she's been on my mind a lot lately. Something niggling me.'

'Not trouble on the domestic front, I hope?'

'Not as such. No, I just need your advice. The thing is, I've come to the conclusion that the time has come for me to – you know, pop the question.'

'Splendid! Another wedding! I'll call the planning people and get them to do another survey, shall I? Then we'll put the marquee in the next field. That'll get them scratching their dim little heads, don't you think?'

'Steady on, Algy. You're jumping the gun. I haven't proposed yet – and that's what I want your advice on. The time. The place. The words. Come on, you're a man of the world. How does a shy, retiring Yorkshire lad go about it?'

'Ah, I see. Well, if you want to put on a bit of a display you know you're always welcome to utilise the cannon, or the MG – or . . . I know, how about Lord Nelson, and my new hunting jacket? I can see it now: you riding into the clearing astride the big white stallion and throwing the fair Ann a bunch of blood-red roses.'

'Algy . . .'

'D'you know, I think I've got a suit of chainmail up in the attic somewhere. Not exactly the knight in shining armour, but in the right area, so to speak.'

'Algy, I am not dressing up as a medieval warrior. And I'm not trying to put on a show. I'm just planning to ask her the big question – and I want some ideas as to where when and how.'

'Well, how about whisking her off to Paris for the weekend? Or Barcelona? Or maybe Rome? On your knees before the Trevi Fountain, and maybe a gondolier with a fiddle to serenade her.'

'Except they don't have gondoliers in Rome, Algy. Listen, they're all nice places, but a bit predictable. I was thinking somewhere closer to home, somewhere in Yorkshire, somewhere – what would you say – authentic. Then if she says yes I can whisk her off abroad for a weekend.'

'I see, and if she says no you haven't wasted several hundred smackeroos. Good thinking, Michael. Well look, if we're talking about God's Own County we're spoiled for choice, aren't we? Fountains Abbey, Malham Tarn, Rievaulx. All gorgeous spots and unspeakably romantic.'

'Or under the whale bones at Whitby. Or how about back to Grassington where we took the MG that time? Of course, the location's only part of it,' I said.

'Really? Something else bothering you?'

'Yes. You know in films . . . I mean, how come the guy always knows what size ring to get? I wouldn't have a clue. Is there some trick to it, something I'm meant to know?'

Algy puffed out his cheeks and shook his head. Then, brightening visibly, he said, 'I know. Why not do what a pal of mine did one time? Sneak off to town with one of her gloves? Give the old jeweller fellows a clue.'

'Y'know, that's not a bad idea, Algy. Yes, I like it. See, I knew you'd come up with something.'

The good feeling lasted as long as it took me to drive home and start thinking about the exams again. I got to Keeper's Cottage just as Ann was returning from town. 'Maybe I should phone them,' I said, looking at my watch. 'Before they shut down for the weekend.'

'Phone who?' she said.

'That blooming exam board,' I said. ' Somebody, anybody. I mean, how long does it take to go through a set of papers and tot up a few scores?'

'Er – depends how many people sat the exam, I'd say. Bear in mind it's a national exam, not just you lot from North Yorkshire.' Ann had adopted a certain tone of voice. I knew what it meant: she'd had one hell of a week, so could we change the subject and crack open a bottle of wine. As she said, there's no point in fretting about something you can't do anything about. 'And anyway, we've had this conversation. They told you it'd be a few more weeks.'

Luckily for me, Ann was on the case. She knew I needed a

distraction, and that's what she'd been to town for. First thing Saturday morning she was up making coffee, hustling me out of bed and down the stairs.

'What's the rush?' I said, as she put a bowl of cereal in front of me.

'Springtime,' she said, flinging back the kitchen curtains. 'The season when the male of the species heads out into the wilderness.'

'Eh? What you on about?'

'This.' She thrust a stainless-steel spade into my hand, then a fork, both of them brand new, with the Yates' price tags still stuck on the handles. 'And these.' She had a collection of vegetable seeds in one hand and pair of gardening gloves in the other.

'So that's what you were up to in town yesterday.'

'My goodness, you're quick. You should be in the CID. So – you ready?' She was looking through the window at an area of rank grass that used to be the lawn, dotted with last year's thistles and this year's dandelions. 'Your own patch of virgin land. How many times have we sat out there on that log and talked about all the things we were going to do with it, eh? And here's your chance to make them a reality. Go on, outside with you. Get digging.'

I was about to tell her I liked it when she got all dominant with me, but thought better of it. I put my boots on, fetched a line from the shed, measured out what I thought would make a suitable vegetable plot, and set to work. And you know what? Once I got started I began to enjoy it. The sun was warm on my back, the birds were singing, a woodpecker was tapping away in the tall trees, and Henry, daft as a brush, was snapping the heads off the dandelions, then chasing a sleepy bee around the gooseberry bushes before wandering off to see if there was any sign of life in the rabbit-warren. Meanwhile I was recalling the lessons my dad taught me, years ago, about double digging:

lift the turf, take out a trench, remove the soil to the far end of your plot; then back to your trench to work it over with your fork before digging the next one. It all came back to me and I was soon in a rhythm. Oh yes, this vegetable garden was going to be the business, something he would've been proud of. I hadn't been going more than an hour before I was seeing giant parsnips, mounds of red-skinned potatoes, cauliflowers the size of footballs, rows of scarlet runners, prizes at the village show – and Walter scratching his head, trying to work out the secret of my success.

'I see you've got the first row dug, then.' I hadn't heard the post van come up the drive.

'Yeah,' I said, wiping the sweat off my forehead, 'it's a start, anyway. Tell you what, mate, you won't recognise this place in a couple of weeks' time.'

'Let's hope you've plenty of wire-mesh, eh? Keep them rabbits off it.' He handed me the usual collection of bills and flyers and left me pondering how much these prize vegetables were going to cost me.

We had a late lunch, Ann and I, sitting side by side on the log as a pair of blackbirds hopped to and fro, pulling worms out of the newly turned earth. 'Isn't this great?' I said. 'Our own little patch of Yorkshire.' I looked past Ann to the space at the other end of the log. I was wondering whether to say what was on my mind, about it being big enough to take a family. Then I thought, no; first things first.

We finished eating, and sat with a cup of coffee. 'Just like summer, what a beautiful day,' Ann said, squeezing up beside me.

I didn't answer. I was summoning up my courage. Here we go, I told myself. Forget plotting and scheming and waiting for the perfect moment. I'm going to do it right now. I've always been one to act on impulse – even if it has got me into trouble more often than not. I stood up, put my cup on the log and knelt down on one knee. Ann leaned back and looked at me, her eyes narrowed with suspicion. For a fleeting moment I wondered whether I was setting myself up for a massive disappointment. What if she turned me down? Just try it, I thought.

Reaching out, I took her hand in mine and looked her in the eyes.

'Ann,' I said, 'there's something I want to ask you.'

Acknowledgements

To my Mother, Aunt June, Frank and Jo, Lynn and David, Rob and Julie and all the staff at 'Twiggys' – all of whom play a part in keeping my sanity (well trying to do). Thank you for your support and friendship. To Kevin Sinfield and Heidi Dyson at Yorkshire Tea for their tremendous and continuing support. Also, to all the serving police officers and emergency services who do such a fantastic job keeping us all safe and supporting my books . . .

And a little bit extra . . .

Readers from all over the world – and people I meet when I do my talks and other events – often ask me about Yorkshire so here are some helpful websites:

www.yorkshire.com
www.visityork.org
www.yorkshiretea.co.uk
www.yorkshirerainforestproject.co.uk
www.nymr.co.uk

Finally, if you want to help a deserving cause – and people you might need one day – the local Mountain and Cave Rescue teams all do a great job. They're volunteers who go out in all weathers and the service depends on donations:

Scarborough and Ryedale Mountain Rescue Team:
www.srmrt.org.uk
Swaledale Mountain Rescue Team:
www.swaledalemrt.org.uk
Cleveland Search and Rescue Team:
www.csrt.co.uk
Cave Rescue Organisation:
www.cro.org.uk
Upper Wharfedale Fell Rescue Association:
www.uwfra.org.uk

Mike Pannett

Have you read the other tales from the Yorkshire bobby?

MIKE PANNETT

YOU'RE COMING WITH ME, LAD

Policing rural Yorkshire is a far cry from Mike's old job hunting down drug gangs and knife crime in Central London. Settled back in his native Yorkshire, however, Mike finds that life as a rural beat bobby is no picnic.

After a crazed swordsman threatens to take his head off, he finds himself confronting a knife-wielding couple bent on carving each other up. When a stag night turns ugly he ends up with the groom, the best man and the bride-to-be all banged up in the cells – and the wedding just hours away. With record-breaking floods and politicians to escort, will Mike find time to woo the woman of his dreams?

Hodder & Stoughton paperback and Ebook
www.hodder.co.uk

Have you read the other tales from the Yorkshire bobby?

MIKE PANNETT

NOT ON MY PATCH, LAD

Mike Pannett used to work the beat in Central London and when he moved back to Yorkshire he was hoping for a quieter life. But it seems the moors and villages of his native county aren't as sleepy as he once thought . . .

A casual remark about a barn with blacked-out windows leads him to an isolated farmhouse and a young girl is attacked at a local theme park. Meanwhile, Mike is still trying to identify and bring to justice the 'Sunset Gang' who are systematically targeting isolated warehouses and shops on his patch.

On the home front, Ann has moved into Keeper's Cottage and taken a Sergeant's post in York – and people are asking Mike what it's like to be a kept man.

Hodder & Stoughton paperback and Ebook
www.hodder.co.uk